# THE SACRED FIRE

# THE STORY OF SEX IN RELIGION

# The
# SACRED FIRE

By **B. Z. GOLDBERG**

With An Introduction by *Dr. Charles Francis Potter*

**THE CITADEL PRESS**     Secaucus, N. J.

First paperbound printing, 1974
Published by Citadel Press
A division of Lyle Stuart, Inc.
120 Enterprise Ave., Secaucus, N. J. 07094
In Canada: George J. McLeod Limited
73 Bathurst St., Toronto, Ont.
Copyright © 1958 by B. Z. Goldberg
All rights reserved
Manufactured in the United States of America
ISBN 0-8065-0456-0

TO

**MAROUSSIA**

# INTRODUCTION

By *Charles Francis Potter*
(M.A., S.T.M., LITT.D.)
(Author, THE STORY OF RELIGION, HUMANIZING RELIGION,
THE FAITHS MEN LIVE BY, THE GREAT RELIGIOUS LEADERS)

In the years since 1930 when Professor Goldberg dared to set forth in popular form his thesis that sex and religion are intimately related, there has been considerable recognition of the existence of that relationship by the observant folk he then awakened. There has been also of late in the minds of the more intelligent laity a growing suspicion that scholarly experts in anthropology, psychology, and "comparative" religion, before Goldberg's time and since, have not spelled out the whole story.

Of course, it has been admitted in scholarly tomes and technical journals that sex and religion may have been inseparable among primitive peoples, and are even now seasonally affiliated in remote regions where dwell "our contemporary ancestors." But these admissions have been couched in academic gobbledygook, usually in French or German scientese, while the more realistic descriptive details of sex customs are still often phrased in Latin, for fear, presumably, that the lay reader might, surreptitiously and immorally, try to fill the prescription himself.

Further and more important, the obvious persistence of phallic survivals and sexual motivations and manifestations in current Christianity and Judaism is a disturbing fact which is seldom proclaimed even in professional media, except euphemistically, and never in "popular" mass-circulation books and magazines.

Sexy books sell — in fact they are the best-sellers — even in, and especially in, Christian countries, *provided* there is no mention, admission, or hint of the sexual elements, influence, and characteristics in and of religion. Once sex and religion are connected and their relationship explained, then the book becomes taboo, which is why such a beautifully written, interesting, and sociologically valuable book as Goldberg's THE SACRED FIRE was an "under-the-counter" title and has for years been rare and practically unobtainable.

The book covers a vast territory: in fact, it is really four books in one, as Goldberg indicates by dividing the volume into four parts, covering the evidences of the erotic motive in (1) primitive religion, (2) classic civilizations, (3) modern monotheistic faiths, and (4) the sects.

He threads his way skilfully through the tangled darks of the worship of the early generative divinities; then describes the colorful customs and ceremonies of the religions of Baal, Aphrodite, Dionysus, Moloch, and Shakti, and goes on to mention sexual influences in Judaism, Christianity, and Islam, finishing his thesis in the fourth book by noting the sexually rebellious nature of sectarian religious leaders from the Manicheans down to the Mormons. And all through the book, one can but admire the delicacy and felicity of language used even in passages where a less skilful or a careless chronicler would be apt to slip into vulgar phraseology.

In fact, the author has caught the intrinsic beauty which is central in both sex and religion, and has portrayed with deep poetic feeling and fervor that common mystic element which is the essence of both ecstasies.

The thrill which a sensitive reader often gets from such a sex-religion study as this is a subtle feeling-consciousness of the beauty of holiness blended with the sacredness of sex. Properly presented, the sacred fire of sex-in-religion excites no nasty thoughts or impulses: rather, it awakens in a person a realization of his unity with all life, a mystic but rational appreciation of evolution through sex. If he be an honest rationalist, agnostic, humanist, or atheist, he may prefer to leave the religion part out. Cosmic consciousness, or awareness of the universe and one's evolutionary relationship to it, may be attained without any connection with established religions.

Truth to tell, it is more often the representatives of a religion who may consider sex "nasty." Celibate priests and eunuchs from ancient times to now have with such frenzy and bigoted fanaticism condemned sexual love that they have betrayed their own abnormal interest in and obsession by the sex impulse. A religion which considers virginity, chastity, and celibacy to be virtues, and condones the normal married state only because "it is better to marry than to burn" deprives its own votaries of the blessings and beauties of the higher religion which finds in natural sex experiences the consummation and expression of union with the divine.

Conversely, it should also be said that the non-religious person who looks upon sex as "dirty" or a mere emotional nuisance is missing an aesthetic value, a precious human experience. One need not be a member of any religion in order to have the higher values of sexual communion. As Goldberg says (page 25) "The very religious term 'adore' is a prime favorite in love's vocabulary. We all know the implicit faiths of lovers . . . how all-pervading and overpowering love may be." Sex in itself, properly planned and experienced, is beautiful, inspiring, and of highest worth.

The chief message of THE SACRED FIRE, however — a thesis which must be continued, expanded and deepened today — is that human love is holy and sex is itself the "sacred fire." It is high time to cleanse of such impure ideas those religions which consider sex experience essentially sinful, to be tolerated only as a concession to human fleshly frailty, even within a long-standing legalized marriage.

The obvious insincerity, inconsistency and patent hypocrisy of certain well known sex-hating, medieval-minded religionists is particularly noticeable when they oppose planned parenthood and the limitation of unrestricted birth on the ground that God told man to "increase and multiply" (when there were allegedly only two people on earth). At the same time, these medievalists exalt virginity, and the very priests who oppose planned parenthood themselves have vowed celibacy, and therefore cannot obey the first command of God to man to increase and multiply and thus replenish the earth.

Another phase of this inconsistency has been touched upon by Goldberg (page 26) but could well be re-emphasized and expatiated upon. He points out how in Christianity "carnal love has become unworthy, profane, and in its place must be substituted spiritual love for the divine being." The result has been that "The religion of western civilization is based on a mystic conception of the union of a human virgin with the Spirit of God."

This doctrine of the Virgin Birth of Jesus, supplemented by its necessary corollary, the Immaculate Conception of his mother by her own mother, to make sure of protecting Jesus from the human sinfulness of his mother as well as from the sex taint of an earthly father, was evidently an afterthought of the early Christian chroniclers. Paul's Epistles, all earlier than the gospels, contain no references to the miraculous birth. Only Matthew and Luke in the late-added "infancy narratives" contain the statement that Mary conceived by the Holy Spirit, or by the overshadowing of the Power of the Most High. Neither Mark nor John, in their gospels, know the Virgin Birth stories. (Although John's treatise or gospel was long thought to be the latest of the four "biographies" of Jesus, the manuscripts recently found in the Qumran Caves near the Dead Sea challenge that dating and impel some scholars to state that Mark may have to move aside from its traditional place as the earliest gospel to make room for John.)

These same "Scrolls" from the caves are also throwing considerable illumination on the angelology of interbiblical and New Testament times. In the light of Essene beliefs, it appears that Paul's "principalities and powers" as well as Jesus' "prince of this world" were angels or intermediate beings or spirits, superintended by such archangels as Gabriel and Michael who had direct access to God. So we are left rather confused as to which "spirit" or angel was God's agent by whom the Virgin Mary conceived. Three are mentioned, Gabriel, the Power of the Most High, and the Holy Spirit.

Moreover, in the attempt to remove the sex-taint from the birth of Jesus (when the theologians were making a god out of him) the patches show in several places in the gospels. It is admitted in the newest (1951) great commentary, THE INTERPRETER'S BIBLE, vol. 7, pp. 252-253, that Matthew's statement (1:16) "Jacob the father of Joseph the husband of Mary, of whom Jesus was born, who is called Christ," "looks like his (Matthew's) own attempt to make the genealogy conform to . . . the virgin birth doctrine," of which "Matthew is a strong proponent." It is admitted also that "Possibly Matthew's source contained some such reading as *c*," c being the reading of a number of manuscripts, generally unknown as yet to the laity but referred to by scholars as the Ferrar Family, the Koridethi Gospels, or frankly as "the naturalistic tradition." These little-known but authentic manuscripts state plainly, *"Joseph, to whom was betrothed the virgin Mary, was the father of Jesus who is called Christ."* This was in the Old Latin MSS, also, before Jerome changed it so that all Latin MSS since his day contain the Virgin Birth version as now found in Matthew's gospel.

Another bit of patch-work in the same chapter: Matthew introduces into Jesus' genealogy (differing radically from Luke's) four women, Tamar, Rahab, Ruth, and "the wife of Uriah," Bathsheba. Why did Matthew omit all the virtuous ancestresses of Jesus and list only those of dubious morality, four females all famous for extramarital or premarital sex affairs? Was the author of this Gospel of Matthew, who wrote especially to persuade the Jews themselves that Jesus was their expected Messiah, trying to defend Mary the mother of Jesus by pointing out that Jewish history and tradition often overlooked sex irregularities in women who gave birth to great men? Rahab the harlot was reputed to have been the ancestress of many great men and women, including besides David and Solomon the prophets Jeremiah, Baruch, and Ezekiel and the prophetess Huldah. But wasn't this Matthew author defeating his own theory of the Virgin Birth by implicitly putting Mary in the same class with these others?

However you look at it, the whole Virgin Birth—Immaculate Conception, with its complex collection of questionable evidence, is an exhibit in the theological museum of unnatural history where are exposed the various attempts of sex-scared celibates to deny the sacredness and dignity of the sexual nature of men and women, or to keep the facts of sex life secret, or even to condemn sex as an evil devilish thing in itself, instead of giving it its proper and honorable place in religion and life.

In most societies today, the connection of sex and religion is so obvious that it is admitted, and the fact taken for granted. But in the various sections of Christendom, that fact remains concealed under many disguises. All sorts of deceptions and subterfuges, euphemisms and rationalizations, are employed. But it is time now to follow the leadership of the author of THE SACRED FIRE, and state even more definitely and with the emphasis afforded by recent discoveries and developments in the fields of psychology, anthropology, folklore, comparative mythology, and the scientific appraisal of the phenomena themselves, his thesis that the sacred fire of life, the *elan vital*, the very dynamic of human existence, is the sex impulse which, properly controlled and directed, and partly sublimated, will give new vigor to old and decadent religions. Religions must recognize its debt to sex in origin and early development, and restore it to a place of dignity within religion, instead of despising and condemning it.

For, after all, life is the only marvel: only life is divine. If you tell me of virgin births and immaculate conceptions and of a god born by the overshadowing of a holy ghost, I will match you by telling you that a tiny protoplasmic living cell has in it the potentialities of all life, and therefore towers in majesty above the petty incredibilities of pious miracle-mongers.

No miracle of holy writ can magnify the importance of the birth of a child, from its conception by the ecstasy of the love of two complementary human beings, through the long months when the germ of life, changing hour by hour and minute by minute, recounts the processes of its evolutionary ancestors, until in due time, by the travail of the mother, there comes into individual existence a tiny being, in whose vibrant life the hopes and fears of all the years are centered.

Religion cannot afford to overlook the existence, importance, and essentially sacred character of the life-stimulus called sex.

# CONTENTS

## BOOK ONE

## FAR AWAY AND LONG AGO

### THE EROTIC MOTIVE IN PRIMITIVE RELIGION

13

BOOK TWO

IN THE TEMPLE OF THE GODS

THE WORSHIP OF THE GENERATIVE DIVINITIES

BOOK THREE

## IN THE HOUSE OF THE LORD

THE EROTIC MOTIVE IN THE MONOTHEISTIC
RELIGIONS OF TO-DAY

The erotic motive in the Christian religion among the Negroes—The religion of the black man as compared with the faith of his white brother—The primitive religion that the Negro brought with him from Africa—The black man's first steps in the white man's church—Psychological differences between the white and the black Christian faith—The elements of longing and love in the Negro religion—The revival as a release from sexual suppression—The erotic symbolism of the primitive religion carried over to Christianity—The strange mixture in Voodoo.

BOOK FOUR

# THE SPIRIT OF REVOLT IN RELIGION

### THE SEXUAL MOTIVE IN SECTARIANISM

The liberator of a people later its oppressor—Korah's revolt against Moses—The spirit of revolt in every generation—Religion's inception in spontaneity—Social aspect of religion—The non-conformist as rebel and as ruler.

Various causes underlying religious revolts—All religious insurrections indirectly related to sex—Reasons for the erotic element in religious revolts—Leaders in revolts highly sexed individuals—Reversion to religion in its original form.

Sexual indulgence among the Nikolaites—The Mormon church and its relation to the sex life.

The devil worshippers—The devil elevated to a divine position by Manes—Sexual gratification in the religion of the Manichæans—The Messalines and sex—The erotic element in witchcraft.

# CONTENTS

# LIST OF ILLUSTRATIONS

# BOOK ONE
## FAR AWAY AND LONG AGO

"... *and thou shalt love the Lord thy God with all thy heart, and with all thy soul, and with all thy might.*"

# CHAPTER I

## FAR AWAY AND LONG AGO

### I

FAR away and long ago a gibbon slid down a tree. Once on the ground he did not feel like climbing up again. Life seemed so much better below than above ; only he realized he had to change a thing or two in his mode of living. He had to walk erect, for instance, rather than crawl on all fours. He had to perfect as well the use of his anterior limbs and to make hands out of them. And so it was that when the gibbon raised his head toward heaven and stretched his arms forward, he himself came to proceed forward as well. He was started on the way to human form.

It was then that the animal that was once gibbon or akin to the gibbon ventured out on its big climb again, not on the branches of a tree, but on the rungs of the ladder of civilization. Man burned the animal bridges behind him, for he saw no other way of living but to make the best of whatever humanity he possessed.

To-day, if you see an aeroplane soaring in the sky, you may know it is all due to that enterprising gibbon that slid down the tree. Had he been content to remain swinging on the branches, that which to-day passes for mankind might have been just another form of gibbon.

### II

Once humanized, the gibbon was driven further toward humanity by the lash of Dame Care. Because he was defence-less against the storm, he betook himself to the shelter of the rocks and caves. Because he was not equal to the demands that his new environment set up for those who would survive, he developed tools and implements. Because he was afraid of the prowling beast, he cultivated a taste for sociability. He took to wandering with his kind so that, with the help of others, he might conquer his foes against whom he was powerless alone. And because he lived in groups, he acquired a desire for the approval of his fellow-creatures and was for ever trying to outdo himself in every prowess his particular group considered worth while.

It was Dame Care that forced the humanized gibbon to trudge along the path of progress, but there were two other mighty forces that drew him to the great kingdom that was to be his. They, too, were his constant companions, leading him into the great spiritual world that he was to inherit. They made his life bearable in moments that were most trying ; they added a drop of exaltation to his cup of drab existence. They were the prizes that were held out to the little schoolboy of civilization, to be his when he made the grade. They were the pillars of fire in the darkness through which the gibbon walked into the promised land of humanity. They were : LOVE and RELIGION.

### III

Both were doubtless very crude ere man first consciously called them by these designations. Love was probably only a physical overpowering of the female in a passing moment of passion, or winning her favour by appearing at an advantage in comparison with his fellows. Or perhaps it was, as it sometimes is to-day, a case of barter. He may have thrown her a banana or a nut, for which she, in return, received him in her chambers.

And religion was probably equally crude in the beginning. It was a mixture of fear and bribery. The strong fellow was dangerous in life and so he was in death. For, although his body returned to nothingness, his double, or soul, did not die but became even more powerful now, unbounded, as it was, by space and time. The man who was a devil when living became a demon after death. There was only one way of fighting him and that was by magic, but even magic was not always effective. It was rarely so in the case of the very strong demons. So it seemed more sensible to appease the evil spirit, to do it homage and to present it with the things it had liked when it was merely human. Religion may have had its origin as humbly as in bribing off the pernicious soul of some rascal in the tribe.

Still, there was something inherent in these prehistoric experiences of love and religion that potentially contained all the elements of which this rare fabric has been woven through these many thousands of years. Crude as the beginnings were, they contained the makings of the great phases of life that these forces came to be.

Even when love was a brief, physical, sex hunger, it embodied something more. Man was the first animal to abolish the rut or sexual season. Early man, like man to-day, was potentially ever ready to mate. He was already possessed of a conscious memory and an active imagination. As he lay basking in the sun after a satisfying meal, his memories probably wandered over his sex experience of the previous day, dwelling upon the particular female that had afforded these pleasures ; possibly upon her co-operation in the attempt to make them more gratifying. He may have felt a certain amount of gratitude toward her, as an intelligent animal might, or he may merely have felt kindly disposed toward her, as we usually are to-day toward people who have shared with us some joy or happiness. In his fancy he may have been reliving with her these intimacies. In short, promiscuous as the original sex life of man was, cruelly and brutally as it may have expressed itself, it still contained the trace of an attitude toward the object of his desire. There was no suggestion of such an attitude toward the meat that stilled his hunger, or the water that quenched his thirst. Out of this attitude grew love, even such great love as that between Abélard and Héloïse.

Similarly, the warding off of evil spirits, which may have constituted early religion, was an expression not only of fear but of awe as well. What man is forced to fear interminably will necessarily rise in his estimation and become an object of awe and adoration. It was true in the past—physical strength was idealized in the primitive world, and the might that induced fear was admired and envied. It is true to-day—man's own self-respect demands that whatever he sets above himself, shall grow to superior proportions, that whatever he subjects his own personality to, shall become idealized and raised to the plane of the superhuman. This explains the metamorphosis of a man to a god—hated and despised by his tribe in life, he becomes a deity for their worship after his death.

Once the demon became an object of awe and reverence, he was idealized, at least in part. He took the form of man's wish-content. All that man wished to be himself, he projected into the object of his reverence. Naturally, he sought, as he does to this day, to follow his idealized personality, not only to do it homage, but to emulate it as well. As man turned the demon into a god he learned to walk humbly before it. Thus, crude, primeval fear that lurked in the human heart before the dawn of the gods already possessed the basic elements that enter into universal religious experience.

IV

Now the two, love and religion, have been inseparably inter-twined all through the history of mankind. We are all aware of the element of religion in love. The very religious term " adore " is a prime favourite in love's vocabulary. We all know of the implicit faith of lovers, how blind they can be to the flagrant faults of the beloved. We also know how all-pervading and over-powering love may be. Like religion, it may bring one to the loftiest heights of bliss and to the depths of despair, so that he may sacrifice everything for it, even his very life.

To a much larger extent, love has been identified with religion. The fervour of religion seems naturally to induce the ecstasy of love. Pagan religious rites generally ended in open sex orgies. Whatever behaviour bonds on the sex impulse existed within the tribe were lifted for the moment. Sex indulgence that was so taboo as to be punishable by death was permitted in religious worship and was entered into with a vengeance.

The Greeks and the Romans followed the pagans in the worship of fertility gods. To this very day, millions of people practise circumcision as a religious duty, a symbolic signature of a covenant

*Phallic symbols in*
*ancient art*

into which their forefathers entered with their God, a signature of an undoubtedly erotic meaning.

The religion of western civilization is based on a mystic conception of the union of a human virgin with the Spirit of God. Carnal love has become unworthy, profane, and in its place must be substituted spiritual love for the divine being. Spiritual love, but love nevertheless. Suffice it only to mention the evangelistic revivals with their sudden conversions, which psychologists are wont to compare with sexual ecstasy, and the highly erotic symbolism in modern religion. The more one studies, not religious dogma or philosophy, but religious living as it is experienced by people all over the world, the more one is bound to nod assent to the sign often seen on the windows of missions : " God is Love."

v

How did love come to religion? Is there a clear distinction between the experience of love and that of religion? How has love fared within religion these many thousands of years of religious development?

There are a number of ways in which man to-day may look upon religion. He may conceive of it as truth divinely revealed to him by his Maker, as is believed by the faithful. He may look upon it as mere superstition, a projection of man's subjective mind—a dog, as it were, chasing his own tail, taking it for something foreign to him—elaborated according to the theory of Sigmund Freud. He may see religion as an innate tendency, the functioning of a special instinct, the interpretation advocated by Professor E. D. Starbuck to the utter dismay of Doctor John B. Watson. Again, he may be psychologically more cautious and, instead of viewing it as the result of a special innate tendency, take it as an outgrowth of other instinctive reactions, such as the herd instinct, agreeing with Trotter ; or the sex instinct, following Schroeder ; or, like McDougal, he may make religion the focal point of several instinctive tendencies, such as awe, admiration, and reverence. He may even agree with Thouless that religion is not so much a thing in itself as a mode of living. This view makes it the outlet supreme for man's all-instinctive craving, the expression of all the urges in his heart, a channel into which he may pour all that is burdening his soul.

However one looks upon religion, he cannot avoid the issue of love, love ever present, ever stirring, ever colouring the very essence of true, devotional, and exalted religious experience.

This book will undertake to trace the path of love in religion. It will follow the stream from its very source, down all its tortuous windings through the centuries : crude sex passion, physical love, love refined and idealized, and love sublimated and æsthetically symbolized. In doing so we may find it necessary to digress here and there in the dimly lighted past. We may have to wade through what to some may seem muddy waters. Still, it will all be for love and religion. Instead of discouraging, it should be a source of lofty inspiration and æsthetic intrenchment. Ours will be a course following the light out of the darkest forest, as it grows ever higher, clearer, purer, and more beautiful.

# CHAPTER II

## PRIMITIVE MAN IN LOVE AND FAITH

*And after the cry of fear*
*Came the sigh of love.*

### IN LOVE

#### I

ERE love was born and faith came into the world man was already there. Wild and woolly he was, crude and beastlike, yet the progenitor of a specie that was to produce civilization and culture, romance and art, love and religion. He was there when Europe was still covered with ice and the mammoth roamed over the land. If we had called on him, we would have had to seek him out in the crevices of some rock, cold and hungry, in hiding from the terrific forces of an environment to which he was hardly equal. What did this crouching, recoiling Old Anthropology Adam think of Love and God ?

His means of expression was necessarily limited ; he existed long before there was an alphabet or any attempt at written record. In fact, even verbally we could not have gotten much out of him. His words were few and as indefinite as the thoughts forming in his brain. And yet, this Old Anthropology Adam, living in inner and outer darkness, felt the urge to express himself and found his medium in art.

Were we to call upon him in a happier moment when he had caught his fish and trapped his prey, when he had had his fill and napped off the process of digestion, we might have found him drawing upon the walls of his cave the outline form of the mammoth, or painting the lion in fast colours upon the roof of his dwelling. Old Anthropology Adam was engaged in art.

What made him decorate the walls of his cave with drawings and paintings ? Was it a vestigal sense of the beautiful that possibly came down the animal line with him ? More probably he was little concerned with beautifying his abode. He may have drawn the lion not so much to put it on the wall as to get it out of his head. He may have been the true artist, pursuing his art for art's sake.

For Old Anthropology Adam was already possessed of a memory and an imagination. In idle moments he had been recalling the things that had happened to him on the previous day. He had been dreaming of his desires and wishes. Such activities served him as a mental stimulus, creating surplus energy

28

that had to find an outlet somehow. For man's mind ever seemed to be like a container of a more or less definite volume. Too full, it ran over and out into the world. Thus it was that Old Anthropology Adam came upon the medium of art, finding it most appropriate to convey his thoughts plastically and in line upon the screen of space before him.

## II

Having found our way into the province of the primitive mind, we might now explore it a little. Old Adam was a realist to the

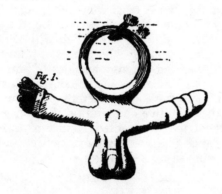

*An ancient amulet*

core. In his art he portrayed objects of his immediate environment. He presented them as faithfully as his primitive technique would permit. And critics have marvelled at his ingenuity in overcoming technical difficulties.

Yet we very soon find him going in for symbolism. He not only presents an imaginary object to the eye, but he gives it a meaning. He intentionally rejects certain details and exaggerates others, emphasizing those that are apparently most important in his eyes. Old Anthropology Adam not only gave us his environment in his art, but himself as well, his own personal interests and urges, his dreams and desires, his very soul.

Now, what was on the mind of primitive man as expressed in his art ? What was the motive that overfilled his being and sought projection into the outer world ? It was love, sex, revealed to him in its concrete, physical form. When he drew the figure of an animal, his interest was centred on the parts that harboured the prime force of nature. When he was representing the human form, he took pains to render these same parts elaborately, in great detail and out of proportion to the entire body. No attempt is noticeable to delineate the limbs carefully or to represent the head realistically. All his attention was centred on the embodiments of that great life-bringing power in nature.

The impression obtains that primitive man used the body as a background for the generative organs, which he took for the chief detail, the leitmotiv. Whatever Old Anthropology Adam was concerned with in his art, his attention was focused on the sex of it. Sex was the prime mover of his life.

In this respect, the artist did in his art only what the singer did in his song and the dance master in his dance. The songs of primitive man concerned themselves with hunting, fishing, and driving spirits away. But far more than with these, were they concerned with sex. Similarly, the dances of primitive man may have represented war and the hunt and death, but, in most cases, they took on a sexual meaning in the course of execution. All other dances seem to have been merely a warming up for the chief dance of the primitive community, the dance that was the exaltation of the tribe, the sacred climax of every important ceremony, the dance that was highly suggestive and imitative of mating, culminating in rank sexual orgies.

### III

What was it that made sex the centre of primitive man's thought, the prime motive of his imagination? Was he conscious of it as the life-giving force throughout nature? He may have been, for he realized his dependence upon the regeneration of nature, upon the green of the fields and the young of the animals for his sustenance. Again he may not, for he was not aware of any relationship between the occasional moment of pleasure with a woman and the offspring so many months later.

It is most probable that Old Anthropology Adam dwelled so much upon sex because it was pleasurable. His drab life offered little bliss and the sex emotion was his chief source of joy and exaltation. All other animals had a rather mechanical sexual life. Generally their mating instinct was inactive ; their existence consisted chiefly in feeding, resting, and physical play. This stretch of sexual inactivity was crossed by a definite season of hypersexuality. Then their entire organism was highly attuned, susceptible to the least attraction of the opposite sex and driven into courtship and intercourse by the lash of a force as incomprehensible as it was uncontrollable. In man these periods of rut were dissolved in an indefinite, general sex activity. This activity was the great diversion in his life except when it was submerged by fear or struggle. Frequently it was also associated with physical contests, as fighting or racing for the female, which added even greater zest to his loving. Is there any wonder, then, that his mind should dwell on it in his idle moments and that it should be the chief content of his memories of the past and imaginings of the future ?

The attitude of primitive man toward sex was not at all like ours. He could never have understood our secretiveness about it or our reserve in speaking of it. Old Anthropology Adam was not in the Garden of Eden, yet he went naked and knew it not. There are many primitive peoples to-day that go about entirely naked. Among others, only the married women go unclothed, bearing their nudity as a mark of their marital state, just as our married women wear the wedding ring. Early man had no secret part in his organism nor was he ashamed of any one of them. His attitude toward his own body may be gleaned from the lullaby the Nama-Hottentot mother sings her babe :

> You child of a strong-thighed father,
> You'll press yet strong oxen between your thighs ;
> You that have such a powerful organ,
> You'll bring many and strong children
> Into the world.

Proud of his sexual apparatus, primitive man could not be ashamed of its function. To him sex was as natural as eating. He ate in public any time, anywhere there was food and he was hungry. So did he satisfy his sexual appetite. The Latin poet, Horace, described this stage of man's love in his own inimitable manner when he said : " He jumped in beastly fashion at the first best female that came his way." The great modern ethnologist, Bachofen, reiterates that originally man " satisfied his natural instinct like the beast without lasting bond with the particular female and before the eyes of all."

There are still those who disdain to think that such was the origin of the love of man. They would rather have him spring from more noble stock that was monogamous by nature. Only in time did he fall and degenerate into the state of promiscuity we find him in, in the past or present. Westermarck is one apostle of this monogamous faith in man and he musters considerable evidence in support of his theory. Still, the consensus of opinion among anthropologists to-day is that originally man was promiscuous in the exercise of his sexual function. Greek and Roman historians speak of races living in promiscuity in their day. Modern travellers have found tribes in Australia and elsewhere, who in their sex life know neither family ties nor privacy, neither constancy nor consideration.

Moreover, the environmental life of primitive man was conducive to promiscuity. The tribal group lived in a circumscribed space. It was no more safe or convenient to go off to a place where one might not be seen than there was a conscious urge to do so. Old Anthropology Adam may have been returning home

*Even primitive man used symbolism*

after a long day of hunting, weary in body and heavy of heart. What could be more pleasant to him than grasping a female and drowning his troubles in the joy of union with her ?

The female was at hand and she dared not refuse. In his moment of passion little thought did he give to the presence of others, nor would he shrink from exercising his sexual function before them if he did. What one man did another would do. Imitation was the spark that set man's heart a-burning. What to us should be a strictly private affair became a social function, a group experience. And whenever the sexual function is exercised by individuals in a group, an exchange of partners will follow. It is true to-day in the so-called " wild parties," and in the orgies of religious sects.

The exercise of the sexual function in the presence of others only added fire to its flame. It intensified a passion already overwhelming the primitive being. It brought additional joys to a signal pleasure in a life of bleak existence. As it was, in addition, free from all restrictions, we need not wonder that Old Anthropology Adam set his mind upon sex. In time, it overran his entire personality. He projected it out of his self in art and dance and song. He shouted it forth in his speech ; for the sounds that escaped him during his mating formed the basis of his language. And old, idealistic Plato tells us that even thinking was a sublimation of man's sexuality. That is why in most languages the word " conceive " has the two meanings of thinking and becoming pregnant. Sex became the way of man's living.

## IV

But the very fact that the sexual function had been exercised openly in the social group caused it in time to be limited and circumscribed. Once sex became a social activity the group took it in hand to make it serve the social unit rather than the individual. Inhibitions were imposed upon the mating instinct not to add to man's pleasure or to make it more orderly and improved. They were there to save man's physical energies for the greater tasks of the tribe in war and peace. They were there to whet his appetite for victory, which would bring the women of the enemy as its reward. They were there to drive man on in his daily grind, for at its close the great accumulated hunger would be satisfied. Harnessing the individual more closely to the work of the social unit, the latter found it imperative to curtail his sexual life.

Thus the sexual function was limited, and any break of the bonds upon sex spelled ill for the entire group. A sexual act committed against the accepted code of morality was in olden times thought to hurt the tribe by causing sterility of the crop, since it offended the fertility gods. To this day in some parts of Europe, adultery is said to bring about a fatal epidemic to children and when infant deaths increase the morality seekers have an easy hand.

Time and experience gave birth to such concepts as incest, which forbade intercourse between mother and son, father and daughter, brother and sister, and other blood relations, varying with different people. Exogamy came into being, by which the males of one group were forbidden sexual union with the females of the same group. Marriages of various sorts—beginning with group marriages and ending with modern monogamous marriage —limited sexual union with a woman, first to a group, then to members of a family, like father and brother of the male, and finally to a single male.

Out of the chaos of promiscuity grew our complicated solar system of kinship, family relationship, and monogamous marriage —as complicated, for instance, as the Mosaic law that one may marry his niece but not his aunt. This remnant of antiquity is still reflected to-day in the pseudo-scientific theory of consan- guineous marriage, for which modern eugenics can find no justification.

But this growth did not take place without pains, nor has it yet reached its completion. We all know of the desperate fight against incest by the servants of Jehovah. Even at the present time, incestuous relationship is not so rare, as the records of criminal courts in any land will show. Methods of escape from the rigid rules were evolved—sort of a back-door entrance, either in space, delimiting definite places, like the Bais or Young Men's Barrack, where all was permitted ; or, in time, like festive occasions, when again all bonds were loosened. Gradually these back doors were closed upon the hinges of civilization. Still, man's heart has not changed. We occasionally hear of an ex- change of wives between families, recalling tribal or clan marriage, and a monogamous marriage is in many places almost as often honoured in its breach as in its fulfilment.

The repression of any innate tendency brings in its wake the desire for some escape. So it was that sexual prohibition gave rise to an erotic tendency in religion. When Old Anthropology Adam found his sexual desire fenced in by social customs and tribal taboos, he, too, sought a way of going around these inhibi- tions. The hand of the group weighed down too heavily upon the individual for him to try to break the law of the tribe. It was the group that made the taboos ; it was up to the group to raise these taboos temporarily at various times. Hence, on all religious occasions, whenever primitive man returned from the hunt or the stream, whenever the tribe gathered for an important event, the taboos were wholly or partially raised.

He may have been in a joyous mood celebrating the advent of the spring-time, thankful for a successful hunt, exultant because of a victory over an enemy, proud and happy at the birth of a child, or even depressed and saddened at the death of a favourite member of the tribe. But no matter what the cause, each of these occasions gave rise to a very definite display of emotion in an appropriate dance ; and, again, no matter what emotion called it forth, the ceremony ended in an orgy in which all bonds were cast aside, all previous joys or sorrows forgotten, while, for a few short hours, love and sex furnished the bliss and exaltation that the primitive heart of Old Anthropology Adam craved.

Even to this day when the Buriats of Asiatic Siberia have a holiday, bonfires are lighted near the villages, around which men and women sing prayers and dance their monotonous *nadan*. Every once in a while a couple leaves the circle and disappears in the dark woods near by. After a time they return to the dance, only to disappear again, but with different partners.

v

Thus, Old Anthropology Adam looked to sex for whatever exalted joys life had in store for him. In the enjoyment of this pleasure he had been very early inhibited and hemmed in. This impressed sex even more strongly upon his mind. It was not only

*An Egyptian phallic altar*

the thing he wished most, but also the point where his desire was crossed. Moreover, sexual experience has always been man's outlet for his other pent-up emotions. Suppressed rage, swallowed pride, hidden fear, all could be relieved in an orgy of drenching sexuality. Hemming in the sexual impulse meant not only penning up man's greatest passion, but also closing the outlet for his other emotions. Modern man must either sublimate his suppressed energies or develop a psychosis. Old Anthropology Adam faced the problem by a double-headed solution. He went in for blood-letting, raising all bonds from time to time as a soul cleansing, and for sublimating his desires in symbolism in his art and other products of his mind—above all in religion. The cruder he was, the more anthropologic he was, the oftener were his blood-lettings and the more simple his symbolism. As he climbed the ladder of civilization, the open outbursts of sexuality grew fewer and his symbolism became more highly involved.

At first, these symbols were merely realistic portrayals of the generative organs. Later, man began to embroider them in his mind—they became something intricate and fanciful. Simple and natural sexual union was clothed with ideas and mental images. More and more it became a thing of the imagination. As these ideas grew, the act itself dwindled in importance, until it was only a ritual.

## In Faith

### I

Old Anthropology Adam lived in a world of fears. His great-great-grandfather, the gibbon, swinging in the tree had been much happier and comparatively free from worry and fright. The gibbon did not know enough to be afraid. Modern man knows better ; he has learned to discount his fears. Primitive man was caught in between. The babe may crawl right into the ocean, not knowing enough to fear the waves. The little child will play on the beach and enjoy the sight of the water, but will run back in horror when the foam of the waves touches his feet. The older boy knows just how far into the ocean he may safely go. Old Anthropology Adam was like the child in his attitude toward the great world about him.

Many things might put terror into the heart of primitive man. There was the blinding flash of lightning across the storm-darkened heavens, followed by the deafening crash of thunder. There were the powerful waters washing away everything before them after the cloudburst. There was ominous night with its strange, screeching sounds coming out of the bush, or echoing in the forests. There was the wail of the wind sounding like the moan of a friend when that mysterious something happened to him—something that made him no longer able to walk, one who would soon lie listless and be carried away to the hills, a prey for the vultures and wild beasts.

For here another mystery was impressing itself upon the dawning mind of Old Anthropology Adam—death. It is a mystery to this very day, in many cases even to medicine. Its puzzling strangeness, coupled with sorrow and grief, overwhelms one still when it occurs in his immediate environment. It was even more of a mystery to primitive man, since it often occurred violently, and the quick transition from a healthful life to sudden death was shocking indeed. Neither was it quite conceivable that the big chief who was the terror of the land might suddenly become as powerless as the slain bison. What, he wondered, could it be that made a person lie down and be almost nothing at all ?

The very same person that became nothing at all may have been seen later, quite as he was before—in dream or delusion. His very dreams filled Old Adam with awe and astonishment. How could he lie down to rest and, while he was lying there, go hunting, trap an animal, and feast on its meat ? Even to-day, in the very moment of waking, many a man finds himself grasping for the object of his dream as if it should be there in reality. Is there any wonder, then, that primitive man should be puzzled over what had become of the food he had been dreaming of ? Like the child, Old Anthropology Adam confused his imagination with his experiences, his dreams with his realities. Yet the two did not tally at all. What was this stuff that dreams were made of ?

All these mysteries that worried the groping mind of primitive man could be allayed by the single idea of " doubles." Such an idea may have been suggested by the shadow of himself which he saw on sunny afternoons or moonlight nights. There was actually a " double " of himself, following him wherever he turned. There was, then, the man one could see and get hold of, and his " double " that one did not always see. But it was there just the same. Now as Old Anthropology Adam was lying asleep under the tree or in the cave, it was not he, but his " double," that was hunting and feasting on the prey. Therefore it did not do him much good when he awoke. For it was only when he was together with his " double " that he was himself and things went well. Once his " double " left him, he might fall asleep or become ill, and if the " double " did not return, he might come to be nothing —that is, dead. It was for this reason, too, that one could see a person even though he was dead. One did not really see him, but his " double," and " doubles " persist for ever.

This " double " idea was extended, not only to humans and animals, but to everything in nature. It was before the time that primitive man learned to consider himself the crown of creation. It was still the day when he did not have the consciousness of being singled out from his environment. Like the child of to-day, he drew no line between himself and the world about him. He was " double " ; therefore, all things were " double."

As Old Anthropology Adam went about building up this idea of " doubles," little did he realize how much trouble it was going to cause him. It proved a sort of boomerang. Relieving man of some of his fears, it came to add many others. Take the case of a very formidable enemy. The enemy died. Instead of being relieved by his death, Adam's woes increased tremendously. He might have been able to cope with his enemy living ; but he was not equal to the " double " now that it was liberated from the body and thereby unlimited by space and time and physical barriers. The " double " might be visible or invisible ; he might be here and there and everywhere within a second. He could strike and do all sorts of mean tricks in the world of darkness in which he operated. The " double " thus became a ghost, and the ghost of an evil man, of a deadly enemy or a cruel chieftain, was a demon. And there were also the demons of nature, such as thunder, hurricanes, and forest fires.

To be sure, there were also good " doubles," favourable ghosts, such as the " doubles," of one's beloved or of the friendly forces in nature. But the harm that the demons might do one by far overshadowed the good that one might expect from the friendly spirits.

Harsh, cruel, and menacing as the environment of Old Anthropology Adam was, it became still harder and even more threatening because of the " doubles," ghosts, and demons that thickly populated it.

## II

Man has always found remedies for his ills, whether real or imaginary. The remedies are on the same plane and appropriate to the ills. Old Anthropology Adam may not have been very cunning ; but he knew how to play off one " double " against another. If there were " doubles " that could come down in the night to do harm to one's cave or hut, there was a rattle—with a " double " as well—of which the threatening " double " was quite wary. Get after the demon with a rattle and he would take to his " double " heels. What was in the rattle that drove off the devil ? Something inherent in it which was as real as the demon, and for all that, the rattle was a rattle and no more. Its power to charm, its *mana* quality, did not distinguish it from other objects used in the hut.

Of course, to us there is not much sense in driving off spirits with rattles. Neither do we see any reason to worry about what a spirit may do. But to those who stand in awe of spirits, the rattle may be a powerful charm. Even to this day in eastern Europe, the peasants expel the devil with incense. If a rattle will drive off a demon and incense will chase the devil away, why should not a horseshoe bring good luck ? Certainly luck is as evasive a phenomenon as a spirit, and the iron of the horseshoe as tangible as the rattle or incense. It is all the same phenomenon which is called *mana*, and so many of the " initiated," civilized people who ridicule the *mana* of Old Anthropology Adam will take very seriously their own superstition of a horseshoe, or of Friday the thirteenth, or of a broken mirror, which is sure to bring bad luck since the breaking has liberated the spirit, that is, the " double " that dwelled therein.

Thus, Old Anthropology Adam found in *mana* one way of counteracting the multitude of untoward forces in his world. Another way of dealing with the world of animal wills and " doubles " was to charm them, just as one charms a snake. You get them to do your bidding by simply knowing how. The spirit of water may withhold the rain, wishing in his anger to dry up the world, to parch and destroy it. But when the wise man, the shaman, the medicine man, the magician, comes out and throws up sand to the sky and the sand comes down like rain, then the spirit of water must give up the rain. This magic way of dealing with natural forces and spirits is a kind of activity-*mana*. Apparently it is a form of persuasion that cannot be refused. Again, one may question the logic of it—compelling the spirit of water to give up the rain for such a small reason—yet it is no more illogical than the very belief in a spirit of water that withholds the rain.

*Mana*, or magic, is a quaint way of dealing with supernatural powers, hardly conceivable to modern man. It is so old that its origin lies side by side with that of man himself. Its sense or motive is hidden from us. We can see in it only the product of a mind groping alone in the haze of muddled thinking. To us, it is a single-handed, mechanistic method of coping with an unequal opponent, but without this weapon man might have succumbed beneath his burden of fears.

As social life developed among humans, man was no longer so helpless. He acquired new ways of dealing with other beings within his social group, and he carried over some of these into his relationship with the supernatural. Instead of depending on sheer, senseless mechanics, it occurred to him that he might obtain the desired result in a more natural manner. He might deal with the supernatural in much the same way as he dealt with his fellow-men. He might impose upon the " double " by threat or win its favour by offering gift or compliment.

This is a social relationship entered into with the " double." It involves an emotional attitude toward the supernatural power. At first, it was crude and mercenary. There may have been neither adoration nor humility in it, but it was the making of religion. Once man entered into a relationship with the supernatural, the affinity was bound to grow in importance and omnipotence as man became more and more dependent upon it. He was started on the way to faith and god. Humble indeed was the beginning of his religious sentiments, but humbler still was the beginning of his gods.

And this is the story of how Nathuram, the rascal, became a god :

Nathuram was a rascal, that everybody knew, although no one had ever learned who he was or where he had come from. Apparently he wandered down from the hills and kept himself in the woods of Rajputana. No sooner did he arrive than he was heard from in an unsavoury way.

First it was the wife of Surenda. She was returning from a visit and was stepping sprightly along the road to Marwar, when she felt something spring at her, gasping in a dreadful way. She thought it was a snake, or perhaps a monkey gone mad. Then she saw the dark eyes, burning like coals in the swarthy head, the large hand with its iron grip dragging her after him into the woods.

When Surenda's wife emerged from the woods, she uncovered her head and walked, not in the middle of the road, but at the side—the path of sinners. Weeping, she reached her husband's door and prostrated herself before him.

Then it was the wife of another, and yet another, until one day, there were as many as five women who had been caught by Nathuram and made victims of his passion. There were many expeditions sent into the woods to capture him, but he was not to be caught.

Finally a little girl of the tribe, the daughter of a priest, was seized by Nathuram and kept for a whole day in the woods. She fainted on her father's doorstep, unable to tell of the torture and the violence that she had undergone. But no telling was necessary. Just one glance at the poor little maiden and they knew— Nathuram.

So all husbands and fathers took an oath that they would not return to their huts until they had caught Nathuram, living or dead. And they got him along the side of a stream as it ran down a short but steep hill. And as they beheaded him, the head of the rascal rolled down the hill, winking one eye and wearing a strange grin. It finally fell into the water, but still it winked and still it grinned.

Wives were safe in Rajputana and so were young girls, and all was quiet again. But no quiet knew the souls of the Rajput. The men could not banish from their minds the wink in dead Nathuram's eye and the grin on his face. And the women-folk of Rajputana were awakened at night by dreadful dreams and nightmares, all brought about by the dead rascal Nathuram. They could almost feel his breath and his grasp about their waists.

And so again the wise men of Rajputana met in council and decided to placate the angry spirit. A feast was prepared in his honour, in which a figure representing him was carried down the hill to the bank of the river, and songs were sung, telling of the powers and superhuman virility of Nathuram, that all the women of Rajputana could not satisfy his sexual hunger.

Seasons came and seasons passed. The young of Rajputana grew old, and the old were no more. New young folks, who had not witnessed the execution of Nathuram, filled the huts. They knew of him only by hearsay. Nathuram's spirit, too, apparently had grown old and less bothersome. No longer did he worry the memories of the men, nor disturb the sleep of the women. Yet the feast of Nathuram continued to increase in importance in its place in the life of Rajputana.

Both men and women liked the songs about the things Nathuram did, and all enjoyed the dances showing in action the life of Nathuram in Rajputana. These dances were executed by the women around a huge figure of Nathuram, a nude monster of sexuality. Time wore off the ill-feeling that the people of Marwar had borne toward the former rascal. He was now the God of Fertility ; barren women looked to him for deliverance from their sterility, and on the night the bride first visited her husband, an image of Nathuram was placed beside her on the couch. Nathuram, the rascal, had become the god of Marwar.

*A demon of love*
(*Adapted from an old English ballad*)

### III

With so many opportunities for god production and the ease with which the gods took root in the mind of primitive man, it is not at all surprising that Old Anthropology Adam had a great many of them. Whatever played a part in his life was food for his thought and cause for mental speculation. If it was strong enough to stir his soul and overshadow his whole being, he carried it right up to the mountain of the gods.

There were gods for the sun and the moon and the stars ; there were gods for the woods and for the river and for the fishes that swarmed therein. And there were people who became gods. In some places, when a man died, an image of him was made and placed along with other divine images of the household—the initial step in the development of ancestor worship.

At first, the god of birth was only one among many on the mountain of the gods. But many factors were driving this divinity to the head of the divine family. True, it did not have the advantage of the first and considerable start the gods of fear had. But these latter were bound to lose as man grew less afraid of his immediate environment, when his fancy ran along more pleasant channels. In fact, the very god of fear was building a temple for the god of birth and generation. For fear was a strain upon man's soul and he had to find relief somewhere. This was afforded him by the god of procreation. Even now, people living under great strain seek relief in sexual activity. All the energy collecting under the strain was released in the channel of sexuality.

Then again, the god of birth and fertility was associated with another great force in the life of Old Anthropology Adam : physical hunger. He wanted to eat, and the hunger for food was as potent as the desire for the life upon which the fear gods were rasping. Birth of the young of animals meant additional food ; besides, it was easier to trap the young animal. The generative force was also the harbinger of spring, when life generally eases up, when the first signs of abundance are manifested. The life of primitive man was chiefly a physical matter and it was the creative force that supplied his needs.

There was still another element in the selection of the generative force as king of the gods. Birth was the opposite of death. The sorrow that came in death was relieved by the joy that a new birth ushered in. The more man pondered over death, the more his thought turned to birth, making it the chief encouraging event in his life. The fact, too, that the father of the clan or family was also the progenitor, or birth-giver, added import to the god of birth, just as the god of birth gave prestige to the birth-giver in the family. One reacted upon the other to their mutual benefit.

Another element that made for the supremacy of the generative divinity was the order of worship. Man served his god in accordance with the function over which the god presided. Putting on masks, making a terrible racket, moaning, shouting, shrieking, all served to let off energy in the service of any divinity. But the erotic dances, representing the activities of the birth god, the songs that we to-day would call obscene, and the physical union of the sexes that became a definite part and the climax of the services to the fertility god, made this particular service a source of unusually pleasurable excitement and exaltation. Not only was the birth god gradually growing in importance through the realization of his powers in the minds of the people, but the very

*Anglo-Saxon phallic figures*

service that the people offered to this god enhanced his value and his importance in their eyes. The god became associated or " conditioned," as the Behaviourists to-day would say, with the most supreme moments of happiness and joy in the life of the community.

Finally the god of birth came to be served at the most opportune moment—the time of spring. Love came into religion when loving was in the air. To-day, " in the spring a young man's fancy lightly turns to thoughts of love." There is a response in the physical organism of man to the great regenerating changes that occur in nature. That is the time when humanity revolts against the bonds, when " freedom rings," and man seeks to escape the prohibitions that social customs have developed about his love life.

So in time, the worship of the generative force in nature came to overlap all other forms of worship and the god of fertility was the leading god on the mountain, in fact, if not in name. The service to the god of generation spread beyond the limits of his temple and into the provinces of other gods. Whoever the god was, or however he was served, the service was an overture, or a preparation—a sort of warming up for the real ceremony which was to follow, the ceremonial dances and songs and other expressions of the sexual emotion that came into the religious sphere through the gateway of the god of birth.

Old Anthropology Adam realized intuitively what is so obvious to us to-day : that the emotion of love and the sentiment of religion have very much in common ; both are to a large extent indefinite, general sensations, arousing the entire organism and ending in an approach to ecstasy ; both are ways of escape from an oppressing environment, a means of relieving mental strain.

*From an old Egyptian urn*

No wonder then that the two have become intertwined and that all other gods partook of the sacrifices that Old Anthropology Adam so generously offered his god of fertility—his god of love.

. . . . . . .

There is a legend that has always captivated the fancy of men and women in all parts of the world. It is the story of the Sleeping Beauty.

A beautiful princess of the blood and of spirit is forcefully held captive in the tower of a castle guarded by dragons or men of evil. In time, a youth appears on the scene, a young prince charming who slays the dragons or evil men, and liberates the princess. Of course, the two fall in love with each other, marry in royal fashion, and live happily ever after.

Some such relationship exists historically between the emotion of love and the sentiment of religion. At first, love was royally free, without bonds, barriers, or restrictions of any sort. In time, organized society laid its hand upon the free exercise of the love passion and imprisoned it. A number of taboos, like dragons, were woven about it. Love was forbidden with certain persons, as incestuous love. It was forbidden with many persons at once, as promiscuous love. It was forbidden in free and open spaces, before the eyes of the people. Love was forbidden altogether unless men ran the gauntlet of capture, barter, or bans. There were ample reasons for all these barriers thus placed in the path of love. Yet they oppressed the spirit of man. His whole being rebelled for his thwarted sex instinct.

It was then that Prince Religion came to liberate the imprisoned Princess of Love. Religion, born of fear and nursed in darkness, raised itself by fusing with love. What was forbidden in ordinary life was allowed in the life of religion. Bonds were broken and taboos raised, once people entered into the temple of the gods. What was desired in lust was sanctified in song and prayer. That which was *kadosh*, taboo, unaccessible, forbidden the very touch or the slightest approach, was purified and elevated to supreme duty by the magic wand of faith. The very mother-in-law, who was not to appear under the same roof or tree with her son-in-law, who must flee at sight of him, could be had for wife as the dessert after a religious feast. The other fellow's wife, union with whom could be had only under sure forfeit of one's life, could be secured at the motion of one's finger during the incantations of the priest. All this only served to strengthen even further the bonds between love and religion, culminating in a marriage that was to be both happy and lasting.

# CHAPTER III

# IN THE FOUNDRY OF THE GODS

*In his own image*
*He created his god.*

## I

THERE is a sacred corner in every dwelling—even the humblest—in the East. Whatever the hut may lack—and it will be lacking in most modern comforts of the home—it will not be without its little shrine. There is sure to be an icon, an image of a saint, graven or in paint, standing on a plain triangular piece of board which is set in between two walls of the house.

Before it there is ever a light burning. The woman of the house will not fail the shrine. The last morsel of bread may be gone from the larder, but never the last drop of oil or piece of tallow to keep the fire burning before the eyes of the saint, who, in turn, will never fail the family of the house. Times may be hard, life scarcely bearable. Starvation, illness, death itself, may stalk within ; but dark as it all may be, the family is never without the consolation and hope that the graven image brings. In the humblest dwelling of the East there is always a light—a light that never fails, physically or symbolically.

There is an eternal light ceaselessly burning before the Holy Ark of the synagogue, there is a light over the altar of the church, there is one illuminating the crescent of the mosque. Similarly, there was a light upon the hearth in ancient times. Whenever man had a light within him, he lit a fire outside of him. So long as there is faith in the world, so long will the light kindled many thousands of years ago never fail.

The universal, eternal light is symbolic of universal, eternal life. Primitive people seem to have felt it, somehow. It dawned upon them as they produced their fire, rubbing together two pieces of wood, one laid upon the ground and the other held vertically upon it. This action being so suggestive and the result analogous to life, the two sticks have been associated with the two life forces and their use has almost universally received a sexual interpretation.

Somewhere, somehow, life began. Whether it was by the word of God : " Let there be " and it was ; whether it came flying across space from another planet ; whether it began as an accidental chemical mixture ; however life came into the world, it has never ceased to be. Living objects perish, life never dies. The life of an individual comes to an end ; families die out, tribes, races ; but the human species lives on, the stream of life never stops. It flows on and on for ever, from its inception in the formative period of our planet, through its tributaries of the countless species of living forms—plants or animals.

When living things were small, consisting of a single microscopic cell, life was continued by growth. The amœba grew so big that it split in two ; it exchanged its single old age for a double life of youth. An amœba could be destroyed but it would never die.

This tiny bit of life grew larger and, in time, when it split, the two parts stuck together instead of separating. It was no longer

*Venus and Cupid fulfilling their
mission of love*

unicellular ; it became a group of cells working together. Then specialization set in. Some parts of the animal undertook its locomotion, others did the digesting, still others concerned themselves with continuing the life that was in the living being. These were the sex cells. Their function was to perpetuate the light of life so that it might never fail.

At first, their work was simple ; they merely grew into another being. Again specialization set in—the sex cells developed variously, becoming male and female. They must now be united before a new creature could come into existence. But they still grew on the same body. In time, the organism had only

one kind of cell, either male or female.  So it was that out of sex
emerged the sex cells and out of sex cells came the sexes.

Prometheus stole the fire from the gods and brought it down
as a gift to mankind.  That fire is still kept burning and will ever
go on warming and enlightening the world.  Venus sprang from
the foam of the sea and is for ever serving those who are in love ; so
life sprang from among the streams and mists of the deep, when
the earth was in its formative state, and is now being continued
to the end of time by the agency of sex.

## II

When Old Anthropology Adam let his mind speculate on sex,
he did not see it as the continuity of life.  This latter idea is of
more recent date, having been borne in on the waves of evolution.

*A Phallic amulet*

It is still rather new to the man in the street.  To Old Adam,
sex was a force bringing new life.  A baby was born in the tribe,
an offspring came to an animal in the herd, new blossoms
appeared upon the branches of the tree, presaging new fruit.
There was someone behind all this, some mysterious force giving
life.  Like all great forces in nature it was a god—a god unseen—
the god of sex and birth.

How did primitive man conceive of this new god ?  His concept
of the sex divinity follows a course similar to the course of the
development of sex in nature.  This new god was originally
neither male nor female, but just sex.  It was the generative force,
not the generator or reproducer.  He conceived it as the sex
organs, the lingam and yoni in union, minus the bodies.  There
was little or no regard as yet for the individuals who bore these
organs.

In India, a smooth, round stone, rising out of another formed
like an elongated saucer, suggestive of the lingam and yoni in
union, represented the powerful divinity, Siva.  A favourite god

in Southern Celebes is Karaeng lowe. He is a powerful spirit
figured under the form of the lingam and yoni in union. In
Celebes, too, images of the generative organs are found on the
posts of houses raised in honour of the fallen warriors. The
Brahmans represent this union by a cylinder hanging from a vase
which is set into a pedestal. The vase represents the goddess, the
yoni, and the cylinder the god, the lingam. Cakes kneaded in
the form of the lingam and yoni were eaten at the marriage rite
of the Greeks. The Bayanzi in the Congo basin mould these
images out of clay and adorn them with feathers.

Representations of the lingam and yoni were current all over
Europe. As late as the sixteenth century these figures, made of
wax, were offered to Saint Foutin at Varailles in Provence,
France. They were suspended from the ceiling of his chapel and
were so numerous that when the wind stirred them, the lingam
struck against the yoni, to the apparent disturbance of the faithful
at their devotions.

### III

Later, man came to seek his god of generation, not in the union
of the sex organs, but in these organs themselves. He deified the
male or female in man and animal. An old Egyptian legend
offers an explanation of how the lingam came to be worshipped :
Isis and Osiris were powerful gods of the Egyptian hierarchy.
They were brother and sister. They were also husband and wife.
When Osiris was murdered by Typhon and his body cut up and
scattered in all directions, Isis went about collecting the parts.
She found all of them except his lingam. For a long time she
continued her search, but never did she come upon a trace of it.
So she finally caused a wooden lingam to be made and this image
she held as very sacred. That is how the lingam, in wood or
stone, came to be so common in Egypt.

Now, man has always sought to elaborate his house of worship.
Pyramid, pagoda, or steeple, do not primarily serve a utilitarian
purpose. They are there to lend glory to the divinity and to
impress the onlooker with the sacredness of the place. In like
manner, Old Anthropology Adam elaborated his figures of lingam
and yoni, not only with artistic decorations, but with bodies of
tremendous proportions and striking appearance. The lingam
and yoni remained the miniature representations of the generative
divinity ; the male and female figures came to be the full images
of the gods of fertility.

Here again the evolution of the generative god followed the
development of sex in nature. As man came to clothe his sex god

with the human form, he had one individual contain both sex organs. Janus of the Greeks was not only double-headed, but also double-sexed, hermaphroditic, like a plant that produces both stamens and pistils in the same floral envelope. Siva, the great god of India, is the Reproducer. He was originally a single

*Brahma created himself double, both male and female*

substance ; but of his own free will he divided himself into male and female.

We find a similar development in the story of Purusa, the Soul of the Universe. At first, Purusa was alone. " He did not enjoy happiness, he desired a second being. So he caused himself to fall asunder in two parts. Thence arose a husband and a wife. From them men were born. But she reflected, ' How does he, after having produced me from himself, cohabit with me ? ' So she became a cow, but he became a bull ; from them kine were produced. Then she became a mare and he turned himself into a stallion. From them the whole family of animals with undivided hoofs were produced. In this manner, pairs of all creatures whatsoever, down to ants, came into the world."

But the hermaphroditic gods were only a transition in the development of the individuals, male and female gods, and, as such, they were short-lived. They persisted into classical times, but only under the veil of mysticism for exotic natures. Creating his gods in his own image, man began to conceive of them as male or female, like the men and women serving them. We now have male and female gods.

The Ewhe of West Africa make an image of red clay which rudely represents the human figure. " It is generally male, rarely female, and always entirely nude. It is always represented as squatting down and looking at the lingam, which is enormously disproportionate. When female, the figure is provided with long pointed breasts and the necessary adjuncts."

In the Babar Archipelago, there is a festival, Upu-lero, in honour of the sun. "An emblem of the generative force of the sun is erected in the form of a standard flying a pennant of white cotton almost five feet long. The pennant is cut in the form of a man, and fastened to it, a lingam and scrotum, an apt suggestion of the orgies enacted below."

At every turn, we run into more of these male and female gods. In the forests of Central Africa, there are little rustic temples made of palm-fronds and poles. Within them male and female figures, nearly life-size, with over-emphasized sex organs, represent the generative principles.

The Roman god, Priapus, was represented in passion, and every bride of Roman aristocracy was supposed to sacrifice her virginity to him. To quote Saint Augustine : " This custom was once regarded as very honest and religious by Roman women, who obliged the young brides to come and sit upon the masculine monstrosity representing Priapus." The Babylonian goddess, Mylitta, or the Greek Aphrodite was represented as a naked woman, the acme of allurement, according to the tastes and standards of the times in art and love.

There is a beautiful legend symbolic of the evolutionary way in which man created his god of generation : The sky was the father and the earth was the mother ; the two were for ever lying in union, the sky weighing down upon the earth. Whatever off- spring resulted therefrom were smothered by the weight of the father. But one day, one of the sons managed to work his way out, so he pierced the sky with his spear, raising it high above the earth. The pair were separated, but they were no longer fruitful. Another son, realizing the cause of the parents' sterility, came and married them according to the rite of the tribe.

Once primitive man conceived birth and generation as a divine process, he naturally looked upon the male and female gods as its joint agents. Consequently, when he was desirous of regeneration, it occurred to him to marry these gods, so that universal birth might follow the divine union, just as the birth of children follows the union of man and woman.

Testimony of this survives. At Calah, the old Assyrian capital, the marriage of the god Nabu appears to have been annually

*At the Altar of Priapus*

celebrated on the third day of the month Iyyar, which corresponds to May. The marriage of Zeus and Hera was performed annually in various parts of Greece. Among the Bambara of the Niger Basin in West Africa, the male and female idols are believed to couple at the time of the annual sacrifices offered before the rainy season. This marriage of the gods may have been accomplished by imitative magic. Without appealing directly to them, or participating in their life, man could perform an act which would be a suggestion the gods were bound to take. In other words, he could marry the gods by marrying himself. Human copulation would bring about copulation of the generative gods, wherever they might be, and thereby bring fertility to the world.

Suggestion was also resorted to by the people of Central America even to the time when the white men first visited them. When planting time came, they were extremely anxious that the sowing of the seed be done in a most auspicious hour for generation. Four days previously, therefore, the men separated from their wives in order that on the night preceding the planting they might indulge their passions to the fullest extent. This intercourse was even enjoined upon the people by the priest as a religious duty, in default of which it was not lawful to sow the seed. Certain persons are even said to have been designated and appointed to join in sexual union at the very moment when the first seed was deposited in the ground.

Even to-day in some parts of Java, when the season of the blossom on the rice is at hand, the husbandman and his wife visit their fields after dark and unite for the purpose of promoting the growth of the crop. It is a form of *mana*, a magical way of getting the generative divinities to do likewise and to bless the world with fertility.

Sometimes the suggestion is extended through persons who seem already to be in favour with the generative gods. Having received the blessing of the fertility divinities, they are in them-selves fertility gods in a small way. Among the Baganda of Central Africa, the birth of twins is the sign of a godlike power of fertility. Some little time after the twins are born, a ceremony is performed which is supposed to transfer the fertility powers of the parents to the plantains. In this ceremony the mother lies down in the thick grass near the house and places a flower of the plantain between her legs. Then the husband comes and brushes the flower away with his lingam. After this, the parents may go through the country, performing dances in the gardens of friends and favoured people, spreading the abundance of their fertility powers.

IV

If man arranged the marriage of the gods we should not be surprised to find him inviting himself to the wedding and partici-pating in it. A ceremony of this nature survives among some of the tribes of Africa. The inhabitants believe in the sun as the male god and the earth as the female. Once a year, at the beginning of the rainy season, the marriage of the two takes place. On this occasion, pigs and dogs are sacrificed in profusion ; and the men and women indulge in saturnalia. During the cere-monies the sun is supposed to come down into the holy fig tree to fertilize the earth. To facilitate his descent, a ladder with seven rungs is considerately placed at his disposal. It is set up under a tree and adorned with carved figures of the birds whose shrill clarions herald the approach of the sun in the east. For all that, the marriage of the sun and earth is too abstract for the primitive mind. Consequently, this mystic union is dramatically represented in public by individuals taking the parts of the divinities, amid song and dance and by real union of the sexes under the tree.

The Oraons of Bengal celebrate the marriage of heaven and earth by remarrying their village priest and his wife. After the marriage ceremony, all eat and drink and make merry ; they dance and sing frank love songs and finally indulge in the wildest orgies with the sole object of making mother earth fruitful.

Similarly, long ago the marriage of the sky god Zeus to the grain goddess Demeter, was represented by the union of a priestess of Demeter and a hierophant. The torches were extinguished and the pair descended into a murky place, while the throng of worshippers awaited in anxious suspense the result of the mystic union, upon which they believed their salvation depended. After a time the hierophant reappeared and, in the blaze of the night, silently exhibited an ear of corn—the fruit of divine marriage. However, their intercourse was only dramatic and symbolical, since the hierophant incapacitated himself by the application of hemlock.

Sometimes only one of the gods needed to be thus substituted as the other one was already concretely represented in animate or inanimate form. When the natives of Bengal marry their male god to the goddess of water, they make an image of the male in wood and immerse it in the water. In this way the two are united and the well which has been thus consecrated will ever be an abundant source of water.

The Indians of Peru had a god in human form done in stone. This idol they would wed to a beautiful maiden of fourteen years. All the villagers took part in the ceremony, which lasted for three days and was attended with great revelry. The girl thereafter remained a virgin and sacrificed to the idol for the people.

Not always, however, did the consort of the god remain untouched in her marriage. The Akikuyu of British East Africa even to-day worship the snake of a certain river and, at intervals of several years, they marry the snake god to women, especially to young girls. For this purpose, huts are built by order of the medicine men who consummate the sacred marriage with the credulous female devotees. If the girls do not repair to the huts of their own accord in sufficient numbers, they are seized and dragged thither to the embrace of the deity. The offspring of these mystic unions are fathered by the god, and there are many youngsters among these people who pass as children of the divinity.

In the temples of Egypt, a woman slept near the image of

Ammon as his " divine consort " and was said to have no intercourse with a man. It was the queen herself usually, since the
kings of Egypt were actually begotten by Ammon, who cohabited
with the queen in the assumed form of the reigning pharaoh. In
Babylon, a woman was kept in the lofty temple of Bel as his wife.
This is how the temple priestesses came into being. In India
to-day, where prostitutes are attached to a temple, they are first
married to a god.

It is not altogether unusual for a priest to represent the god in
his conjugal activities. In tribes where virginity is sacred, it is
the god who is to deflower the maidens. He operates through his
priests, who charge a fee for this divine service. Poor girls who
cannot afford the fee may grow into spinsterhood, since no one
will marry them unless they have been deflowered in the temple.
A vestige of this rite we could find in Europe down to quite
modern times in the so-called *jus primæ noctis*, the right to the bride
for the first night, which belonged to the lord of the manor.
Every maiden living on his land was to offer herself to him before
she joined her husband. Sometimes he would relinquish this
right for a price ; at others, he would insist upon it.

Not every marriage of a human with a god ended in happiness.
Sometimes it was fatal to the maiden—like the bee, once he mates
with the queen, he must die. So it is in the Maldive Islands,
where the Prince of the Sea is worshipped. On the shore, close
to the water, there is a temple with a window looking out upon
the sea. Every month lots are drawn and he upon whom the lot
falls must give up his daughter to be married to the prince. She
must be a young virgin. After being adorned in many ways, she
is taken into the temple and left there for the night. When she is
found in the morning, she is a maid no longer—and dead.

## V

The substitution of an image or a human in the marriage of
the gods for one of the partners served to separate the divinities
by sexes in the minds of the people. If the human being was
married to a god, it was, to be sure, to represent a divinity ; the
emphasis, however, was not upon the god present by human
surrogate, but upon the one that remained in its full mystic glory.
When a woman was married to a god, it necessarily became a
worship of the god. When a man was married to a goddess, the
emphasis was naturally on the latter and the services by degrees
came to be the worship of the female principle.

In time there grew up a multitude of gods of fertility, representing the male and female principles. At first, the same fertility god

may have served the purpose of all living beings, plants, animals, and man. In time, even here specialization set in, although the boundaries were never clearly drawn. There were gods that brought the spring and saw to the fertility of the fields. There were those that looked after the reproduction of animals. Others were concerned with fertility among humans, while still others fanned the flames of passion and love.

As the custom of marrying the gods became universal, colouring the entire religious experience, other divinities also assumed, in time, a sexual meaning. Gods sprang up out of the sexual experience of man or were sexualized with all the erotic paraphernalia carried over from the worship of the generative divinities. Faith became love.

Old Anthropology Adam long walked in the darkness. When we first hear of him we find him already carrying a torch of light to blaze his way. It is a torch of light and fire, the eternal fire, the fire that never fails—the fire of love. Within this flame the base metal of crude religious belief has been refined and forged into the beautiful institution of the present day, and this same refining process has, in turn, purged the fire itself.

Just as sex deepened the religious emotion, added joy to the religious experience, and lifted it up to ecstasy, so did religion add to the crude sex experience the element of spirituality, adoration, and devotion, that made love the great erotic and overwhelming spiritual experience that it is to-day.

# CHAPTER IV

# THE SPIRIT OF LOVE IN GOD AND MAN

*Even as the passion of man*
*Is the love of the gods.*

I

AS you look upon the map of Europe, you notice a strip of land hanging down like an old man's whiskers into the Mediterranean waters. This is the troublesome Balkan peninsula, mother of many conflicts, including the last great war. Further down, the whiskers grow thin and scattered, splitting up into tiny bits. This is the land of the ancient Greeks, the clever people who stood at the gateway of the continents, collecting all that came out of the East and sending it forth into the West, retouched a bit here and there, with the attached label " made in Greece."

Among the numerous things the Greeks collected were also gods. Many a Greek divinity when scratched will be found to hail from some country back east, or from an island in one of the seas not far off. It may have seen better days on the banks of the Nile, in the streets of Babylon, in the bushes of Ethiopa, or in Cathay. But its locks were evenly trimmed and its nose straightened à la Greek.

Like all good collectors, the Greeks had a sense of order. They could not let all these gods roam aimlessly about Hellas. So a mountain was dedicated to the folk that were divine, where they might live their own lives with as little interference in the affairs of man as man deemed necessary. All gods were delegated to Mount Olympus.

Once on the mountain, they went about their lives much the same as the humans in the valley below. There, god struggled with god for power or love, the vanquished undergoing torture or eternal imprisonment. There, they loved and suffered, their hearts eaten away by jealousy ; there, they also loved and were happy, basking in the sunshine of bliss. On Olympus they were born, grew up, begat children, and there, some of them perished, like the mere humans at the foot of the mountain.

Fate and luck played their parts above as well as below. Some of the gods, for all their divine presence, cut no figure at all, while others dominated, not only their immediate family, but the very length and breadth of Olympus. There was Hera, mother of gods, not much of a figure in the feasts and festivities on the mountain, yet a kindly creature, in whose arms her many children might find peace and protection. Yonder was Aphrodite, charm-

ing in her beauty, sprung from the foam of the sea when Poseidon
was good-naturedly at play. There was Pan, the merrymaker of
the divine dwelling-place, stirring the heart with love and laughter.
There was chaste Artemis, athletic goddess of the hunt ; Hermes
with his winged feet, fleet messenger of the gods ; and the swart
and limping Hephæstus, their mechanic, hammering out the
heavy armours on his smoky forge. And there was Pallas Athena,
goddess of wisdom and learning, sprung fully armed from the

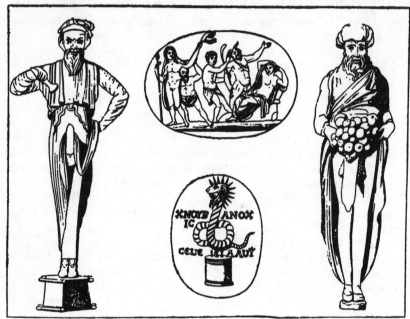

*Figures of Pan*

head of Zeus, best loved of all the gods and goddesses, but most
cherished by the intellectual Athenians.

One could go on indefinitely naming the worthies among the
gods, not to mention the lesser lights sauntering about and in
between the mighty on the Mount. Yet, to one who knew his
way among them, they were not so numerous after all. Many
were the names entered on the Divine Register and many the
passports held by the Keeper of Records of individual divinities.
Yet, in their essence, many were much the same, changing only
with time and locality. Gods like Fascinus, Tutunus, Mutinus,
Liber, Bacchus, all bore different names ; but they were all one
god. They were the same as Priapus, a naturalized citizen on
Olympus, having been born in Lampsacus on the Hellespont.

Once we leave Hellas and wander about lands and continents peopled by man and god, the aliases among gods are by far greater than among men. The very same lady, fanning the embers of love in the hearts of humans, whom we know as Venus, was called Mylitta, or Milidath, by the Assyrians, which to them meant genetrix, mother. To the Persians she was Anahita, and the Arabs called her Alitta. The Chaldeans knew her as Delephat, the Babylonians as Ishtar, the Saracens as Cobar. In the Bible we read of her as Assera, or Astarte. Wherever she was and whatever her name, she was female, young, beautiful, desirable, guarding over the passion of sex and over the sentiment of love.

Thus, setting out on our venture among the gods, we must be guided neither by name nor by origin. Our criterion should be the function of the divinity—the thing he was supposed to do for mankind, in return for which he was rewarded in worship.

## II

Many were the favours that the worthies on the Mount were bestowing upon man below. Whatever he found in the world about him, whether it was a ready cave or a ripe fruit, man took it as a gift from the gods. All that he got by his own effort was also accredited to the divine powers. Were they not guiding him along the path of success, steadying his bow and properly setting his net? Pious people to-day see "the finger of the Lord" in many things happening about them. Old Anthropology Adam was even more god-intoxicated. His world was absolutely god-controlled.

Man may ever have been the ungrateful creature he is now reputed to be. Yet he was never an ingrate to his god. He always returned full value in worship, prayer, and sacrifice for the favours that the higher powers bestowed upon him. If Zeus had ever called the gods and people together for an accounting, the final balance would have shown a divine indebtedness to mankind, rather than the contrary.

Among all these divine gifts there was one that man even more fully appreciated ; one might say, over-appreciated. It was that awe-inspiring power that ushered in new life, birth, generation. Whether it was a new stalk breaking out of the black soil, the first quiver of a new leaf upon the limb of a tree, the thud of a new-born dropping in the herd, or the first cry of a babe on the bed of hides in his cave—it delighted man's heart. It overwhelmed him with its shroud of mystery no less than with the boundless joy he felt, yet could not explain.

Standing there at the scene of regeneration, Old Anthropology

Adam had neither benefit of priest or of sacrament, nor the thought or the knowledge of religion as such. Still, there he was, a worshipper before what was to be later revealed to him as "divine presence." He was awed, mystified, rejoicing, adoring. Above all, he was exalted, well on the way toward the state of ecstasy, in which his heart seemed to be melting away in happiness ; a state man was later to conceive of as entering into communion with the "all", the cosmos, the universe, God.

Of all that man received from the hands of the gods nothing was so highly prized as the gift of love and none was more readily and with greater exaltation repaid in its own kind. The generative god served man via sex ; man worshipped him in return sexually. The god whose will it was to bring abundance to the earth would be glad to see man, his humble servant, seeking in his own small way to enhance abundance about him. The power whose function it was to cause births through the union of the sexes would feel flattered to see humans in union. It was a way of realizing the will of the god among men. It was akin to our belief that a righteous God would have righteousness prevail in human society—a realization of the Kingdom of Heaven upon earth. Sex worship thus became the appropriate recompense, reward, blessing—however one may designate the religious attitude—for the revered god of love and procreation.

Like all forms of religious service, the worship of the creative power was not only pleasing to the god, but it also enraptured man. It carried with it the usual pleasures accompanying the exercise of the sexual function. Furthermore, by its fusion with other mental components entering into the religious attitude, passion became fired and all-embracing. Grief and pain often intensify passion ; fear, awe, and devotion are oil on the flame of love.

Still, sex worship did for man even more than that. It was the redeemer of his imprisoned soul. It provided an outlet for those sexual passions which the race had known in its infancy, but which later had apparently been driven out of heart and mind. Memories of them may have lingered on, as they had not been entirely effaced from the earth. At all events, the desire was there, smouldering beneath the heap of suppressions.

Once, man was a free agent sexually. He could mate with any female that came his way. Now, he was in chains. Sex worship came to break the fetters and, if only for a brief space of time, to bring back to man the freedom that had been his. What was forbidden at large in the bush not only was permitted, but, in fact, became a duty in the temple of the gods.

### III

When, in the temple, man was free to do as he pleased sexually, he pleased to do it with all the freedom possible. Venturing far out across land and sea to India, we come upon a people, Kauchiluas by name. On the day of a festival we may follow them along the crooked path through fields of corn until we reach the woods. Further, we cannot go. Beyond, it is only for their own and for the initiated. Yet we do know what is happening there.

The Kauchiluas enter the temple individually. Here the sexes separate, the males proceeding further inside, while the females remain for a few minutes with the priest. They remove their bodices and deposit them in a box held by the divine representative, each receiving a number or check for the bodice deposited. Presently they join the males and the service is begun.

There is song and prayer and dance. As the ritual advances, hearts beat faster and eyes dilate in the glimmer of the burning fire in the front. Then the priest marches about the temple with the box of bodices offering it to each male, who takes one. The woman who has the number corresponding to that garment thereby becomes his partner for the remainder of the service. She may be a stranger, a young girl, or an old woman ; she may be his own sister, or his very mother. Whoever she is, it is her most sacred religious duty to join with him in the fulfilment of the last sacrament of the worship—the union of the sexes. This rite is exercised in communion within the temple and is accompanied by shrieks and wild exercises of an orgiastic nature.

This service was engaged in by all present, by the most devout and pure-minded women, by persons who were otherwise as modest and chaste as any group of men and women to-day. To them, this promiscuous union was a sacred and solemn observance ; yet, while it lasted, it was an overwhelming passion of sexual fury.

The bodice of the Kauchilua woman was the magic wand that converted an act strictly interdicted as a deadly sin into a sacred duty. There, in the temple, all the veneer that social custom had placed upon the exercise of the sexual function was removed. Accompanied by prayer and song, they reverted to the original form of sex relationship, absolute promiscuity.

The Kauchiluas were by no means the only people to dispose of all their sex taboos in worship. There were many such cases in all parts of the world. It was the same at the sacrifice of the Cartavaya to the Indian god Krishna. Again, it was a feature of the Soma-sacrifice in the Vedic ritual. Among the Nicaraguans, who were otherwise a people unusually strict in sex matters, the women could choose any man they might wish in their annual festival. In the frenzy of religio-sexual excitement, their choice was neither discriminating nor limited. In fact, the more strict a people was in matters of sex, the more likely the individuals were to break out in orgy at their worship. This we see in the story of the tribe of Tarahumare.

Here we have a peaceful, orderly, and reserved people. Whether dancing or singing they never lost their decorum and ever behaved with great formality and fitting solemnity. In fact, their self-control so impressed the traveller, who first came upon them, that he did not hesitate to state that " in the ordinary course of his existence, the uncivilized Tarahumare is too bashful and modest to enforce his matrimonial rights and privileges ; and only by means of the national drink *tesvino* is the race kept alive and increasing."

Yet there was a place in their ceremony when formality and solemnity gave way to what the writer·quoted above describes as " debauch." For this very drink of *tesvino* was an essential part of the worship. It was generously imbibed at the close of formal services, and, as the intoxicant was becoming effective, men and women entered into open promiscuous sexual relationship in which they engaged until wellnigh dawn.

Without *tesvino*, religious worship could not dissolve the chains of sexual constraint for the Tarahumares. Among other primitive peoples, it also failed in this 'liberating function in at least one respect : incest. Promiscuous as the worshippers in the temple were, they still observed the taboo on incestuous relationship. Contact between parent and child persisted in the orgiastic rites of secret sects past and present, but it was banished from the temple of the gods. However, all other forms of sexual promiscuity as a feature of religious worship continued for many thousands of years.

IV

Sacrifice is one element that early found its way into the worship of all gods. Its origin was humble indeed. It may have been a bribe to a menacing god to stay his hand, a gift to a supernatural power to secure his favour, or a reward to an obliging divinity who did man's bidding. Again, it was sometimes just a fine for an act displeasing to the gods, imposed upon a person by his own guilty conscience. However it originated, the concept of sacrifice grew with the human mind. It gathered intellectual and emotional values as it rolled along the path of human progress.

As fear gave way to love in the heart of primitive man, and he came to adore his gods rather than to look upon them in dread and horror, sacrifice began to take on a devotional aspect. The dominant note became that of homage. Just as the lover enjoys bringing a gift to his love and is exalted by the very act of giving, so is the devotee happy to offer what is nearest and dearest to him to his god out of sheer love for the divinity.

In the worship of the generative divinities sacrifice also came to play its part. Here, perhaps even more than in the worship of other gods, it secured a hold upon the people to an overwhelming extent, more for what man got out of it directly than for what the gods might offer in return. For sacrifice in sex worship came to be another outlet for the collected sexual energies of man, diverted from their natural course through the numerous social inhibitions.

Although the sacrifice to the gods of generation was to be sexual, it could assume several different forms. It could be the product of the sexual union, the first-born. Like the lover who brings his beloved a gift and is himself first treated to it by the grateful recipient, primitive man offered to the generative god the first gift of new life received through his influence. The first-born was also the thing man waited for so long, the object that was most precious to him. In many a corner of the world, the first-born—whether crop or fruit or animal, not even excluding human—was sacrificed to the divine being. The Phœnicians offered the dearest child, the first-born, to propitiate their god. In Exodus we read that "All that openeth the womb is mine," and in old Judea the first-born was commonly considered an object for sacrifice. Even to-day the first-born Jewish child, if it be a son, rightfully belongs to the descendant of the tribe of Levi, the priesthood of the temple. The father has to redeem the first-born from the *cohen*. Thirty days after the birth, a ceremony is performed which is called "the redemption of the son" and in which the father gives the *cohen* anything of value. The latter receives it in lieu of the boy. After the transfer is made, there is a jolly party and a feast according to the means of the parents. In practically all cases the *cohen* returns the ransom before he leaves the house.

Just as the fruit of the sexual union was offered in sacrifice to the god of fertility, so did the agents in this process, that is, the organs of procreation, also become material for sacrifice. Both foreskin and hymen are the appropriate parts to be rendered to the divinity. The hymen is the guardian at the gateway of generation. Its presence is a sign that no generative services have as yet been brought by the female individual. It is destroyed in the very process so dear to the god of fertility. It is, therefore, ·acred to the god and must be sacrificed at his altar.

The Roman bride offered her hymen directly to the god of generation, Priapus. To his temple she repaired with her parents and the groom. The latter waited in the ante-room while the young maiden alone entered into the sacred chamber of the temple. There, in the representation hewn out of marble, was Priapus himself, a strong, nude male, in passion. The youthful bride embraced him in fear and trembling, and when she left the sacred chamber, she was a virgin no longer.

A similar custom prevails even to-day in some parts of India. A writer, who was long a sojourner there, relates :

" Many a day have I sat at early dawn in the door of my tent, pitched in a sacred grove, and gazed at the little group of females stealthily emerge from the adjoining village, each with a garland or bunch of flowers, and when none were thought to see, accompany their prayer for *pulee-pullum* (child fruit) with a respectful abrasion of a certain part of their person on a phallus."

To the westerner, watching stealthily, it was, perhaps, a quaint, erotic scene. To the maidens about to enter matrimony, this was a solemn sacrifice of their hymen to the god within whose power it was to bless them with many births, assuring them of the love of their husbands, or to curse them with barrenness, causing them to be hated and despised.

Among very primitive peoples the god was personified in the ceremony, not by an inanimate object, but by his priest. In many places, this divine representative acted openly, even demanding a fee. Again, he played the part of the god under cover, in the dark of the night. So it was that some brides believed they had actually consorted with the divinity, while others realized, perhaps, that it was with the priest. But the priest here became impersonal. He was no longer a mere human but rather the divine representative upon earth. He played a rôle similar to that of the modern priest when, as the confessor, he takes the place of Christ in forgiving the sins of the contrite penitent.

The custom of having the priest act as the representative of the god is practised in India even at the present time. It is not uncommon for a husband to accompany his wife to the priest and to remain a reverential spectator of the act representing the union of god and woman. In certain parts of the country, there are definite days each year on which women call at the temples to receive from the priests the sacred blessing that they are unable to obtain from the god of creation through the medium of their husbands.

Where a king or lord assumed a theocratic function, as was usual in ancient times, it was customary for him to substitute for the god at this hymeneal sacrifice.   In our own times, the Justice of the Peace claims the right to kiss the bride first.   He is entirely ignorant of the fact that therein he merely claims a mild substitute for the first right to the bride that should be his according to ancient custom.

In the male, there is nothing to correspond to the hymen, which so symbolically represents the transition from virginity to the realm of sex experience.   Still, the foreskin is the nearest to it.   Like the hymen, it undergoes a change in sexual intercourse. Again, like the hymen, it can be removed with pain, yet with little danger to the life of the individual.   We thus have the circumcision operation at the time of puberty as the sacrifice of

*A Hindu goddess offering a lingam*

the male agent in the sexual process.   This ceremony is performed among the Jews on the eighth day after birth ; among the Arabs at the age of thirteen ; but by other peoples in various parts of the world as a tribal rite of initiation corresponding to the modern confirmation ceremony.

The sacrificial meaning of both circumcision and hymeneal rupture becomes even more apparent in the perversions of some religious sects.   Among those people who live religion very intensely and vividly, we find the true intent of the rite unmitigated by the consideration of individual well-being and the interest of the group.   We see it in the actual incisions in the female organs, such as removing the clitoris, or in the infibulation of the labia minora.   We see it again in the castrations following great religious excitations in both ancient and modern times.

In the heat of religious passion, the avid worshippers of Cybele lost all sense of reality and ran about like madmen with furious eyes and streaming hair.  At times they joined in wild, fantastic dance amidst the cries and shouts of drunken song.  Again, they broke up and rushed about through the woods, falling upon each other and flogging themselves relentlessly with iron chains.  And all the time they carried burning torches or brandished sacred knives.

For hours the drunken, furious orgy went on and in the excitement of the dance, drink, and flogging, they forgot themselves completely.  In the pain and frenzy of the approaching ecstasy, they thrust the knives upon their bodies in the name of the goddess.  Unconscious of the resulting anguish, they continued their mad dance and waved about the severed portions of their bodies, while the blood streamed from the gaping wounds.  When the fury had died away, they approached the altar to present their goddess with the spoils of their virility.  They had made the great sacrifice for her and now they were to adopt woman's dress and serve her in the temple—eunuch priests.

### v

As religion develops and love ever plays a larger part in it, the idea of sacrifice becomes more and more sacred, the sacrificial object ever growing in holiness.  Hence, once the agents of the sexual process were offered in sacrifice to the generative divinity, it is only natural that they came to be looked upon as something sacred.  When one took an oath in olden times and, as we do to-day, had to put his hand upon a sacred object, he placed it upon his genitals.  When Abraham is stricken with age and desires his servant Eliezer, who is also the Elder of his household, to swear that he will take a wife for his son Isaac, not from the daughters of Canaan, but from Abraham's own people, he says :

" Put, I pray thee, thy hand under my thigh and I will make thee swear by the Lord, the God of heaven and the God of earth. . . ."

The thigh was a generic term for the organ of creation.  In the Bible, one refers to his descendants as those " who came out of my thigh."

Travellers tell of a people whose priests on various occasions go about uncovered so that the worshippers of the generative divinity may pay the lingam the homage usually paid when sacred objects are exposed to the veneration of the pious.  In Canara and other districts of India, the priests went about naked in the streets, ringing the bells that they held in their hands.  It was to call out the women to the religious duty of piously embracing their sacred organs.

The old idea of the sanctity of the lingam survives in the Christian attitude of reverence toward the Holy Prepuce, the foreskin of Jesus. Until very recently, there were twelve such prepuces extant in European churches, and many a legend was woven about them. One of these, the pride possession of the Abbey Church of Coulomb, in the diocese of Chartres, France, was believed to possess the miraculous power of rendering all sterile women fruitful. It had the added virtue of lessening the pains of childbirth.

Where the sanctity of the organs of generation had worn off, there still existed a certain attitude toward them—akin to sacred. The genitals were taboo. They were out of the range of usual experience, not to be touched or mentioned by name. The Mosaic law had no pity upon those who violated this taboo.

" When men strive together one with another, and the wife of one draweth near to deliver her husband out of the hand of him that smiteth him, and putteth forth her hand and taketh him by the secrets, then thou shalt cut off her hand ; thine eye shalt have no pity." The punishment was to be so severe because she had touched an object that was most taboo.

In many parts of the world, among savages, to uncover oneself before a person is to curse him. In Russia and other places in Eastern Europe, one expresses spite or defiance by making a fist with the tip of the thumb extended between the index and the middle fingers. This is called a " fig " and is symbolic of the male genital. Although, when used as suggested, it may be very effective in producing the desired result, very few people are aware of its original significance. As late as the latter part of the eighteenth century, in Naples, this same figure was used as an amulet and worn to guard against the evil eye.

VI

There was yet another sacrifice that man could offer to the god of generation—the sacrifice of coition. Just as he created his god in his own image, so did he bestow upon him that which he himself cherished most. Respectable old Herodotus was shocked to find that all people, with the exception of the Greeks and the Egyptians, cohabited within their temples.

In principle, the first sex experience was to be with the god himself. There was involved in it the sacrifice of the hymen as well as the first act of coition. In the absence of the god, his priest or temporal representative could fill his place. There were yet other surrogates, such as the stranger and the group as a whole.

In a world where the group is small, every one is known, and travellers are rare, a stranger becomes an oddity. His coming and going are veiled in mystery. So it was that he came to be looked upon as a divine emissary, a possible angel in the flesh. To the Jew of the Middle Ages, every stranger was a potential Elijah the prophet, in disguise. To the Christian, he was possibly the wandering Jew or a reincarnation of Christ or some saint. To the Easterner, the stranger was a sacred man, and that accounts for the famed hospitality of the Orient. The same halo hung about him already in primitive times. What was due to a god was frequently given to the stranger and what was expected from the divinity was looked for in the possible gift some passing traveller might bring.

No wonder, then, that the virgin coition was also to be performed with a stranger. We read of maidens, among primitive peoples, being brought to the altar of the generative goddess at least once before their nuptials, to be sacrificed to a stranger. This did not at all detract from their value in marriage. In fact, to this day a husband in the Kamerun has small opinion of his wife if she has had only limited sex experience before her marriage, for " if she were pretty men would have come to her."

Among the American-Indians, when girls enter into womanhood, they are taken to a hut, painted, and made to cohabit with strangers while songs are offered to the goddess Iteque. Similarly must the Santal girl, once in her life, cohabit with a stranger in the temple of Talkupi Ghat. And when we reach the stage of so-called temple prostitution, it is the stranger again who takes away the prettiest girl, the girl that is first to be initiated.

Not only the stranger, but the group as a unit may take what rightfully belongs to the gods. A vestige of this attitude we have in the popular concept of *vox populi, vox Dei*—the voice of the people is the voice of God. We have it again in the unusual theological powers which a conclave of ministers will assume for themselves. A hundred rabbis will void a marriage vow against the rule for divorce. A church council will decide upon substantiation and the figure of the cross.

The tribe as a whole may delegate to itself the privilege that accrues only to the god. In Serang a maiden must herself provide the food for her wedding-feast. Yet she has nothing with which to get it but her maidenhood. So she calls at the temple and there, after prayer and song, she is ceremoniously bathed and clothed in a skirt of fibre. Now she is at the service of every man until she has collected as much as she needs for the feast.

At the feast, a pot filled with water is covered with a leaf. An old woman takes the index finger of the girl's right hand and thrusts it through the leaf. This symbolizes the fact that her hymen has been broken. The leaf is then displayed on the ridge of the roof. It is a sign for the old men of the village that it is their night, and during that evening, they all have access to her room.

Herodotus tells us that among the people of Lydia, the bride, on her wedding night, accorded her favour to all the guests for which they, in return, presented her with gifts. Possibly our custom of wedding presents is a forgotten hang-over of such rewards to the bride for her amorous favours, just as our privilege of kissing her may be a mild form of another and more severe claim upon the newly wed maiden by all the members of the clan.

It was not only the first coition that became a sacrifice. Any sexual union, if executed within the temple and under the auspices of the divinity, might be offered to the god of generation. Soon, any man, a lonesome stranger or a tired soul, weary with the burdens of life, could come to the temple to find escape from worldly troubles through the gateway of love. He had only to pay the god for the privilege of representing him, and the union in which he joined was then but another sacrifice of coition. Hence, we find the widespread custom of the duty upon every woman, at least once in her life, to come to the temple and to give herself to anyone for a donation to the god. Little did it matter how humble or how noble she might be ; she must offer herself to the first bidder.

We are told by Herodotus that once in her lifetime every woman born in Chaldea had to enter the enclosure of the temple of Aphrodite, sit therein, and offer herself to a stranger. Many of the wealthy were too proud to mix with the rest and repaired to the temple in closed chariots, followed by numerous attendants. The greater number seated themselves in long lanes on the sacred pavement. The place was thronged with strangers passing down the lanes to make their choice. Once a woman had taken her place there, she could not return home until a stranger had thrown into her lap a silver coin and had led her away with him beyond the limits of the sacred enclosure. As he threw her the money, he pronounced the words : " May the goddess Mylitta make thee happy."

A similar custom prevailed among the American-Indians. Among the ancient Algonquins and Iroquois, as well as among some South American tribes, there was a festival during which the women of all ranks extended to whosoever wished, the same privileges that the matrons of ancient Babylon granted even to the slaves and strangers in the temple of Mylitta.  It was one of the duties of religion.

In the course of time, this custom passed out of existence.  No longer could the group take the place of the god in the sacrament of sex.  Yet it continued in a different form.  What the group could not do as a whole with all the individuals participating in it, some individuals representing the group could still do for the god of generation.  Instead of the entire group joining in promiscuous sexual union, certain individuals were selected by the group to execute the act on behalf of the entire assemblage.

In those temples in India where there is no general sexual union, there is still a ceremonial performance of coition by a chosen couple.  It is carried out in a so-called " vacant enchanted place," which is rendered pure by sprinkling it with wine.  Secret charms are whispered three times over the woman, following which the sexual act is consummated.

When Captain Cook visited one of the Pacific Islands, he and his party invited the natives to a religious ceremony.  In return, the natives performed a rite of their own.  After the usual Indian ritual, a tall, strong young man and a slight girl of about twelve stepped forward and, upon an improvised altar, joined in sexual union, the elder women advising and assisting the young girl in the performance of her amorous duty.  The entire audience stood silent as they looked on in solemn reverence.

Various were the forms that the sexual sacrifice assumed in the temples of the gods.  In one case, it may have been just the hymeneal offering of the first union in sex.  In another, it may have been a union at any time during the life of the woman.  In still another, the sacrifice was to be repeated annually, or every time a certain festival was celebrated.  These variations were effected by the religious institution itself, the priests, and the social traditions of the group.

Still other variations found their origin in the different attitudes of the individual women.  One woman may have brought the single sacrifice more out of necessity than out of inner desire.  To her, it may have been a painful duty of which she was glad that no more was required.  To another woman, the one sacrifice may have left only greater desire for a repetition of the worship.  In terms of our modern psychology, this distinction would be one of sexual sensibility and erotic propensities.  To the primitive man, the distinction was in degree of piety.  It was the extent to which one was devoted to the god and ready to serve him.

Five times a day the Azan is chanted on the balcony of the minaret.  It is the call to the faithful Moslem to wash his face, hands, and feet, and bend down in prayer.  North-light, meridian, and sunset are reminders to the Jew to "listen that the Lord is his God, the Lord is One." Morning, noon, and evening the Angelus bell tells over and over again to the faithful Christian the story of Christ's advent upon the earth and reminds him of the worship he owes his God.

There are those whose lives are merely intermissions between acts of worship. There are others whose worship is a rare and thin sprinkling over a secular existence. This was true in primitive times as it is to-day. There were women whose sexual sacrifice at the temple was an incident of small significance in their lives. There were other women who were devotees of the divinities, bent upon serving them continually. In time, such persons came to be

*A Hindu god in copulation*

the priestesses of the god and acquired as much dignity in the temple as the priests who performed the rites of worship. He who chanted the incantations or carried the idol was no more entitled to the dignity of the priesthood than she who honoured the god in her own sentient flesh.

There were priestesses who devoted themselves entirely to the god, sleeping in the sacred chamber and never leaving the temple. Their lives were given wholly to the divine being. They offered themselves directly to him, foregoing all the joys of secular living. There were others who did not cohabit with the god directly, but with his representatives, the stranger, the passer-by, anyone who might call in the divine name. They were offering themselves in sexual sacrifice. The procreative god was served by the act of procreation performed in the temple. The priest partook of the sacrifice of the first-born. The priestess partook of the sacrifice of coition. In the latter we have the origin of the institution of temple priestesses, which has so shocked the prudes of later times.

VII

The execution of the sexual union as a sacrifice to the gods gave rise to a very important and almost universal institution of pagan religion. We know it by the unsavoury name of prostitution,—temple or religious prostitution. Perhaps it was unsavoury at the time the Roman writers were preserving it from historical oblivion. Whatever we know of it, we owe to writers who belonged to a later culture and who looked at it adversely, if not with actual disgust ; who saw it in its disintegrating, degenerating ugliness, when it was dying a shameful death.

In its inception, however, there was nothing degrading about it. To the primitive man, it was both honourable and pious. He looked at it in some such fashion as this :

Sexual union is a pious act pleasing to the gods. Every woman is enjoined by the god to sacrifice at least one such union in his honour. The god being divine and physically absent, a surrogate is necessary to receive the sacrifice. He may be a priest, a stranger, or a group. Whoever the surrogate is, he who is thus honoured must himself bring an offering to the god ; he must show his appreciation of this privilege by contributing his mite for the divine needs. In our own plain, prosaic words, we might say : he must pay for it. Now, let us remember : pay, not the woman, but the god for partaking of her sacrificial favour.

When the priest was the surrogate, no one was to inquire how he squared it with the god. Presumably, he repaid it in prayer and worship. Sometimes, it was the woman herself, or her family, who provided the recompense which was due from the priest. Whenever the surrogate was not of the god's human family, that is, not of the priesthood, he contributed to the upkeep of the god's house in coin or in gift from field or forest.

When the man threw the coin to his choice of the women aligned at the temple and said : " May the goddess Mylitta make thee happy," he was not buying the woman's body. He was participating in a religious ceremony in which his share consisted not only in uniting with the woman but also in bringing an offering to the god—in this case, a monetary one, since the priests must live and the temple of the divine being must be kept up.

In fact, one may question the justice of applying to this institution the term " prostitution." By the latter we seek to signify a sexual union in which one of the partners fulfils his part for reward or material gain outside the field of sexuality. It is the motive that determines whether a sexual union is prostitutional or not. Certainly, the woman who came piously to the temple, waiting in prayerful mood to be chosen by anyone at all, be he ever so unattractive physically, and receiving for herself no monetary or material compensation,—certainly, this woman cannot be called a prostitute.

True, in its later development, this institution of sacrificial sexual union did assume a semblance of prostitution. As time went on, the temple priestesses easily outnumbered the priests. In some temples, there were as many as a thousand of them.

Our churches and synagogues are built in locations where they may be most easily accessible to the public. A modern house of worship will not disdain to advertise its services so as to attract a greater number of worshippers. The pagan temples followed a similar course in their attempt to attract a large attendance. They were even more concerned with it, since the economic factor here played a greater rôle. The human family of the god was large and their material needs were considerable. In consequence, their temples were built on cross-roads and, in cities with a port, not far distant from the docks. For it was the traveller, most in need of the sexual sacrifice, who was sure to call at the temple. It was he, too, that was to be favoured, and in many cases, when a woman came to offer herself at the temple, she was to do so only to a stranger, as he was possibly a divine representative.

With so many priestesses and so many worshippers, the service had to become systematized, the fee or monetary sacrifice definitely fixed, and the share of the priestesses in the proceeds justly apportioned. No wonder, then, that to infidel eyes this looked more like a brothel than a house of worship. Did not any man call there, just as he calls on a legalized house of prostitution, pays the fee, and takes a woman in sexual embrace?

But the fact that the services of the temple priestesses had been so definitely systematized need not be deprecatory of the temple priesthood. System is a necessary feature in any large human institution, religious as well. Our worship to-day is only too well systematized. Nor need we be shocked by the payment offered for the services of the priestesses, since it was really the sacrifice of the male. The priestess offered her sexual function to the god, the man offered his coin. In fact, both were offering coin in addition to the sexual union, for the temple was receiving the payment from the male on account of the female. She was as much a partner to the monetary contribution to the temple as she was a partner to the sexual intercourse.

Even her sharing the fee with the temple need not be surprising

*Venus in a phallic shrine*

considered from the pagan viewpoint. When the farmer brought his first-born to the temple, it was sacrificed to the gods ; yet, only a small part went to the god directly, that is, was burnt at the altar. The greater portion was returned to the donor and he was supposed to feast upon it in the temple court. And a goodly portion went to the priest. Just as the priest received his portion of the sacrificial lamb, so did the priestess receive her part of the fee for the sexual sacrifice. The one is no more prostitution than the other.

After all, the term prostitution is psychological in nature. There is nothing inherent in the physical union of the sexes to make one prostitutional and the other legitimate or respectable. It is the way in which society looks upon a sexual union and the way the partners feel about it that determines whether it is prostitutional or not. In those times and places where the institution of temple priestesses was established, society did not look upon it as prostitutional. Quite to the contrary, it was the most respectable and pious vocation a woman could select, or have selected for her by her parents or guardians. Nor did the temple priestess view herself as a prostitute. She saw herself a servant of the god, possibly bringing more joy and gladness to the divinity than to herself.

## VIII

There were several paths by which a woman found her way to the temple priesthood. She may have come as a virgin to marry the god, where such marriages between divinities and humans were performed. In this case, she was wedded to the god according to the rite of the tribe. After being initiated by the priests, she was the divine spouse and could, therefore, receive all his worshippers. The priests, in addition to consecrating her to her love-life, may have trained her in the art of love. In proportion to her amorous talents, her fame and fortune grew to the extent that she was paid by lay married women for private instruction in the *ars amandi*.

Again, she may have come after her marriage, preferring the exalted erotic life in the temple to the cheerless existence of a primitive wife in servitude. In that case, she approached the divine dwelling-place, bearing upon her head some such gift as a coco-nut and a packet of sugar. She was received by the priest and given cakes and rice to eat. After her consecration, she was assigned to temple duty, such as sweeping and purifying the floor by washing it with cow-dung and water, and waving a fly-whisk before the god. In the meanwhile, she was instructed in the art of the sexual sacrifice by priest or priestess and, in time, she assumed her place before the god of generation.

More often, perhaps, she was brought to the temple by her father or brother, at an age when she was not yet old enough to have an opinion in the matter or to understand its significance. Her father may have had a guilty conscience ; perhaps he had broken his marriage vow. He may have committed adultery, and the punishment for this would be visited upon the entire tribe. The tribe, in turn, would wreak its vengeance upon him. It were best to mend things before it was too late. So he took his female child, possibly not more than five years of age, and brought her to the temple in expiation. It was not much of a sacrifice, girls being of little account anyway. In addition, it conferred an amount of distinction—one was somehow associated with the priesthood.

Occasionally, she got there by accident. Times were hard for the tribe ; somehow the god or goddess was not pleased with the worship of the people. Then, a number of girls were collected and, *en masse*, admitted to the temple so that the divine frown might disappear. In another case, all may have been well with the tribe. Gods were pleased and man grateful. Once more, girls were consecrated to the divinity. Xenophon dedicated fifty courtesans to the Corinthian Venus, in pursuance of the vow he had made beseeching the goddess to give him victory in the Olympian games. Pindar makes Xenophon address the priestesses thus :

" O, young damsels, who receive all strangers and give them hospitality, priestesses of the goddess Pitho in the rich Corinth, it is you who, in causing the incense to burn before the image of Venus and in inviting the mother of love, often merit for us her celestial aid and procure for us the sweet moments which we taste on the luxurious couches where is gathered the delicate fruit of beauty."

However a girl came into the temple, she had a long period of training before her. This training was neither in religion nor in sex, but primarily in the graces of love-making and companionship. For the vocation of the temple priestess was complicated, indeed. She was catering not to the Western man, but to the man of the East whose loving was as refined as it was intricate.

To the Occidental man, love is either highly spiritual—romance and chivalry, or purely physical, mere sexual union. The prostitute of the West answers the call of his physical love. She receives her guest in the dark and only for a brief moment. The man comes to her when his passion runs high ; the minute the passion is spent he leaves. The Chinese or Indian prostitute is first of all a companion and an entertainer. She will delight her guests intellectually by conversation, or artistically by playing or singing ; she may dance and she may serve tea. What follows is a relationship gradually drifted into, not an act bought and paid for.

The temple priestess is, therefore, trained for Oriental lovemaking. For ten hours each day these little girls are instructed in singing and dancing. From the age of seven or eight to fourteen or fifteen, they dance six times daily. They are taught, too, to acquire charm and poise and to make their bodies attractive through the use of fine clothes, sweet-scented powders, and delicate perfumes whose exotic fragrance enhance their allurement. Their minds are also trained and they become delightful conversationalists.

A pen picture of the priestess in action is offered us by Savarin : " The suppleness of their bodies is inconceivable. One is astonished at the mobility of their features, to which they give at will an impression agreeable to the part they play. Their indecent attitudes are often carried to excess. Their looks, gestures, all speak in such an expressive manner that it is not possible to misunderstand what they mean. At the commencement of the dance they throw aside, with their veils, the modesty of their sex. A long, very light silken robe descends to their heels enclosed by a rich girdle. Their long black hair floats in perfumed tresses over their shoulders ; a gauze chemise, almost transparent, veils their breasts. To the measure of their movements, the form and contours of their bodies are successively displayed. The sound of the flute, of the tambourine and cymbals, regulates their step and hastens or slows their motions. They are full of love and passion ; they appear intoxicated ; they are Bacchantes in delirium ; then they seem to forget all restraint and give themselves up to the disorder of their senses."

The sexual sacrifices by these priestesses were usually carried on in the ante-rooms of the temple but sometimes, also, outside, in the court or out-buildings, or even along the banks of the sacred rivers. The price was always considerable. In India, in comparatively recent times the sacred fee was from ten to forty dollars, while the Nizam of Haldabad offered a thousand pounds sterling for three nights. Stories of Egypt and Greece indicate that the fee was considerable. King Cheops, impoverished, sacrificed his daughter to procure the necessary funds for the pyramid he was building. Flora, a priestess, was the benefactress of her town, erecting at her own expense a statue to the father of Crœsus.

To what extent favours were highly paid for in antiquity may be gleaned from the following anecdote of a famous courtesan, Archidice. A young Egyptian became infatuated with her and offered her all his possessions for one night of love. Archidice disdained his offer.  In despair, the lover besought Venus to give him in his dream what the beautiful Archidice refused him in reality.  The prayer was answered and the young Egyptian had the dream he so much desired.  When Archidice heard of it, she had the young man arrested and taken before the judges to make him pay for his voluptuous dream.  The judges decided that Archidice should, in turn, pray to Venus for a dream of silver in repayment for a fictitious lover.

In India, there were even wandering troupes of priestesses led by old women, former servants of the temple.  Raynal describes their activity :

" To the monotonous and rapid sounds of the tom-tom these Bayaderes, warmed by a desire to please and by the odours with which they are perfumed, end by becoming beside themselves. Their dances are poetic pantomimes of love.  The place, the design, the attitude, measure, sounds, and cadences of these ballets, all breathe of passion and are expressive of voluptuousness and its fury.

" Everything conspires to the prodigious success of such women —art and the richness of ornament, the skill with which they make themselves beautiful.  Long dark hair falling over their lovely shoulders or arranged in pretty tresses is loaded with sparkling jewels, glittering among natural flowers.  Precious stones flash from their jewel-decked necklaces and tinkling bracelets. . . . The art of pleasure is the whole life occupation and only happiness of the Bayaderes.  It is extremely difficult to resist their seductions."

The institution of temple priestesses was widely spread and quite extensively developed.  Strabo said that there were as many as a thousand of them at the temple of Corinth.  There were nigh twelve thousand such priestesses in Madras in quite recent times. There was not a country in which the institution was not present in some form.  It was a natural development out of the sex worship which was universally followed.  Beginning with a god of generation and reaching a stage of sexual sacrifice, a priesthood for the sacrifice was a natural and logical consequence.

IX

There was another way in which man sought to tap divinity by his sexual emotion.  To our eyes it would seem most unholy, as pitiable as it was unnatural.  And yet it was there, exercised in all the piety and seriousness man is capable of.  For not only did man create his gods in his own image but he also served them in his likeness.  The man whose sex life was contrary to nature, set upon members of his own sex, served his generative god homosexually.

The Armenian father who brought his daughter to the temple of the goddess to be there consecrated as a priestess, often brought a son along as well. The son, too, was consecrated and his service was just as much a sexual sacrifice. The priest of Cybele who castrated himself in religious frenzy assumed feminine dress not without a purpose. He continued in the service of the temple and like the priestess served man for the required fee. There were male priests serving males in the temples of all the gods. The homosexual priest had a special designation in both the Hebrew and Babylonian languages. *Kadosha* was the name applied to the temple priestess engaged in sexual worship ; *kadosh* was the word for the male in the same service.

In Tahiti, there were special divinities for homosexual worship. It was the god Chin himself who instituted homosexualism in Yucatan and sanctified it. His priests, therefore, wore feminine dress. What Chin was in the primitive world for the homosexual man, Mise, Pudicitia and Bona Dea were for the homosexual woman in antiquity. In these services artificial lingams were used by the women worshippers. There were divinities, like the Phrygian Cotytto, that were homosexually worshipped in some places by men and in others by women. And at the service to Demeter at Pellene not only were men excluded but even male dogs so that there would be no disturbing element whatever for the rites to be performed.

Among the Santees, an American-Indian tribe, if a man had a nightmare and dreamed of the terrible goddess, the moon, he had to appease the divinity by putting on feminine dress, serving as a woman and offering himself to men. In other tribes, the medicine men had to be effeminate and always wore the dress of women. In old Japan, according to Xavier, priests were to have sexual relations not with women but with men. Arabic travelling merchants reported, in the ninth century, that the Chinese resorted to pederasty in the worship of their icons. Leo Africanus tells of an order of women Satacat in northern Africa that served the gods in tribadistic fashion.

Even the gods resorted to homosexual practices. Zeus, their very father, came down from Mount Olympus attracted by a rosy-faced, bright-eyed youth. It was Ganymede, the most beautiful of mortals, whom the god, disguised as an eagle, seduced and carried away to the Mount. There, Ganymede became the object of love among the divinities for whom he acted as cup-bearer. And Zeus, to compensate the boy's father for the loss of his son, sent him a team of beautiful, light-footed horses.

The key to this strange way of serving a god must, as already indicated, be sought in the homosexual tendency that we find

*Siva as the Hermaphroditic God, the eye in the centre of his forehead symbolizing the union of the two creative forces*

creeping up throughout the entire history of man. There were special lupanars for boys in Greece which were frequented by both men and women and were subject to the same tax and regulations as other lupanars. Dufour tells us that " Rome was filled " with male hierodules who " rented themselves out like the girls of the town. There were houses especially devoted to this kind of prostitution and there were procurers who followed no other business than that of renting out, for profit, a hoard of degraded slaves and even free men." Some of the greatest men of Rome, especially among the Cæsars, though not infrequently among the poets as well, were publicly known to be homosexual. They frequently gave themselves to men for gain—monetary or political. There seems to be no people on earth that did not know of this sexual relationship. In fact, it seems to have come down the animal line with man, for this very practice is found even among animals. It still is not uncommon. Less than a century ago, there were legalized brothels of men for homosexual practice in Paris just as there had been in Greece and Rome. The late Doctor Ivan Bloch described a ball of homosexuals in Berlin. There were some thousand of them ; some in men's clothes, others in the dress of women, and still others in futuristic attire. At present, in America, homosexualism seems to be on the increase, especially in the artistic circles.

How did man come to prefer a member of his own sex to a person of the opposite one ? This is a very interesting question but it need not concern us here. Suffice it to say that at first man's sexual nature is indefinite. It is a vague, blind yearning that has to be set to a person and to a sex, and that is conditioned by first associations and experience. There are environmental and social conditions that give man's instinct a homosexual turn. These obtained in the past as they still do to-day. That is why the homosexual tendency was ever present, running parallel with the so-called natural instinct.

Was homosexual worship merely a reflection of homosexual living ? Quite likely it was, although by a stretch of the imagination one may derive it in another way :

Originally the gods were hermaphroditic and were, therefore, worshipped by the union of the opposite sexes. As the hermaphroditic divinity separated itself into god and goddess, the worshippers, in some places, may also have separated by sexes, the male serving the god, the female the goddess. When members of one sex exclusively worship a generative god, their service is well in danger of becoming homosexual. Still, it seems more simple and doubtless more psychological to assume that homosexual man preceded the homosexual worshipper ; and that even in homosexualism man only offered to his god what was dearest to him and all-embracing in his life.

.    .    .    .    .    .    .

On the shore of the island of Cyprus, in the waters of the Mediterranean, there once was a townlet called Amathonte. It lay well in the shade of Mount Olympus, yet it dared to defy the gods.

Its women were modest, reserved, contemptuous of all carnal pleasures. They covered their bodies and were disdainful of the flesh. One day, Venus was washed upon their shore. As the women came down to see her, they noticed her nudity and treated her with scorn. So when Venus came to her own, she descended to punish the women of Amathonte. She called them together and ordered them to prostitute themselves to all comers, so that they might glory in the very flesh they had so disdained. The women had no other recourse but to do as commanded by Venus.

*Images of Venus, in bronze and lead*

Still, they did it so reluctantly and with such distaste as to defeat the purpose of the goddess. Then Venus came down again and turned these women into stone.

And this was the end of the women of Amathonte, the women who denied the call of the flesh. They who feign would live were turned into stone while life went on. For in time, in this very city of Amathonte, a temple to Venus was erected, and other women came to live there, women who instead of denying love lived to worship it, who instead of rebelling against the flesh lived to triumph in it.

And amid the stones that once were women, the song of love was heard, love, natural, physical, permeating the entire existence of mankind. And woman's rebellion against sex defeated its own purpose.

There was yet another revolt against sex—by man ; and this is the story of Siva and his lingam :

Siva was a great god. With Brahma and Vishnu, he was master of the universe, his own function being generation and aiding new life to emerge out of death, like the spring out of the arms of winter. It was Brahma himself who said : " Where is he who opposes Siva and yet is happy ? "

But the great god Siva himself was not happy, for he was bereaved of his mate and he was tired and weary. So he wandered

*Indian temple, showing lingam and yoni*

about the land and came to the forest of Daruvanam, where the sages live—the sages and their wives.

And when the sages came out to see the great god Siva and noticed that he was haggard and sad, they treated him with scorn and only saluted with bent heads.

Siva was tired and weary and said nothing but : " Give me alms." Thus the god went about begging along the roads of Daruvanam. But wherever he came the women-folk looked at him and felt a pang at the heart. At once their minds were perturbed and their hearts agitated by the pains of love. They forsook the beds of the sages and followed the great god Siva.

And as the sages saw their wives leaving with Siva, they pronounced a curse upon him :

" May his lingam fall to the ground."

Was it the effectiveness of the curse, or did Siva himself shed his lingam in affliction at the loss of his consort ? Whatever the cause, there it was—his lingam—sticking into the ground and Siva himself gone.

As the lingam fell, it penetrated the lower worlds. Its length increased and its top towered above the heavens. The earth quaked and all there was upon it. The lingam became fire and caused conflagration wherever it penetrated. Neither god nor man could find peace or security.

So both Vishnu and Brahma came down to investigate and to save the universe. Brahma ascended to the heavens to ascertain the upper limits of Siva's lingam, and Vishnu betook himself to the lower regions to discover its depth. Both returned with the news that the lingam was infinite : it was lower than the deep and higher than the heavens.

And the two great gods both paid homage to the lingam and advised man to do likewise. They further counselled man to propitiate Parvati, the goddess, that she might receive the lingam into her yoni.

This was done and the world was saved. Mankind was taught that the lingam is not to be cursed or ignored ; that it is infinite in its influence for good or evil ; and that rather than wishing it destroyed, they should worship it by offering it flowers and perfumes and by burning fires before it.

Whether it was the goddess Venus or the god Siva, whether it was the feminine principle or the masculine, the worship of the god or of the goddess came as a punishment for sex ignored. Love suppressed, offended, and imprisoned came to be rescued by the gods of religion.

# CHAPTER V

## LOVE'S HIDDEN WAYS

*Beyond light and shade,*
*Beyond thing and thought,*
*There is love forever lurking.*

### I

ON the cross-roads of the Balkans, near a city called Naissus, an illegitimate son was born to an innkeeper's daughter. The boy's arrival in the world hardly raised a stir at the very inn of his mother. Yet he came to rule over a mighty empire and to shape the destiny of Europe. As if to reflect upon his parents, this boy was named Constantine.

Up from obscurity Constantine climbed. He fought his burdensome way through Roman soldiery in the East. On the banks of the Danube his star began to rise. He was made a tribune. He became a Cæsar. He made himself an Augustus. Slowly, slowly it all came about. It required patience to wait until a superior would rise to greater heights and vacate his place. Prudence was necessary that neither envy nor suspicion be aroused in filling the place vacated. And courage was needed when the ripe moment came to make the move so decisively that it would weather any storm.

Patience, prudence, decision, brought this son of a woman innkeeper of Naissus to the very waters of the Tiber—at the head of an army. But there was the end. Across the bridge lay Rome with Maxentius and his army, two hundred thousand strong. Beyond Ponte Molle no one could go. Constantine saw Severus try it with disastrous result—Severus, the very man in whose footsteps he had followed on his climb in the East. He watched Galerius make his attempt to cross the Ponte, Galerius whose star had sailed out of the East westward across the heavens—the celestial path his own star followed. Galerius never came to Rome again. The hopes and aspirations, the very lives of these Augusti lie buried in the sands of the Tiber shore.

It was just like Constantine to halt at Ponte Molle and—wait. But one day, Constantine had a dream—a dream at noon-time. On the horizon in front of him he saw a flaming cross ; the familiar triad, which the poor, persecuted men and women called Christians always carried about them. In the flame of the burning cross he read : " *In hoc signo vincas* "—in this sign you will conquer.

When he came to himself, his patience was gone ; his prudence thrown to the wind ; only decision was left, his decision to cross the bridge, however unequal his army might be to the forces of Maxentius.

So Constantine had a cross made, and bearing the sacred emblem he passed over the Tiber and took Rome. And the son of a woman innkeeper at Naissus sat upon the throne of the Cæsars with the name Constantine carved upon it. When he left this throne, heeding the call from a still higher one, fame came and added " the Great " to his name.

Constantine was the first Christian Emperor, the founder of the Holy Roman Empire, and the father of papal power at Saint Peter's. Who knows what might have become of the growing yet already disintegrating band of Christians had not Constantine joined them at this time ? The faith of the cross had been saved by the vision of the cross appearing to a mighty man of Rome.

True, Constantine was just then in need of a faith. He was facing the crucial point of his career, the critical moment of his life. And everything was against his favour. Considering the actual situation, common sense would have made the ardent leader stop at Ponte Molle. All his courage and energy, fired by ambition and his overwhelming desire for power, could never have carried him across the bridge in the face of such odds. Yet, there was one source out of which a hand might appear to lead him. There was still something that could save him. It was faith ; the force that takes away the very sense of reality and taps the energy of the subconscious, the mystic nature in man. Faith— the power that makes so many superhuman heroes, men who defy nature and life itself to attain their goal.

Faith, a new faith, Constantine needed, to make his own cause the cause of the faith, so that he might fight his own battle in the name of God and for his religion. " When thou goest forth to battle . . . thou shalt call in the name of God. . . ." Constantine may have saved Christianity, but Christianity surely saved Constantine.

Now, he may have heard long before of those poor, ridiculed bands of men and women who called themselves Christians. He may even have been acquainted with the ideas and rituals of this new group coming out of the East. Yet no amount of knowledge or rational persuasion concerning Christianity could have given him that reliance and self-confidence needed to cross the bridge. Mere thought, abstract idea, imageless belief, never carried one off his feet. The Sermon on the Mount might or might not have aroused Constantine's admiration ; the vision of the fiery cross conquered worlds for him. The symbol of Christianity was more effective than Christianity itself.

A symbol will rouse men and women and carry them over all

sorts of obstacles, beyond their apparent limitations. A striking example of its efficacy is to be found in the mascot. Everyone undertaking a hazardous task "trusts to luck." He has no solid reason for believing that things will take a good turn in his enterprise; but he hopes for it. It is the will to win that instils the hope of victory and inspires confidence in the ability of the individual to carry the project to a successful end. So far, it is all abstract and cannot very well hang together. What is lacking is a concrete basis for this sentiment of trust and confidence, and belief in luck. This is offered by the mascot. The elk, or dog, or rabbit, taken along on a dangerous voyage, on an airflight, or to a football game is supposed to assure the luck that is hoped for. And any man may commit this intellectual sin and accept the superstitious premise, not because he believes in the

*The Persian Triad*

mascot's power to charm, but because it offers an object upon which he can collect and focus all his hope and confidence.

Deep in the heart of every man there is a strong feeling of nationality, but whether his nation be large or small, as an abstract thing, it is hard for him to visualize it and to love it in itself. There is a symbol, however, that offers him something upon which to centre his devotion. It is the flag, the emblem of the land he loves and honours. His entire thought may be taken up with the problems and duties of business and life; he may have little time to think about his country. But once an appeal is made to him in the name of his flag, he will drop everything for it. It exerts such a hold upon him that he may gladly face death itself to protect it.

The cross and the crescent, the emblems of two great religions, convey to their followers thoughts that transcend the limitations of language. And the faithful, in turn, love these symbols of creeds that are in themselves highly abstract. The very cross that means so much to a Christian may convey an entirely different idea to a man of another belief. In the times of the Inquisition, to save his life, a Jew might bend before his executioner and kiss his boots imploring surcease from torture. Yet, he would not kneel or touch the cross with his lips. The former was simple humiliation ; the latter was to him a symbol of betrayal of God and people.

In religion, symbols play an important rôle. The symbolic object offers many sensations, every one of which helps to keep the idea that is symbolized in the foreground of consciousness. A symbol is the hold that a man can obtain on an abstract thought, the peg upon which he can hang his heart, the funnel through which he pours out his soul.

II

If it is difficult for us to-day to grasp a purely abstract idea, how much more difficult must it have been for the man of primitive times ? His mind was less organized, his notions more confused, and his thinking heavily befuddled. Watch a steamer sail out of a haze on a misty morning and you will see man's thinking slowly emerging out of primitive mentality. Watch the steamer making shore on a foggy night and you will observe the primitive mind groping for a way to give a meaning to the multitude of impressions hammering away at him from all corners.

Imagine Old Anthropology Adam struggling toward the concept of a generative force in nature. Its manifestations showered upon him at every turn : spring, warm weather, green grass, flowering fields, budding trees, fresh products of the land, births of animals, the increase of fish in the streams. There were births in his own hut and there were times when he himself seemed reborn as well. He felt the sharp, sweet pang of romance, and his whole being was attuned to mystic forces beyond his power of comprehension. What a leap from all these varied impressions to a single thought of regeneration !

Thrown amidst these phenomena of life, death, and rebirth, primitive man was unconsciously groping in the dark of his ignorance, seeking a symbol, a unifying element for all that was going on about him. Lost in the woods, he was searching a way out into the open. In the language of to-day, he was attempting to give a meaning in a single concrete form to the various phenomena of generation about him. This process was gradually and unconsciously working out in the primitive mind, clarifying his thought and giving it definite expression, just as our ideas become definite and fixed in our minds very often while we are apparently not thinking at all.

One such clarification was light. In the dark, all things seemed to ebb away. All nature seemed to have sunk into a languid inactivity, while man himself was lost in sleep. Whatever lay awake at night was a source of danger and of fear. Darkness was an enemy. Darkness was death.

As the sun creeps above the horizon a new day is born. Everything begins to stir : the birds chirp and the horses neigh. When the sun rises, man may leave the dark, damp cave and bask in sunshine. He feels as if new life has come to him. As the days grow longer and the rays of the sun become more intense, all nature seems happier, the fields yielding their crops and the trees their ripening fruit. Consequently, this heavenly body may be that common denominator in all manifestations of generation, so gropingly sought after by primitive man. Just as the father is both generator and provider of the family, so may the sun be generator and provider of all life upon the earth.

To the sun, the author of life, the power behind all generation, primitive men sought to render homage by identifying him with the principle of good. They personified the sun in such divinities as Brahma of the Hindus, Mithra of the Persians, Osiris of the Egyptians, and Adonis of the Greeks. We, therefore, have sun worship all over the world, in some places in its pure form, in others in a form merged with other symbols.

Some superstitions prevailing until very recent times point to the erotic element of the sun. It was believed that if a young woman walked naked through a field of corn in the intense sunlight of midday, she would become pregnant. In the same way, some Slavs still hold the belief that a woman may conceive by standing naked in the moonlight ; the moon like the sun being once taken for a deity.

Again, it may not be the sun itself that is behind creation, but the light of the sun, its rays, the fiery ball sinking below the edge of the world at the approach of night. That is fire, the great mystery that consumes everything like the crocodile, yet aids man in combating darkness and in driving off the beast. The fire built by man is only a small part of the great fire of the Universe that makes for life and generation. Just as it sustains life, it may also generate it. And just as it generates, so does it consume, transforming everything it touches into ashes and smoke. Fire is the beginning and end of things. It is the basis of all the generative manifestations that the spiritual hand of primitive man was groping for. Its worship became another universal religion.

Fire and sun came to serve man as symbols of the generative

force ; but even they were abstract. The sun is distant and cannot be touched. One cannot even look at it when it is at its zenith. It is difficult to visualize its action upon the earth, or to see in the concrete its generative quality. Fire, too, is intangible. The young child tries to grasp the flame before him. He reaches for it, but it only burns his fingers. Fire is something that is nothing. God appeared to Moses in the form of a fire upon the bush. Yet Moses could not tell what God was, and when he asked, the answer came : " I am that I am," a very slightly illuminating reply. Had God appeared in the form of a bull, like the god of the Egyptians, Moses would not have been puzzled.

In consequence, both of these representatives of the generative manifestations had to be reinforced with more concrete symbolic aids. There were animals about man doing in their own way for themselves what the sun or fire was doing for the universe. There were the bull and the goat, both of which came to their high positions in the religions of the world because of their supposed superior virility. They performed sexually oftener than other animals in primitive man's immediate environment. And in the period of rut no other domesticated animal could compare with them in sheer brutal strength and in the blind urge that would not stop at self-destruction in its hunt for the female. The strength of the force of rut fills us with awe even to-day. The sight of an aroused bull making for the cow or of a stallion rushing upon the mare is an exhibit of so tremendous an urge that it cannot fail to impress.

The generative force exemplified by these animals introduced the animal symbols as aids to the higher symbolism of the sun and fire. In time, these symbols, just because they were more concrete, overran the entire worship. There are religions in which the bull or goat or serpent is the basic element and the sun or fire has almost entirely vanished from the minds of the worshippers, lingering only in rare and half-forgotten rituals.

When the Bijagos of Africa were attempting to represent in the concrete their generative deity, they took the goat as its representative on earth. Similarly, the old Aryans of Europe had their spirits of the woods, Ljeschie, depicted with the horns, ears, and legs of a goat. The woods were ever swarming with life : grass and trees, birds and beasts and insects. There was always something creeping, flying, humming in the woods. This seething life, this bubbling-over of the forests, must be the spirits of life, Ljeschie. And only the goat could justly symbolize the generative powers of the divinity.

Dionysos, the Greek and Roman version of the Eastern god

of generation, was personified as a goat. This god was born, died, and came to life again to annually resurrect all nature, just as he himself had been resurrected. He was known as the " one of the Black Goatskin."

The sacred goats were usually kept in the temple with considerable care and tenderness. At Mendes, there were sacred stalls for them back of the room containing the altar. As the ceremonial progressed and the worshippers worked themselves to a pitch of excitement bordering on ecstasy, the goats were let loose among them. There was a scramble to touch the sacred animals. People struggled with one another for the opportunity to give them an humble kiss of homage. In this state of excitation, amidst song and revelry, attemps were made to join in sexual union with these living symbols of virility. There were he-goats for the woman worshippers and she-goats for the males. Those who were not fortunate enough to have the animal impersonations of the generative divinities had to be satisfied with human substitutes. And general sexual promiscuity followed the festivities and worship.

Not always, however, was the life of the sacred goat so happy. Often enough this animal became all the more sacred in its death and was offered up as a sacrifice to the generative god. Just as man offered his own generative organs, or parts of these organs, to the divinities, so did he sacrifice the entire animal that symbolized for him the very essence of these organs.

Kali was an Indian goddess, who knew everything that was going to happen to the humans in the huts and villages of India. She was kind enough to impart her knowledge in the form of prophecy to the priests in her temple. Yet she would not descend to her earthly dwelling-place unless a goat was sacrificed upon her altar and her priests sucked the blood of the animal while it was streaming from its cut neck.

The fate of the bull in the faith of the primitive peoples was not much different from that of the goat. There were occasions when the bull was eaten alive so that the worshippers might draw directly to themselves a part of his living force, for this animal was a powerful phallic emblem signifying the male creative power. At the Dionysian mysteries, bulls were torn apart and their flesh devoured while still warm. Dionysos himself was often represented as a bull as well as a goat. In Achia, the priests of the goddess of the earth could not commune with the divinity before they had offered her the fresh blood of a bull.

However, there were places where the bull was kept with great care, led a long life of comfort and ease, and, at death, received a distinguished tomb. There was the sacred bull of Egypt. In excavations at Serapeum, near Memphis, in Egypt, the tombs of over sixty of these sacred animals have been discovered. In these tombs, one usually finds a careful statement of the age of the animal, its place of birth, its mother's name, and the date when it was enthroned. Even the plain bull, without any official connection with god or temple, was held in great esteem. All these animals that died a natural death were carefully buried in the suburbs of the city, and their bones were afterwards collected from all parts of Egypt to be interred in a single spot. When the bull lost his life in religious duty, such as in sacrifice to Apis, all the worshippers beat their hearts and mourned his death.

*The Serpent the Sacred Image of the Solo-Phallic Cult*

The worship of the bull was not confined to Egypt and Greece. In India, Nandi—the sacred white bull of Siva—is still the object of much veneration. For the Persians and the Jews this animal, the personification of virility, served as an important religious symbol. And it was reverenced as well by the Assyrians, the Phœnicians, and the Chaldeans.

Like the bull and the goat, the serpent came to lend its aid in presenting to the human mind the force of generation in the world. Because it annually sheds its skin, reappearing in a new body as it were, this animal has for ages been looked upon as the emblem of immortality and reincarnation. The serpent, it is said in the Bible, is " more subtle than any of the beasts in the field " and therefore carries away the biggest prize. Not only has it become an erotic symbol, but it was, at one time, almost a universal religion in itself.

The American-Indians had their serpent mounds, and the Druids reverenced their sacred snakes. The mystic serpent of Orpheus, the Midgard snake of Scandinavia, and the brazen serpent of the Jews give testimony to the universality of this religion. There are even to-day some quarter of a million snake worshippers in India alone. A carved serpent curled up in an oval may still be found among the decorations on the ark in the synagogue. There were serpent ceremonies in Europe long after the advent of Christianity. Within recent times, live serpents were burned on the Eve of Saint John in the Pyrenees. The

*Greek medal*

Ophites caused a tame serpent to coil round the sacramental bread and worshipped it as the representation of the Saviour. The very traditions of Saint Patrick driving the snakes out of Ireland and of the expulsion of serpents from France indicate the struggle of early Christianity against the worship of the serpent-lingam.

What is it that singled out the serpent of all the animals for such a prominent place in the symbolism of religion ?

On the one hand, it was the particular impression the serpent was making on the primitive mind. Its noiseless walk aroused both suspicion and mystery. Its peculiar gaze and its knowing look, along with its supposed power of fascination, won the serpent the designation of " intelligent fish " from time imme-morial. Its name in some languages means life ; it also stands for wisdom. It was the serpent that opened the eyes of the first human pair that were born blind. The serpent is the teacher of man in wisdom, but its wisdom is generally taken to be misguided and applied for evil purposes. It was evil in the minds of some primitive peoples ; it is evil in the faith of Zoroaster ; it was so conceived in the Biblical story of Adam and Eve.

In Sunday school, we learn of the serpent in his glory. He did not crawl over the surface of the earth but had legs to stand upon. In fact, he walked erect like Adam and Eve and was equal in height to the camel. He could talk and was in the habit of conversing with the first woman on earth. He was clever enough to meddle in the life of the first humans and to offer them the benefit of his counsel.

To be sure, it was bad advice ; slyly he induced Eve to desire the fruit of the forbidden tree. Gently and cleverly he pointed the way to disobedience of the divine command. And as the woman slid downward, she pulled man down with her. It was by the guile of the serpent that Adam and Eve were driven out of the Garden of Eden to a life of toil and pain. Like Samson of a later day, the serpent itself shared the ruination it caused. By the fall of man, it was crushed and left to spend its days crawling upon the earth.

There is more to the story than is told to the Sunday-school class. The serpent was in love with Eve. He had seen Adam and Eve in their conjugal act and was animated by a passion for the woman. He hoped to get Adam out of the way and to take Eve for himself. The serpent is the first illicit desire of sex, the first thwarted passion of love, the first struggle of the male with the male for the female.

There is another reason for the serpent's place in religious symbolism—its resemblance to the lingam. They who ascribed the life principle to their own organs of generation were impressed by a living animal so suggestive of the male generative organ. So they deified the serpent and associated it with the sun-father gods and the generative divinities in general.

Like all male gods, the serpent came to be considered as a source of generation. A married woman needed only to enter a place where Tamburbrin, the eel-like creature was, and she would become pregnant. In the temple, a serpent might assume a human form and bless the women worshipper with his divine sexual presence. The offspring resulting from this union were known as the children of the snake. In the execution of the sexual function, however, the priest represented the serpent.

Just as we to-day associate the generative powers with youthfulness, so did the primitive men ascribe to the serpent not only generativeness, but the capacity of eternal youth as well. Utnapishtim, living beyond the mountain Mashu, past the wonderful park and across the Waters of Death, knew the secret of immortal life and perpetual youth. Gilgamesh, a hero of Elam, who became a god in Babylonia, set out to learn this secret. After a series of supreme difficulties, he ran the gauntlet of scorpion men and obtained the thing he so desired. But a serpent in the pool deprived him of the plant that rejuvenated old age, and itself became the guardian of the treasure. Out of scorpions the secret came to Gilgamesh; to a serpent it returned. The serpent is in itself the fountain of youth.

Once this animal symbolizes virility and youth, it is promptly exploited by men anxious to impregnate women. At a religious festival in Bengal, the men march entwined with snakes, while the chief has a rah-boa, or python, round his neck. It is a march like many others in which the males strut out like birds before the females, in display of their conjugal strength. He who kills a serpent even accidentally may be burned alive, for he has exposed the virility symbol to humiliation and insulted the men of the tribe.

Naturally, it was the women who were to show the greatest reverence to the serpent. It was their homage to the lingam, the sign of their subjection to the male sex. In India, there are wives of the snake as there are wives of the other gods in the temples. In Malabar, the serpent inspires certain women with oracular power, if they are perfect in their purity. In another place, the oldest woman enjoys the distinction of carrying the image of the serpent in the processions. This woman must lead a celibate life, since she is dedicated to the snake. Like many generative divinities, the serpent is worshipped by women with libations of milk; they are bestowing upon the snake their motherly gift.

If the serpent is a god and a source of fertility, it is only natural that he should be looked upon as a father as well. And a father he is for many of his worshippers. The rattlesnake men of Moqui claim to have originated from the snake, and snakes they will become after death. The Black-snake men of the Warramungas believe that they embody the spirits of snakes, which their ancestors, genuine serpents, deposited in a certain creek. The Moquis of America claim descent from a woman, who gave birth to snakes; in consequence, reptiles are freely handled in their snake dances, the purpose of which is to secure fertility of the soil.

In Papua, the natives have given thought to the animating principle of human beings. What is that something that gives life to a growth within the woman's body and causes it to eventually emerge as the new born? Why, it is Birumbir, of course. Birumbir is the embryo, as we might call it, operating within the uterus. And how does Birumbir get there? It enters the vulva in the form of Junga, and the Junga is inserted by an eel-serpent-

*Ornament from Puzzuoli Temple*

like creature called Trombuir. Translated into our scientific tongue, it is as if we said : life is brought into the womb in the form of semen introduced by the male organ. In the picturesque language of the Papuans, the lingam is the serpent-like Trombuir.

Now while Trombuir may enter the yoni of a married woman and impregnate her, it cannot do so to virgins. In the latter, the entrance is closed. Some special ritual must be observed by the woman and the tribe before the serpent or lingam may find its way to her. This is the origin, perhaps, of the universal stories of serpents guarding a treasure or dragons watching over hoards of value. It is symbolic of the masculine desire held in abeyance before the taboo on the virgin is raised. Having appeared on the scene as the mere physical representation of the lingam, a sort of living pillar, the serpent by its own attributes grew to much larger proportions and took on deeper meaning. It came to signify both wisdom and virility and to express the male protest and the masculine anticipation at the gate of the eternal feminine.

### III

It should not surprise us at all that just as animals came to reinforce generative symbolism on account of their virility, man's own virility should also come in as an additional element in the symbolism of generation. Primitive man was greatly occupied with his own organs of reproduction. He offered them in sacrifice to his gods ; he operated upon them for his own salvation ; he was ever conscious of their virility. No wonder, then, that they became for him the symbols of generation in the universe. Just as the sun was the father, so was man's lingam the father, and just as the moon was the mother, so was the yoni. Not only were these organs themselves symbolic, but anything suggesting them became emblems of the generative divinities. The lingam is in the shape of a rod with a round head ; so any object of this form, stone or wood, might become such a symbol. The yoni is an oval opening ; so any oval figure might represent the female divinity of sex. By further simplification it was enough to draw a vertical line to suggest the lingam and a horizontal one to signify the yoni, while the union of the two was represented by the cross.

The erotic symbol in religion was naturally a concomitant of the erotic religious thought. In fact, the two were elements of the same formative process. The thought affected the symbol, and the symbol influenced the idea. We should, therefore, expect the development of erotic symbolism to follow that of erotic thought. Just as man originally saw the generative process not by sexes but in the actual union, so did he seek to symbolize the generative force by the actual union of the sex organs. We find such images in Africa and Australia. We come across them in India and Japan. We can observe them carried in procession to the temple of Persephone. There are collections of such amulets in some museums with the notice that they were in use as late as the seventeenth century in Southern France and Italy.

Upon the altar of the Hindu temple, there is a sacred object of deep meaning. It is what the cross is to the Christian and the tablets or scroll to the Jew, and more. It is a cylinder hanging from a vase which is set into a pedestal. The pedestal is symbolic of Brahma, the basis of all that is in the universe, the fundamentals of reality. The vase stands for Vishnu, the goddess, the female principle ; and within it is the cylinder, representing Siva, the male god, the lingam. Highly involved as the Hindu trinity is, its symbolism is simple. Here we can see the foundation upon which the Hindu mythology has developed. It is the representation of the sexual organs in union.

Close to three millenniums before the Christian era, a Chinese emperor, Fu-Hsi, was given to creating religious symbols. He invented the pa-kua, eight symbols consisting of broken and unbroken lines ; the broken lines were symbolic of the yoni, while unbroken ones represented the lingam. Here again we have the two sexual principles together.

In the mythology of both Japan and China, there is the Queen of Heaven, Kwan-yin, whose name means : yoni of yonies. She is represented as seated upon a lotus, which, in turn, is a symbol of the womb, and immediately over her is her lord, Shang-ti. Below the two of them the emblem of fertility is placed. This same queen of Heaven and lady of plenty, Kwan-yin, is sometimes represented as a fish goddess. Then she is shown holding a lingam and swimming in a phallic sea.

Seeing the generative process in the union of the sex organs, primitive man came to conceive of it as essentially hermaphroditic in nature. And so the scarab, because it was believed to be double-sexed and capable of fructifying itself, became a sacred emblem. It was symbolic of the generative force of nature. In Egypt, it was the emblem of Khefera, god of creation, father of gods and men, creator of all things and the rising sun. In times of famine and poverty in medieval Europe, the people resorted to an old symbolic service to secure divine aid. In some places the " need-fire " was kindled by two naked men, who rubbed two dry sticks together, an action in itself symbolic of the sexual process. With the flame they lighted two fires between which the cattle were driven to insure fertility in the herd. In other places the monks kindled the fire in the presence of the faithful. Near the fire they raised the image of the lingam.

The ceremony was a form of magic. It was an appeal to the heavenly powers to engage in the process of fertility and bring an abundance of crop. The fertility powers in nature were definitely shown what was expected of them by the kindling of the " need-fire " ; it was a symbolic union of the sexes. The sexual union,

*Kwan-yin, the Oriental Queen of Heaven*

then, was the purpose of the ceremony. Still, at its end an image of the lingam was raised. Of the two sexes represented in union, one emerged separated, individual, with a place for itself in the ceremony. It was the development of the god of sex, male in this particular case, from the divinities representing the sexual process. Religious symbolism, therefore, had to seek ways of representing the individual agents of sex—heretofore represented together.

Of the two agents of the sexual process, it was only natural that the female principle should first occupy the primitive mind. The female is directly associated with the birth of new life. It is the mother who brings the child into the world and it is she, too, who nurses the young. In sexual symbolism we might, therefore, expect the female principle to be most often represented. As a matter of fact, however, there are comparatively few female symbols, while there is an enormous number emblematic of the male organ. The reason for this is often given as the difficulty in representing the female generative organ ; the male organ, on the other hand, invites representation. However, this is insufficient reason. The symbol did not always represent the organ realistically. It was often only suggestive. If no difficulty was encountered in representing the lingam by a straight line, there is no reason why it should not be possible to represent the yoni by curved lines or an oval. There were many ways of suggesting the yoni that called for little effort or technique.

The real cause for the paucity of female symbols must be sought not in the technical process of representation but in the ideals motivating the social group. In a social system dominated by males, where the women are held in subjection, it is small flattery for the males to have the feminine principle worshipped in the temples. Man, dominating the social group, could not declare himself divine, but he could attribute a divine significance to the lingam. When masculinity is worshipped, the male naturally assumes greater importance. Consequently, the male principle was all the more dominant in countries where women were held in subjection. As the women were more and more enslaved, especially in the western world, the religious symbolism grew more masculine. Man forced woman not only to serve him but to worship his virility as well.

IV

The female principle began its symbolic history crudely enough. Centred upon the mother idea, it only sought to represent motherhood. Just as there was an individual mother giving birth to

individualized life, so was there a universal mother giving birth
to new life universally. The universal mother was represented
by the individual mother. Such a mother was Oma-Oma of the
Hindus. She was a goddess, yet greater than all gods ; for she
was before gods came into existence and before existence itself.
In many early religions the mother goddess was the supreme
deity, the male gods playing only a secondary part.

The individual mother was represented by the figure of a

*Maya, the Hindu goddess, forcing*
*from her breasts the nourishment*
*of all creation*

woman with her breasts and genitals greatly exaggerated, or even
by the images of these parts alone. There were female breasts
and genitals upon the supporting columns of almost every temple
in antiquity. Similar carvings were found over the doorways of
the Christian cathedrals in Ireland, where they served as a
protection against evil. In the Cossit library of Memphis,
Tennessee, there is a Mexican idol in the form of a woman with her
yoni fully exposed ready to receive the lingam. There is a goddess
on the Slave Coast in the form of a pregnant woman, who is

invoked against barrenness. Another African goddess, Odudua, is represented as a seated mother holding her child, and the walls of her temple bear carvings of the lingam and yoni. There are goddesses imaged with babies growing out of their fingers, toes, and all parts of their bodies, and goddesses possessed of many breasts, like the many-breasted Artemis. Out of this idea of motherhood, grew the mother-child symbolism that was so common in the art of ancient times and that later developed into the beautiful Madonna paintings of Christian Europe.

As the idea of mother dissolved into the more generic idea of femininity, the artist jumped a step. He no longer sought to represent the mother or female herself, but to draw or sculp an object that would suggest the female figure or genital. What was it that made the artist give up realism for impressionistic symbolism? It may have been a growing sense of refinement which makes us speak, at times, by indirection or use sarcasm where we might scold and abuse. Again, it may have been the helplessness of the artist in presenting a realistic picture, or his sheer laziness.

Crude draftsman that primitive man was, he may have found it difficult to carve the vulva in true detail. Often, all he succeeded in doing was to hammer out a figure in the form of a horseshoe, the very figure that is nailed to so many doors in various parts of the world, as an emblem of luck. Mighty few of those who live in such houses know that the horseshoe is only symbolic of the yoni and that by nailing it to their doors, they follow out a custom older than the history of their race. Another female symbol of this kind is the Greek delta or the Hebrew dalet, a pointed triangle in form, which also means door.

Another attempt to re-create the yoni was the pointed oval. We may find it yet over the portals of ancient temples in Yucatan, and we can come across it anywhere in India. A profile view of the yoni would suggest the crescent, the sacred emblem of the Moslem, the symbol of Selene, the moon-goddess who appears in similar form in the sky. Selene stood for lunar periods associated with the periodicity of women.

Any oval or fissure may represent the female generative organ. There were oval stones with a cut in them to which women came to pray and to find solace. The *asherah* so often mentioned in the Bible was originally an accidental stump of a tree and later the trunk of a tree with its branches purposely cut away. It had an opening or a fissure, called the Door of Life. Around this door, there were thirteen tufts of hair representing the thirteen periods of a woman in a year. Above it, there was an emblematic representation of the clitoris.

The filled oval suggests the egg, which itself has generative powers. The oval-egg shape admits a number of objects into the female symbolism of religion. Among these, we find the peach in China and Japan.

There is still another line of female religious symbols—symbols that came to be what they were because of their resemblance to the female organ, not in appearance, but in function or activity. Just as the mother harbours the new life, so might any object housing things be symbolic of the mother. The ark, for instance,

*An Oriental divinity*

is a female symbol. The story of Noah's ark is really the story of a dream fulfilled, the dream of returning to the mother to escape from a disappointing reality into the protecting womb of mother-hood. The ark was the container of the Tablets of the Covenant of Moses, the Book of the Law, and other sacred objects of the Hebrews. A tabernacle is also a container like the ark, and in the Roman church Mary is called the tabernacle of God. Mounds and pyramids came to be symbols of the female principle, and taking a dead pharaoh to his tomb upon his demise was actually returning him unto the universal mother whence he came into the world.

By a similar analogy, woman came to be symbolized as a bridge between God and man. Like Prometheus, she steals life from above and brings it forth upon the earth. She is the intermediary between the divine and human, and as such, she is symbolized by objects suggestive of a bridge or crossing. One of these is the altar, which, in India, is called " yoni."

Similarly, the apricot, bean, barley, vesica piscis, comb, cave, and various other things developed as suggestions or symbols of female organs of generation, just as did the circle and the ring. The part of the latter in our marriage ceremony is clear enough, although few people give it a thought. The act of putting on the ring is only the reverse of the function of the consummated marriage. It would thus be more appropriate if the groom put his

*The Sheela-na-gig found on
ancient Irish churches*

finger through the ring held by the bride. Whatever it was that reversed the process, the reversal brought an additional meaning to the ceremony : it were as if until the wedding, the ring, or yoni, of the bride was not recognized because it was not functioning. By giving the maiden the ring, the groom calls upon her for the functioning of the yoni.

v

If there are many symbols for the female principle, those that represent the male force are countless, indeed. The first attempt to represent the latter was a man with a lingam greatly enlarged, or the lingam itself, of enormous size, detached from the body.

We have already taken note of such figures in African temples. In the religious festivals of Egypt, the image of Osiris was carried in the processions. This figure was one cubit in height and the length of its lingam was also one cubit. The woman of Rome reverenced waxen reproductions of Priapus with the lingam enormously disproportionate and movable at will. When the Protestants took Embrun in 1585, they found there the image of Saint Foutin with an exaggerated lingam which was reddened by the libations of wine that had been poured over it by women needing its aid.

Not only were such phallic figures to be found over gateways and doorways of churches and public houses, but the image of the lingam itself, detached from the human organism, is frequently met with. There were such figures at the entrances to the houses of worship among primitive men. In the largest and richest temple of Syria, at Acropolis, there were two immense figures with the inscription : " Bacchus has brought these phalli for Yunon, his mother-in-law." The lingam detached was known in Latin as Mutinus, Tutinus, and later as Priapus. In the convenient form of an amulet, it was called Fascinus.

A red lingam was often the sign above the door of legalized houses of prostitution. Both the Greeks and the Romans used to place an image of this organ upon their graves. It was an affirmation of the belief in eternal life in the very face of death. Was not Priapus referred to as " saviour of the world ? " At Trani, in Italy, a lingam was carried through the streets in religious processions. It was called *il santo membro*. Idols representing it were so common in Christian times that there was a special penance for performing incantations to the lingam. Hot cross buns were originally phallic in form—a reproduction in dough of the generative organs. Finding it impossible to break the people away from this custom, the early Christian fathers ordained that these buns be marked with a cross and accepted in Christendom.

In antiquity, the woman received an amulet from her husband on their wedding-day, and she was supposed to wear it round her neck. It was a bejewelled lingam bearing the inscription : " When they join." Phallic amulets were particularly common in Naples, where they were worked into the designs of vases, rings, medals, and even precious stones. A lingam amulet was often nailed to a tree for the protection of the countryside. In France, a *fesne* was a lingam amulet said to work magic. In Japan to-day, the young man gives an amulet to his beloved. It is a box containing a realistic representation of the lingam in ivory or metal. When a corner of the box is pressed, it opens and the lingam emerges by means of a delicate spring. In Isernia, full-sized reproductions of the lingam were offered to the memory of the saints, Cosmos and Damian ; and this very day, in Naples, one may buy such an image with a serpent curled about it. Sir Joseph Banks, writing in 1786, describes some of the phallic amulets he observed in the same city :

" On the 27th of September at Gernia . . . an annual fair was held which lasted three days. The situation of this fair is on rising ground, between two rivers, about half a mile from the town of Gernia. In the most elevated part there is an ancient church with a vestibule. . . . This church is dedicated to Saints Cosmo and Damiano. On one of the days of the fair, the relics of the saints are exposed and afterwards carried in procession from the Cathedral of the city to this church, attended by a prodigious concourse of people. In the city and at the fair, exvoti of wax, representing the male parts of generation, of various dimensions, some even of the length of a palm, are publicly offered for sale.

" There are also waxen vows that represent other parts of the body mixed with them, but of those there are few in comparison with the number of Priapi. The devout distributors of these vows carry a basket of them in one hand and hold a plate in the other to receive the money, crying aloud : ' Saint Cosmo and Saint Damiano.'

" If you ask the price of one, the answer is ' pui ci metti, piu merito '—the more you give, the more the merit. The price of a man is fifteen Neapolitan grains and of a litany five grains. The vows are chiefly presented by the female sex ; they seldom are such as present legs, arms, and the like, but most commonly the male organs of generation . . . At the time, a woman presented a figure of the male organ of generation in that state of tension and rigidity which it assumes when about to discharge its functions, she said : ' Santo Cosmo benedette, cosi voglio.' Blessed Saint Cosmo, let it be like this.

" The vow is never presented without being accompanied by a piece of money, and is always kissed by the devotee at the moment of presentation."

Leaving the field of complete realistic reproduction of the male principle and entering upon its symbolic representation, we find that anything suggestive of the lingam may become a symbol. There is the pestle, for instance, still generally considered as the male in distinction to the mortar which is the female. In olden times, these objects played a greater part in the daily life of the people and their sexual meaning was consciously accepted as such. There is the mushroom with its bell-like, enlarged

prepuce.  There were the pillar and the post universally considered as sacred not to any particular divinity, but to all the gods.

Moses operated with a rod when he was vying with the
servants of Pharaoh in magic power.  Some of us still pay
for the services of a " divining rod," which is said to locate
water or mineral veins.  There is the concept of the " staff of
life " in modern mysticism just as the Tree of Life figures
mystically in the story of Adam and Eve.  There is a forked
stick used in mystic ceremonies and perhaps there is something

*An early Priapic statue*

of this rod-lingam meaning in our custom of carrying a cane.
Possibly that is why the cane is more of a man's companion in a
love escapade than it is an aid in walking.

In Japan, the term *wo-bashira*, or male pillar, is applied to the
railing of a bridge or a balustrade of a staircase, and to the end
of the tooth of a comb, since they all in some way suggest the
lingam.  Our own Maypole comes down from post and pillar
worship, associated with May festivities—the spring fertility
celebrations of ancient times.  The custom of distributing prizes
from the Maypole is suggestive of its fruit-giving or gift-bringing

powers. At the same ceremony, the gathering of the seed of the male fern further points to a connection between the Maypole and the sexual life.

Along with the rod belong the bow and arrow which are likewise lingam symbols. Above the Assyrian grove, there was a winged figure, the celestial bowman, who was implored by all those desirous of vigour. Cupid, too, has his store of arrows always with him, a symbol of reserved virility ; his bow, relaxed or taut, signifies this power spent or conserved.

The symbol of the lingam is also the father of the statue in religious worship. The primitive forms of Mercury, Hermes, and Troth, all lingam gods, were hewn in stone. These stones had no facial sculpture nor hands nor feet. They were sometimes in the shape of a lingam, but more often simply upright pillars, vaguely suggestive of the human figure. They were considered sacred and were erected upon cross-roads or used to mark the boundaries of properties. They sometimes faced the altars upon which sacrifices were offered to the gods. We still can find traces of such works in stone in the round towers of Ireland.

In time, these stones underwent modifications. At first, only the head was carved upon them. The Hermæ—fertility gods of antiquity—were represented as square pillars with bearded heads. Later, both head and bust were formed on the stone, which descended lingam-like to a square base. Such were the Ameonic statues. Gradually, the part between the head and the base was also humanized, and what was once just a lingam became the trunk and limbs of the human body. The stone representation of the generative gods followed closely the development of the generative deity.

Some notion of the worship of the lingam may be gleaned from the sacred books of the Hindus. The priest was first to go through a series of ablutions like our baptismals ; then, dipping the utensils of worship in perfumed water, repeating the while the sacred word *om*, and invoking the favour of Nandi, the sacred bull of Siva, he was to " bathe the lingam with perfumed water, the five products of the cow, clarified butter, honey, and the juice of sugar-cane, and lastly pour over it a pot of pure water, consecrated by the requisite prayers. Having thus purified it, adorn it with clean garments and a sacrificial string, and then offer flowers, perfumes, ornaments. Thus worship the lingam with the prescribed offerings, invocations, prayers and honours, and by circumambulating it and by prostrating thyself before Siva, represented under this symbol."

The Roman lingam divinity was also worshipped by offerings

of flowers, fruits, and libations. It was likewise served in some places with honey, milk, and myrtle, the symbol of an amorous attitude ; with roses in spring, ears of corn in summer, grain in autumn, and branches of olives in winter. On all these occasions the lingam was decorated with garlands by the women, and prostrations came in for a very important part of the worship. From passages in the works of Maimonides, famous Jewish physician and medical authority of the twelfth century, we get the impression that, in his day, prostration was associated with

*As the god of love developed*

exposing one's self, for to expose one's self was an act of humility as well as a display of a sacred object. As kneeling is a vestige of prostration, its former use in expressing one's amorous feelings was symbolically appropriate for the occasion.

VI

Many were the symbols that were called by the pious to represent the male principle of generation, but only a few were chosen. Few succeeded in becoming universal symbols and forming almost a religion of their own. The tree was one of these few ; and tree worship was once a universal religion.

Like the rod or the pole, the tree graphically represented the lingam. But it also suggested the generative organ functionally ; standing erect, rooted in the ground and stretching skyward, withstanding all assault of the weather, the tree emphasizes power and virility. Bedecking its branches with green leaves and bearing fruit, it was generative in no mistakable manner. The tree was, then, a living image of the lingam.

The ancient Hebrews were so averse to idolatry and figurative religion that they forswore even lay sculpture. Still, they held a venerable attitude towards the tree. In the Garden of Eden, there were two trees, one giving knowledge and the other eternal life. Both were forbidden to Adam and Eve. Yet, Adam, incited by Eve, tasted of the one and became wise ; that he might not taste of the other and live forever, he was driven out of Eden to trudge his wearisome way over the length and breadth of the earth.

What was that Tree of Knowledge that brought so much woe unto mankind ? In Christian theology the notion crept in that it was an apple tree. It was over an apple that Adam tripped and fell for all eternity. According to the Hebrew tradition, however, it was not an apple tree but a fig tree, a ficus or syca- more. It was the triangular fig leaf that covered the nakedness of Eve, the triangular form being in itself the symbol of the nakedness of all her daughters. The fig, universally considered a symbol of the virgin yoni, was the appropriate fruit for the lingam-tree to bear. How much more significant is now the seduction of Adam by Eve in getting him to partake of the fig-yoni she offered him ? We can thus better understand our excessively criticized ancestor who yielded to a woman.

When Abraham chose to express to Jehovah his humility and devotion, he planted a grove at Beth-El, which forever after was to be a " house of God." Thousands of years later, the children of Abraham were looking for a symbol to place upon the flyleaf of a sacred book. Again they found in the tree the most appro- priate emblem. The Hebrews and the Greeks were not friendly to each other, yet they both were friendly to the ficus tree. The idol of Bacchus was always made of the wood of the ficus and the most sacred object in the Bacchanalian procession was a basket of figs. Upsala is far away in cold, wintry Sweden, yet it possessed a grove in which every tree was divine. In the flatlands of Lithuania there were sacred groves until late in the fifteenth century, when the people first embraced Christianity. He who cut a branch in such a grove would either die suddenly or become crippled in one of his limbs. To the Finnish people, the holy groves were so sacred that they would not permit a woman to enter them.

The old Finns had their Veddas called Kalawala. In them we find the story of an acorn. The acorn fell to the ground and was covered by the sand. Then it began to grow. It grew big and yet bigger; tall and yet taller. Finally it assumed such immense proportions that it became a menace to the world. Just then a hero came to the rescue of the universe. He appealed to the mother, the windspirit, who sent out a giant to overcome it. Then it was discovered that the tree possessed the power of bestowing good.

And Zoroaster told his Persians that there was a tree of life called Harn. It grows upon a mountain and is nourished by a spring near by. It is zealously guarded by Ferœdin, the door-keeper of paradise, against Ahriman, the evil spirit who wants to possess it. This tree assures those who die in the faith that when the bugle sounds they will come to life again. This tree, too, is possessed of detective qualities, revealing thieves and murderers before they commit their evil acts.

As the tree was a bearer of new life, it came to be taken for the father of the race. The ancient Mexicans believed that their ancestors came from the seed of the sacred palm. Hesiod tells of Zeus creating a race of daring people out of ash trees. Virgil speaks of people of his day that traced their racial origin to the trunks of trees.

Being the father of the race, it was only natural for the tree to possess a self, like god or human. It could be spoken to or argued with. Before the Fiji Islander tasted his coco-nut he politely asked the tree's permission. When a durian tree in Selangor does not bear fruit, the local sorcerer will take a hatchet and deliver several telling blows on its trunk, saying : " Will you now bear fruit or not ? If you do not, I shall fell you." To this the tree will reply through the mouth of another man who has climbed another tree near by, " Yes, I will now bear fruit ; I beg of you not to fell me."

There were male trees and trees that were female. To make a grove fruitful, the trees should be married. A Hindu would not taste of the first fruit of his mango tree until he had married it to a tamarind or a jasmine near by. This tree wedding was an expensive affair, for the more Brahmans that ate at the wedding the greater was the glory to the owner of the grove. A family was known to sell its golden and silver trinkets and to borrow all the money it could get to marry its trees with due pomp and ceremony.

If a tree may be married, one need not wonder that it may become pregnant and as such are blossoming clover trees treated in the Moluccas. No noise may be made near them ; no light or fire carried past them of nights, and everyone must uncover in their presence. All these precautions are taken so that the pregnant tree may not be frightened and drop its fruit too early by miscarriage.

Since trees are so fruitful, man applies to them as a source of fecundity. A barren woman, among the Maoris, will therefore

*Ancient English artifacts*

do well to embrace a sacred tree, for by so doing she will conceive. If she embraces the east side, she will give birth to a boy, if the west side, a girl will be the result. In Slavonia, a barren woman will place a new chemise upon a fruitful apple tree on the eve of Saint George's Day. Next morning, before sunrise, she examines the garment, and if she finds that some living creature has crept over it, she believes that her wish will be fulfilled within the year. Just as the tree is helpful to man, man may sometimes be of aid to the tree in its function of fertility. In the islands of Amboyna, when the crop appears to be scanty, the

men go naked to the plantations by night and there seek to
fertilize the trees precisely as they would impregnate women.

That the celebration of the Maypole is related to this primitive
tree worship has already been indicated. A few customs of the
May Day celebrations will bear out this statement. In some
parts of Russia, the pole is dressed up like a woman. In other
Slavic countries, a young man is clothed to represent the groom.
Here the sexes seem to have become confused, the Maypole
becoming a female rather than a male symbol. This is probably
due to the position in which it is kept ; it is usually, in these
countries, a long trunk brought in from the woods on two small
carts drawn by horses. The pole being long, only its ends rest
upon the cart so that it resembles a narrow slit between two
comparatively broad bodies. Consequently, it may have been
taken as a symbol of the yoni. Generally, however, the Maypole
is set up erect with its head decorated with garlands and hence
it prevails as a symbol of the lingam.

The ceremonies connected with the Maypole were erotically
appropriate indeed. Philip Stubb decries woefully the licence
in the May Day celebration of England in 1553 : " On Whit-
sunday all the young men and young women, husbands and
wives, and old men as well, run wildly into the woods, hills, and
mountains where they spend the night in pleasant pastimes and
revelry. In the morning they return bringing with them a birch
and branches of trees. Some twenty or forty oxen, each one
having a nosegay of flowers placed on the tips of its horns—in
themselves symbols of the lingam—bring home the Maypole
decorated with flowers and herbs and painted over in variable
colours. Behind the Maypole follow two or three hundred men
and women, and often even children, with great devotion. The
devotees strew the ground round about with flowers, bind green
boughs around the Maypole and set up bowers and arbours
near by. Then they fall to dance about it like the heathen at the
dedication of the idol . . ."

What transpired during the night of revelry in the woods and
mountain ? Mr. Stubb offers few details save that he heard it
" credibly reported (and that viva voce) by one of great gravity
and reputation that of forty, three-score, or a hundred maidens
going to the wood over night there have scarcely the third part of
them returned home again undefiled."

There are various reminders of the old tree worship among us
even now. We still celebrate Arbor Day. We plant a tree
upon solemn occasions, often in memory of the dead. We ceremoniously erect a pole for the flag. Jews still shake the *lulov* on
the Feast of Tabernacles. Christians have their palms on Palm

Sunday and evergreens for Christmas. Both the pillar and the tree are still with us—their erotic significance aptly concealed yet invariably present, however modified.

.　　.　　.　　.　　.　　.　　.

In the land of India, there is a great spirit hovering over two drops of water. One of the drops is white and represents the masculine world. The other is red and symbolizes the feminine element in creation. The two are separate and yet not unrelated, for both are touched by the great spirit Kama, love fluttering over the deep of sex.

Kama, then, is the great force that holds the universe together. But it is not the greatest. For as the drops of water are drawn closer together by the attraction of Kama, they often unite, and their union calls forth a spirit even greater than Kama. The union of the sexes brings down Kamakala, the highest deity of them all, that has the sun for its face, fire and the moon for breasts, and the Hardhakala for organs of generation.

This was the way the old man of India told his tale of love and its place in the world. Of course, it could all be said much more plainly and bluntly, but primitive as the Indian man was, he had the sense for the beautiful and he sought to speak as beautifully as he thought.

There were moments in the life of primitive man when he felt saddened and depressed. There were others when he was expansive and elated. There were times when he felt his heart melting away in a sweet longing for the unobtainable, in a vague attempt to fathom the unfathomable and to become at one with the great power behind nature and life. It was then that he turned to imagine beautiful tales and to conjure up figures and shapes that would express not only the thought in his mind but also the way he felt as he was thinking it. It was then that mythology and religious symbolism came into the world.

Years rolled on. Ages came and passed. Man changed in diverse ways, yet fundamentally he is ever the same. He is ever reaching out for what cannot be obtained, like the child on his way to meet the horizon. Yet his ways of going about it have changed with the times. He may ever be trying to symbolize the same experience, but his methods of doing so have improved with the evolution of his mind and tastes. Kama and Kamakala may be the divinities he is ever seeking to portray, yet his portraiture is ever becoming less brutal and more refined, poor in concrete representation, but richer in suggestive detail.

And even for this fact the people in the East have a fitting symbol :

In the solemn ceremonies of the Lingayats in India, the high priest holds a lingam in his left hand, while he worships it in the required sixteen ways.  During all this time the disciple stands by a reverent observer.  Then the high priest places the lingam in the left hand of the onlooker, enjoining him to view it intently. " Look at it," he says, " it is the highest thing in existence.  Look at it and you will see your own soul."

And just because man's own soul was mirrored in his sex worship, it is so rich in colour, so fascinating in detail, and so fragrant with the aromatic flower of the human soul—its sentiments of love.

# BOOK TWO
## IN THE TEMPLE OF THE GODS

# CHAPTER I

## A DAY WITH BAAL

*—within his palm*
*Was the mystery of life and the joy of living.*

**I**

LET us raise our anchor in the calendar and recklessly sail out into the infinity of time. It is high noon and before the chain is pulled in we are already at the French Revolution. We witness an ill-humoured mob angered by hunger and blinded by the sudden glare of sunlight. Passing the Place de la Concorde in Paris, we see this furious mob beheading its king and abolishing its god. Another start and we meet the *Santa Maria* with Columbus on board, ordering about his crew of fifty-two, on the first voyage to unknown lands where people might be free and start anew. A bit yonder, we see the smouldering flames of the Inquisition in which people who did believe burned those who did not believe in the faith we have just seen abolished.

As the day draws to a close, a blazing sun is setting into a sea of darkening blue. Our path becomes gloomy and grim. Man is forced into the strait-jackets of superstition and enveloped in fear. Here all believe and everything is believed in. Over and above all hovers hate with its malicious gaze and gnashing teeth. The air is thick and the compass is straggling. We seem to have struck a whirlpool of time with no way out. We are passing the Dark Ages.

Sailing onward into the night we feel the hours crawl by. In the darkness we see a huge oven with an immense fire, which was made by the children of the East as a foundry for civilization. Into the oven have just been thrown many a savage tribe of the West. There, in due course of time, they are to be forged into civilized peoples. Meanwhile, the chimney is belching forth thick smoke and dark flames, its soot covering the face of the earth.

Still further into the night we sail until streaks of light begin to cut the darkness. A new star rises in the east—the star of a man who surrendered his life on the cross to gain a place in the heart of the world. Again we move onward, passing a mountain beautiful, the divine abode, where a god may do as a god will with a humanity looking on. Further still, we witness a fire upon a bush that will not burn. This is the fire everlasting, eternally illuminating the Holy of Holies of three faiths of man.

On we advance through the night to greet approaching dawn.

A diffused light is spreading over the sky, while out of a purple horizon the glowing sun rises to shower its golden bounty upon a hungry world. Soon we are in the midst of daylight comforting and cheering, opening to the children of the earth all the treasures of Mother Nature. We are in the land of Baal, the god of the universe.

Go east or west ; turn north or south ; there will always be an altar to Baal, an altar to the god most high, who holds within his palm the mystery of life and the joy of living. On the summit of every hill and under every green tree Baal is worshipped— the god whom people knew long before they had heard of Jehovah, the divinity whom they loved long after they had learned of the one and true God.

For Baal was a god, an only one and true. Other gods' names were never spoken, but names they had. Baal had no name. He had neither father nor mother ; nor did he spring from the sea. Unlike Jesus he came from no definite place. Unlike Jehovah he was not interested in one particular people. Unlike Allah he was not satisfied with one prophet.

Baal was the one great abstract god of antiquity. He was the mighty force in nature that mystifies us no less to-day than it did the men of ancient times. He was the power that gave life and that took it away. He was the sea of life with its tides high and low, ebbing away of nights and rising over its boundaries in the morning. Baal was the greatest god of all, but what was Baal ? How could one fathom this infinite mystery ? Primitive man, limited in his thinking and circumscribed in his imagery, sought a concrete form for the mightiest of the gods. So he looked into the mirror of life and in the image of what he saw therein he created his Baal.

The god may have hailed in the downpour of the rain or twinkled in the dewdrop upon the unfolding leaf. Baal was in the substance that quenches the thirst of man ; in the liquid that impregnates Mother Earth and releases the new life within her womb even as the semen of the male impregnates the female and causes new life to sprout. Again, he was reflected in the waters of the spring. At a spring Abraham and Lot swore each to go his way. At a spring the patriarchs met their wives, and the rulers of Judah were crowned kings. The ancient spring of Gihon, known to-day as Bethesda, the Virgin's fountain, is still held in reverence in Jerusalem. In Mecca, the Zemzem spring continues to well in supreme sanctity.

Again, Baal may have risen toward the clouds with the towering tree, majestically spreading its leaf-hidden limbs and bearing fruits for man and beast. The tree grew in watered places, immersed in the liquid life-substance like the lingam in its life-bringing function. Some trees were the mainstays of life. The date palm was one ; by its fruit is supplied many a community with its daily bread, as the father provides the sustenance for the family. The fig tree was another. It also furnished food for the hungry and, in addition, it offered shelter from the blaze of the sun, like the mother caring for her young. Both in appearance and in service the tree was the life-giving and the life-bringing force.

Baal may also have come forward with the rising sun as it brought light and warmth to a world lying in the cold embrace of darkness. He may have appeared in the form of Shamash, the sun god, kissing Mother Earth with his sunshine and penetrating her with his rays in celestial, conjugal union.

The god may even have ascended with the rolling hilltop as the uniting element between the universal father and mother— sky and earth, even as the lingam among the species created by this universal pair. Olympus or Horeb, Lebanon or Sinai may have been reincarnated as the Baal of the mountains. There may have been a Baal in the erect stones, whether among the twelve at Sinai, the Black Stone at Mecca, or the stelæ of Persia. There may have been a Baal in the lion and the wolf, the bull and the goat. There were other things and places in which the god might be found. Wherever there was a clear suggestion of the function of Baal as the fountain of life, wherever life was being generated or its generators were in evidence, there was also a manifestation of Baal incarnate.

However different its representations, the meaning of Baal was ever the same. However the god appeared, he always did but one thing : he brought new life, he caused the birth of plant and animal and man. Consequently, the worship of Baal was practically the same all over the world. He was rewarded for his blessings of fecundity with the first products of his function. The first fruits and the firstborn were sacred unto him.

But there were times when things went badly with Baal and he appeared to have lost all his generative power. Nature seemed to die and even he succumbed with it. All this was temporary, of course ; it was the winter season of the year, which would be succeeded by the spring, when Baal would resurrect himself. Still, while it lasted, it was a time of sadness and mourning. Man grieved for his god and abstained from all pleasures. He even denied himself food and drink, and to show his solidarity with Baal he abstained from the exercise of the function he shared, in his own small way, with the god. He refrained from sexual union until Baal revived.

Baal was served most appropriately, however, when he and man were in a happier mood. It was then that the worship took the form of a feast. Man brought to the temple of the fat of the land for the glory of the god and his own pleasure. He freely imbibed of the wine which Baal first taught him to use. Finally, he indulged in the act, the function of which is the province of Baal, the act that makes for the happiness of one generation and the advent of another. The god of fertility was worshipped in the union of the sexes.

## II

All through the night the roads were crowded with pilgrims. Some were coming in chariots, with slaves rushing ahead to herald their arrival, and others following behind so that no commoner might approach the conveyance. There were other pilgrims straggling along on foot, resting now and then underneath a tree by the wayside. There were princes of the blood and emissaries from kings. There were beggars in tatters, blind and lame, hopping along the road like a swarm of flies, a scourge upon a land that would forget all misery and woe.

Among the dregs of the world and the glittering stars there was the spirit of youth marching along the trodden road to the Hill of Promise. There was the unkissed maiden, blushing in her golden innocence, as she was making her first visit to the temple of love. Her heart beat fast in anticipation, like the fluttering bride first leaving her father's roof for the greatest experience of her life.

There was the lightsome steps of the boisterous lad, who, heretofore imprisoned in a tiny village, was having his first, full breath of freedom as he started along the way. His joy lay beyond the pebbled road leading up to the Sacred Hill. There was the lingering course of the dreamy youth, absorbed in a fanciful world of his own creation, which he conveniently located upon the sacred knoll. There was the old man, dozing away in his oxen-drawn cart, burdened with memories of happier visits. Another cart carried a portly matron looking wistfully eastward toward the Sacred Hill, the only place where her heart was ever gladdened by forgetfulness and joy. In her hazy mind, she wondered what might befall her on this year's visit. Last year she had been almost overlooked, and yet, there were years when all eyes were upon her, when she was the first to leave the line of women waiting to be selected by the worshippers.

All during the night the roads were crowded with pilgrims. Rich and poor, old and young, saddened and joyous, all were going up the rising hill to give thanks and to pray, to sacrifice or to be sacrificed on the altar of the great master of the universe —Baal.

Nor were they coming empty-handed to the house of their god. Everyone was bringing a gift in accordance with his means. The princes and the emissaries of kings were trailing behind them oxen and chariots to be turned over to the priests, in which they might, at dawn, rush eastward to meet the rising sun, the daily reflection of Baal. The husbandman was leading the first-born of his herd and the farmer was carting along the first products of his soil and the first fruits of his trees. Others were carrying in the pockets of their girdles gifts of silver or of gold and sacred trinkets and coins, all of which were offerings not displeasing to Baal's servants in the temple.

However much each sacrifice meant to the particular individual, however difficult it had been to provide it, he was bringing it happily in the most generous of moods. He was offering it to the All-giver, to the very source of gifts—to Life itself.

III

A cool breeze came out of the north. Strips of blue cut the paling sky. Day was breaking. The travellers quickened their pace. Zest was added to their steps, for out there in the haze and the mist was the Sacred Hill for which their hearts had been yearning these many hours and days and weeks before. They could hardly see it, but they were conscious of what was happening there during the late hours of the night. On the Sacred Hill, all were a-mourning now, mourning for Baal.

While Baal was a living god of life, his own active life was not continuous, any more than are growth and generation upon earth. Baal himself had his ups and downs ; every year he died and was mourned by his worshippers. Women attired themselves in mourning and went about with streaming hair and bared breasts. The men, too, mourned in their own way, and all were to shave their heads as an additional expression of their grief. Those women who would not cut their hair must sacrifice their bodies when Baal came to life again.

This was the last night of mourning, each pilgrim reminded himself. There, in the temple, the priests must now be taking out the gilded wooden cow from her chamber, where she had been resting for the whole year with a golden sun between her horns. Seven times they would carry her around the temple with torches in their hands, while outside every house on the Sacred Hill burned lamps of oil. It was thus they besought the goddess Ishtar to go down to the " house of darkness, where dust lies on the bolt of the door " and to release from the arms of death the life-god Baal.

As the anxious pilgrims hurried on, their entire thought turned toward the temple ; they fell into a familiar rhythm, the rhythm of the song of Ishtar that they had remembered since their first visit to the Sacred Hill.  The song depicted the death of nature, while Ishtar was on her way to revive the god of life ; when Ishtar was away, the song went on :

> " The bull did not mount the cow
> Nor did the ass leap upon the she-ass.
> The man did not approach the maiden.
> The man lay down to sleep upon his couch
> While the maid slept by herself."

These were the only lines they could remember, yet the rest of the story they knew full well.  Not so easily did Ishtar succeed in bringing back the god Baal into the world of the living.  She had to go through the seven gates of hell, and, at every gate, she was required to surrender of her divinity and of her vitality. When finally she found Baal, she was almost dead herself.  She needed the sprinkling of life-giving water to rise and to be able to carry the gods out of the depths.  But as Ishtar rose to the upper world her vitality increased.  At each gate she received anew the attributes that had been taken from her on her entrance. The goddess was rejuvenated and exuberant when she appeared with Baal upon the soil of man.

Now the temple lay before the anxious travellers and their hearts beat fast at the sight of it.  Within, the worshippers must now be anointing the effigy of Baal, after they had washed it with pure water and clad it in a red robe.  As they recalled the odour of the incense always burned on this occasion, they caught themselves mumbling the chant :

" At his vanishing away she lifts up a lament,
 ' Oh, my child ' ;  At his vanishing away she lifts up a lament,
 ' My Damu ' ;  At his vanishing away she lifts up a lament,
 ' My enchanter and priest ' ;  At his vanishing away she lifts up a
     lament.
At the shining cedar, rooted in a spacious place
In Eanna, above and below, she lifts up a lament.
Like the lament that a horse lifts up for its master
She lifts up a lament.
Like the lament a city lifts up for its lord
She lifts up a lament.
Her lament is the lament for a herb that grows not in the bed.
Her lament is the lament for the corn that grows not on the ear.

Her chamber is a possession that brings not forth a possession,
A weary woman, weary child forespent. . . ."

A soft breeze came out of the east, seeming to spread the light
blue strips over the heavy sky. Dawn was breaking, and, at dawn,

*At a Baalic festival*

Baal was to come to life again. The travellers were eager in
anticipation. They wished to arrive on time. They must be on
the Sacred Hill when the rejoicing over the resurrection of Baal
began.

They were already crossing the bridge, for the Sacred Hill was
surrounded by a moat filled with water, an artificial stream

serving the priests in the temple as well as the worshippers. Here they were to bathe and to cleanse themselves, for when they entered the most sacred chamber and faced the statue of Baal, they would have to present themselves naked before their god. Some stripped themselves and went seven times under the water ; others were satisfied with symbolic ablutions, merely washing their feet and hands and sprinkling their bodies with the sacred fluid.

At the gate of the Sacred Hill, there was a priest to inspect those who came to serve Baal, to see that there were no lepers among them and that the sacrifices they were bringing were of the worthy kind. There were beggars standing at the gate clamouring for alms ; merchants of all kinds were offering their wares, including votives in metal and dough—images of Baal in the form of the generative organs. There were vendors of wines, grapes, and pomegranates, for all these things were equally sacred to the god. There were, too, the money-changers and money-lenders ever preying on those in search of pleasure.

A marble stairway, covered with a bower of roses, led to an enclosure paved with blue stones. There, various fruit trees were to be found : pomegranate, almond, cypress, and myrtle. Out of this enclosure an oval opening led into the chamber of the sacred tree, where an enormous cedar reached toward the sky, erect, like the object it was meant to symbolize. Another stairway led to the vestibule of Baal, where two phallic pillars, crowned with fresh garlands, stood guarding the entrance.

The room was very lofty with a vaulted lacework ceiling through which one might gaze at the starry heavens to learn the fate of man. There were pillars and serpents enshrined in niches in the walls, and in the centre of the room, before an altar, there was the image of Baal, hewn in stone. He was sitting upon a throne, within a shrine. He had a long beard and wore a high-pointed headdress and a flowing robe, which reached to his ankles. The roof of the shrine was supported by a column in the form of a palm tree, standing immediately in front of the sacred deity.

IV

Only a few laymen ever entered this vestibule, the holy of holies of the great god. It was there that the high-priest worshipped, offering incense before Baal's statue or sprinkling blood upon the corners of his altar. Ordinarily, the prayers he offered were not for an individual but for the people as represented by the king and for the needs of the State. Yet it was not impossible that someone of high rank might be personally in need of Baal, and then the high-priest intervened in his behalf. Perhaps the wife of some man of royal blood was in difficult labour, and who but Baal could open the " gates of her womb ? "

In such cases, the individual knelt outside the sacred chamber while the priest offered a prayer in this fashion :

" O Baal, lofty judge, father of black-headed ones, as for this woman, the daughter of her god, may the knot that impedes her delivery be loosed in presence of the godhead ; may the woman bring happily her offspring to the birth ; may she bear ; may she remain in life, and may it be well with the child in the womb ; may she walk in health before thy godhead. May she be happily delivered and honour thee."

Still, if the king was in need of Baal, he might enter this sacred chamber, for he, the king, was really an offspring of the god and a priest in his own right. In that case, he came with his offering, first asking Baal not to mind any possible imperfections in the sacrifice :

" Heed not what the chief offering of this day may be, whether good or bad, a stormy day on which it rains ; heed not that something unclean may have produced uncleanliness at the place of vision and rendered it unclean. Heed not that the lamb of thy divinity, which is looked upon for vision, be imperfect and with blemish. Heed not that he who touches the forepart of the lamb may have put on his garment for sacrifice as arshati ; or have eaten, drunk, or rubbed himself upon something unclean. Heed not that in the mouth of the seer, thy servant, a word may have been passed over in haste."

Uneasy lies the head that wears a crown, and the king's visits to the temple were as often filled with worry and anxiety as with desire for bliss and ecstasy. When he came to seek advice or to beg favours from the god, he was perhaps least in festive mood. His days and nights of rejoicing were those when he returned from battle with a train of prisoners and spoils, to share his gladness with his Baal.

But the public little concerned itself with matters of State. The plain people were bound to their own bits of soil, and cut loose only when in the house of their god. They never penetrated into the holy of holies. They never saw Baal himself, seated upon his throne of glory. They communed with their god only through his ministry. They knew him through the priests who received them in the outer room of the temple. There were the altars where all their sacrifices were made. There was the odour of fresh blood and manure, mingling with the fragrance of oils and perfumes. There they saw life destroyed, torn up and flowing away, down the declining floor. There, they heard the call of blood and their own blood answered—fiery liquid circulating in their veins.

There, too, they saw life, new life on its way toward creation. They saw it dedicated, hallowed and suggested in the images about them and in the dances of the priestesses within the enclosure. Life was in the song the priestesses sang, the song of the lingam that praised the powers of Baal. Life was in the air.

To this enclosure they all came, all who travelled the long night through, with the love of Baal in their hearts. Here they turned in their calves, the first fruits and the ears of corn they had gathered from their fields. Here they gave unto the god the first taste of the bounties that he had bestowed upon them, but they, too, shared in these sacrifices. They feasted on what was left after the priests had taken their portions. After the fast, the meat of the lamb was delicious indeed, and the wine was like sweet nectar. Food and drink brought them into that state of bliss and oblivion in which they could all the more appreciate the lovely young priestesses dancing about like sunbeams on the meadow of a late afternoon—dancing the dance of youth and love . . . Love, the god of the universe, Love, the heart of Baal.

The end of the sacrifice approaches. All are weary : Baal, his priests, and his worshippers. Weary, perhaps not so much on account of labours lost as because of pleasures anticipated. Everybody is waiting for the great moment. The final sacrifice is brought. The dead lamb lies upon the altar before the sacred cedar. Its blood has been sprinkled upon the leaves of the tree and upon the ground that covers its roots. The sound of the flute is heard. It is the signal for the chief priestess to arrive. All eyes are turned toward the figure of a bull in the eastern corner of the enclosure, to the triangular door behind it.

Again the flute is heard and a bell is rung. The door opens. The Kadishtu appears. All hail her : " The Kadishtu, the Kadishtu, blessed be the Kadishtu." But the Kadishtu is unmindful of all this welcome. Her eyes are closed tightly ; her face is in contortions ; every muscle in her neck and arms is taut. As if floating in the air, she slowly approaches the opened lamb upon the altar. Her arms are extended ; the fingers of her outstretched hands quiver. She touches the sacrificial lamb. The priest dips his finger in the blood and places it in the mouth of the priestess. She tastes the blood and opens her dilated eyes.

Trembling, she thrusts her hand into the cadaver and tears away the bleeding heart. As the blood gushes forth upon the

altar and streams to the floor, the Kadishtu places the heart of
the lamb upon the sacred platter. And at once the worshippers
break forth in song, praising Baal, the god of life, the god of
blood.

From all sides of the room priestesses arrive, dancing across the
enclosure and out into the open upon the Sacred Hill. They are
followed by the male worshippers with burning faces and devouring eyes. The songs grow wilder, the contortions of the bodies
more frenzied, while the drum and the flute fill the air with
passionate tones that steal into the hungry hearts of dancer and
worshipper.

The dances break up in chaotic revelry. Priestess and worshipper join in the merry-making. Tired, drunk, half-swooning,
the dancer is still conscious of one thing : somebody will touch
her navel—she must follow—but the coin ; he must first give her
a coin, the coin that is sacred to Baal.

As she is trying to seat herself, hardly able to stand upon her
feet, a worshipper touches her. She rises as if awakened from
sleep. She follows him blindly into a tent, where both priestess
and worshipper consummate the final crying prayer to Baal, the
prayer of love.

*Anubis as the guardian of the Dead*

# CHAPTER II

## A NIGHT WITH APHRODITE

*She was the beginning and the end,*
*And the stretch of life between.*

### I

WE are leaving Baal with the setting sun and following the spreading shadows down to the chambers of Aphrodite. Baal will ever dwell in our memory associated with daylight and sunshine, with gladness and the joy of living. Man showed himself naked before his god. He had nothing to hide, nothing to crouch before. In the temple of Baal, he stood squarely upon the ground, filling his lungs with the breath of life and extending his arms in welcome to the entire world. In Baal, man's ego opened to include the universe.

Aphrodite we shall learn to associate with night and darkness. Aphrodite was so great a mother that all her children appeared puny and insignificant before her. Man came into the world out of a woman and was forever longing for his native land. In Aphrodite, he hoped at least symbolically to return whence he had come.

There were two ways in which man could realize himself: one was to absorb the universe within him; the other was to dissolve himself in the universe. Baal was the first attempt, Aphrodite the second. Consequently, Baal was the god eternal, but Aphrodite was eternity itself.

Baal was light; Aphrodite was darkness. Darkness was at the beginning of creation; darkness will be at its end. It seems to be the natural, permanent condition, with daylight its only break. Baal-Shamash, the sun-god, rises every morning from his nightly hiding-place and, seating himself in his chariot, drives across the sky—a chariot of fire over a field of darkness. But as he reaches the horizon, he returns· to his abode, and night, no longer disturbed, continues to prevail.

Baal-Shamash is a god and immortal, yet once a year he dies, only to be resurrected and to return to life again. Aphrodite never dies. It is she who goes down to the lower regions to find the god and to bring him back into the world of the living. Baal is the living god; Aphrodite is life itself. Baal is the green leaf, the stalk sprouting out of the ground; Aphrodite is the black soil that holds within itself the force of life and its secret, the source whence all comes and to which all returns in the end.

We are drawing close to Aphrodite, the eternal feminine. As

we look upon her through the eyeglass of thought and understanding, we see the goddess complete in herself. She is both male and female—a bearded face with full maiden breasts ; in female dress yet with a sceptre in her hand, the lingam symbol of the male. Aphrodite knows no sex, but sexuality. They who come to worship her must hide their sex. Males come in female attire and females in the clothes of males. The greatest glory they can bring to Aphrodite, the overpowering devotion to the goddess that only the chosen ones attain, is to physically efface their sex. When the human being reaches the stage in which he is neither man nor woman, then he is in closest tune with the spirit of the great goddess of love.

However, that was the goal of only a few pining souls. The vast number of Aphrodite's worshippers had nothing further from their minds than to mutilate themselves. They saw another way of communion with their goddess. The sexes in mating resemble Aphrodite ; they attain that supreme unity which is the harmony of nature and the creative force of life. For originally life was but one sex ; only in time the unit was broken into halves, each longing for the other. When the two find themselves and reunite, the original union is restored and happiness is born.

And yet, very few were conscious of these thoughts as they carried their sacrifices into the chamber of Aphrodite. They merely came to her like children calling upon their mother. There, under the roof of the goddess of creation, they heard the call of the creative force and responded to it. There, heart longed for heart and flesh hungered for flesh. And as the call was sharp and the hunger beyond control, they loosened all bonds and plunged head and heart into the sea of love.

## II

On our way to the chambers of Aphrodite we must first pass out of the city, for her temple lies beyond the gate. Her abode is a city in itself, with streets, houses, parks, and shrines, enclosed within a thick stone wall. It is a wall of demarcation between two different worlds.

Outside the wall, life is toil, worry, restraint. Without, one is variously preoccupied with his dry, daily labour. He is limited in activity, in movement, and in relationship with fellow-men and women. Outside, there is a world of hard, drab reality. Inside, life is one great love-feast welling with the pleasures of sense. Man appeared at his best with the best he had when he entered the gate of the wall. He cast aside all care and lifted all restraint.

Inside, he felt like a captive prince returning in triumph to his father's domain. Within, there was sheer joy, bliss, one prolonged state of ecstasy, out of which he woke reborn to a new life.

As we enter the city of Aphrodite, we see the inside of the stone wall lined with trees and shrubbery, among which little huts of two rooms each are arranged in a circular row. There are exactly twelve hundred such huts with twelve hundred priestesses, a hundred for each sign of the Zodiac, and all are on the Sacred

*Roman sculpture, from Nimes*

Ring of Aphrodite, goddess of love and passion. Each hut is the abode of a priestess, an humble yet sacred servant, who has dedicated her life to the great function of her goddess. The door of the hut is of red metal ; over it hangs a lingam, a hammer stuck into an anvil, the symbol of the eternal union. Above the knob is inscribed the name of the priestess. To the right of the entrance is her reception-room and to the left an alcove where the worshipper may spend the night.

From all parts of the world the priestesses came to these huts upon the Sacred Ring to serve their goddess. Their skins were of different colours and they spoke in various tongues, calling their idol by distinctive names. Yet, there they were in the same place of worship, bedecked with the same jewels, anointed with the same oil and exhuming the fragrance of a perfume adopted by custom, all to honour Aphrodite.

They were maidens when first brought there, childish in figure and pure of heart. Little did they know of the meaning of Aphrodite's divinity or of the service they would have to render. There was only the vague desire to be a priestess, to devote one's life to the divine being.

When accepted by the high-priest, the maiden was dedicated to Aphrodite and deflowered with the sacred knife, so that her virginity might not displease the goddess. Then she was entered in the school of love where she was taught to dress, to arrange her hair, to use perfumes and sweet-scented powders, and to arouse the passions of man. In time, she found her way to a room on the Sacred Ring.

The more closely the priestess devoted herself to the temple, the further away she moved in thought and memory from her own country and her very family. She was a maiden reborn in Aphrodite and consecrated to the pleasures of sex. Torn away from a life in which she had been rooted, she was not allowed to take root in another, but was left adrift in the sea of passion. The offspring that might come to her were taken away to be raised as servants in the temple. Seldom did she know what became of her child. When she died, her remains were hurriedly removed from the Sacred Ring so that death might not blot the holy ground of life and creation.

### III

The origin of the temple priestess was hidden in obscurity. Her end was shrouded in darkness. But in between, there was a span of life in glaring sunlight. No wonder, then, that there were so many young women clamouring to be accepted in the feminine priesthood. The poor woman, with no chance whatever to rise to distinction, saw therein the opportunity to climb to loftier heights. The adventurous woman, destined to live on the plane of life to which she was born, found there a chance to get out of the rut and to advance in the affairs of men as well as in their estimation. Many were the maidens awaiting their turn to enter the shrine of Aphrodite. But greater were the numbers pensively turned away by the eunuch priest. Boundless was the love of Aphrodite and great the lust of man, but the temple grounds had their limits.

Even among those that were accepted, favour and fortune played their hands. Only a small number of them were consecrated at a time, and only a few could see their own huts in the near future. Great, therefore, was the strain that weighed down upon the virgins as the day of dedication drew near. Many a sleepless night did they spend in wondering whom fate would choose and what this great dedication might be like. Many were the rumours current among them, yet they hardly conceived what they all meant. The rumours only irritated them and fired their imaginations.

On the morning of the dedication everyone was stirring early. For hours they carefully prepared themselves. There were baths and sacred ablutions. There were ointments to be applied and perfumes to be used. Each maiden was to be ready to meet the goddess, to meet her as a lover with all the amorous preparation of the Orient. They were finally seated in the corridor, waiting to be offered to Aphrodite. And as they waited, a priest walked slowly about them, chanting the Song of the Lingam :

" Virgins, anoint yourselves with the costly ointments. Sweeter yet than the Lotus be your fragrance. The sacred moment is drawing near. Aphrodite the glorious is awaiting you. She, the mother of love and passions, is ardently pressing upon your purple lips and mouth.

" Virgins, anoint your bodies with the costly ointment. Give yourselves to the Lingam—only once in your lifetime. After this holy act you will forever belong to him.

" Give yourselves to the Lingam.

" Virgins, do you feel it ? The Lingam is coming down upon you. With longing pain he is filling every beating heart.

" Virgins, do you feel it so deeply ? The Lingam overwhelmed you. He broke the flower—softly, like the rays of the Sun-god, the Lingam is melting away.

" Sweet is the Lingam's boring kiss. His kiss is sweeter than honey. Once it reaches the heart, the senses take to flight.

" Virgins, give yourselves to the Lingam."

The virgins took up the refrain, " Sweet is the Lingam's boring kiss," and followed the priest to the inner shrine. The room was long and narrow. Its walls were decorated with bas-reliefs of suggestive themes—women overpowered by animals upon a field growing the lingam and the yoni, bacchantes embracing tigers ; monstrous bulls rushing upon virgins. A great multitude of beings, they were all driven together by the irresistible force of overwhelming passion. The male reached out, the female opened herself, in the fusion of those great creative forces.

Within this room the virgins now were, their bodies veiled in their streaming hair. Marching in pairs, they approached the altar, where they prostrated themselves and then drew back in reverence. Again, they marched about the room to form a circle around the altar. They were to be the living witnesses of the most sacred rite of Aphrodite : the sacrifice of the virgin.

As if coming from nowhere the fumes of incense filled the room. In the distance sounded the longing tones of the flute, remindful of pastures and shepherds, of a horizon at which Father Sky kissed Mother Earth. Then the clang of metal cut through the haze of incense. It was the priest making ready for the sacrifice. The goddess of love, through her minister, was now to receive a virgin into her fold.

And outside the circle of maidens, in a corner of the room, the representatives of womanhood were preparing the human partner of Aphrodite, the maiden that would soon be a maiden no longer. Yet, she was not to offer her maidenhood to a man, not even to a priest, but to the sacred golden knife ordained by the goddess herself. The young virgin, delicate, childlike, was placed upon a gilded table, her head resting upon a cushion of silk inscribed with a lotus. The guard of honour, a number of priestesses who were themselves recent initiates, came in their priestly attire to act as sponsors for the new member of their order. They encircled the gilded table, leaving room for the priest at its end.

Somewhere in the distance a horn was sounded. It was to announce that the high-priest was coming. All eyes brightened, all cheeks flamed. Hearts throbbed in anticipation and delight. There was a flutter in the room but no one stirred.

As the head of the guard of honour touched her feet, the virgin closed her eyes. There was neither fear nor apprehension in her face, but the happy expression of ecstatic delight.

The priest raised the golden knife. The rest was a dream, a trance in which virgin, priest, and priestesses participated. They awoke only when the girl was carried out upon the gilded table to an ante-room. They awoke tired, exhausted, yet happy, from an experience that was not to be had by mere mortal.

## IV

We are now approaching still another of the sacred shrines of Aphrodite, enclosed within tall shrubbery in the heart of the

Sacred Ring.  It is the shrine of the chosen priestesses.  No male
ever crossed this threshold, not even priest or eunuch.  Here, at
last, a goddess found peace and privacy with the intimate servants
of her own sex.  At last, the pure feminine element, in communion
between goddess and woman, found expression in a service undisturbed by strangers and undefiled by profane man.  Aphrodite
may not have required this feminine service, but her priestesses
were urgently in need of it.

All her life the priestess was serving others.  From the moment
she entered the temple she acted as a bridge between man and
her goddess.  Over her and upon her, man reached out for divine
communion ; she herself never communed.  Through her, souls
rose to heaven ; her own soul remained hovering over the deep.
She was to divine the slightest caprice of each male who called
upon her in the name of Aphrodite and to satisfy him with all
her artistry.  No one ever heeded any caprice or desire of her
own refined and supersensitive self.

Hers was the life of an actress, ever upon the stage.  From
early morning until late at night she was performing, doing her
part with all the talent at her command.  For all the years of
her study in the school of love, like the master player, her fingers
were ever at the keyboard.  She was practising with the flute
and tom-tom and cymbal : playing pieces to soothe man's nerves
after the strain and worry of the day, pieces to arouse his longing
for companionship and intimacy, and pieces to awaken his desires
and passion.  The low, soft notes she accompanied with warm,
half-suppressed sighs.  And from her languid eyes came tender
glances of love.  At first, she may have been retiring and bashful,
then desire and impatience crept into her expression, and finally
she gave herself to the studied gestures of the voluptuary, dancing
a pantomime of love as she did so.

At every moment of the day the priestess was conscious of her
beauty and its pearl, her bosom.  This she enclosed in gilded
wooden breast-shields, elaborately set with sparkling jewels.  But
through the veil that covered her breasts, their palpitations and
soft undulations were visible and, with her sighs of passion,
contributed to the general voluptuousness.  She was ever study-
ing the effect of her perfumes, the charm of her long black hair
falling in waves over her ivory shoulders or collected in tresses
and ornamented with jewels and fresh flowers.  Like the fortune-
teller, she was to divine from the twinkling of an eye, or the quiver
of a muscle in the face of her worshipper whether she was proceeding along the path of love to which he was accustomed, the
love that pleased him most and called forth his greatest devotion
to Aphrodite.

At times, she was called upon to give delight, not to one individual worshipper, but to the pious congregation at the gate of the shrine. She then appeared at the door of the temple in soft, flowing veils which slowly, almost invisibly, faded away from her body, and she stood before them statue-like—a perfect nude veiled only in the soft waves of her hair. For a brief moment the amazed and panting onlookers were overwhelmed with admira-

*Greek medal*

tion for her god-like figure. Then, like a dark cloud passing over the sun, a purple curtain was drawn before her and she disappeared in all her nudity.

Again, she may have appeared on the steps of the temple where her body, resplendent in the sunlight, shone like marble. This time she advanced to the shore of the bay, where amidst throngs of fervent admirers sending up shouts of enthusiasm, she entered the waves to honour her goddess—the goddess born out of the

foam of the deep.  Withdrawing from the waves, she returned as
Aphrodite born a second time.  And as she stood for a moment
upon the golden sand, her body, glistening with drops of water,
appeared as a pale pink statue against a curtain of vivid blue.

But it was all for man and all for Aphrodite.  The priestess
was fulfilling a mission ; herself, she was hardly a partner to all
her experiences.  In the midst of the greatest joy she may have
brought to man, she herself was often in sadness.  She had been
instructed not to seek her own personal pleasure.  She had
been taught to disregard the personal element, the individual of
the opposite sex.

There are footsteps.  A knock upon her door.  Someone is
coming.  She is not to consider who or what he may be.  He is
a worshipper at the altar of Aphrodite, and she is his priestess.
She is to dedicate herself to his sex, not to him.  And yet, only
human as she is, how can she refrain from looking at the person,
at his face, or listening to his voice ?  Is not sex itself a bordering
on love ?

From the time she came out of the school of love, she was a
bundle of nerves, ever seeking new sensations, new sources of
passion and luxury.  She was the priestess of Aphrodite, yet she,
too, was human ; she, too, needed a god or a goddess for her
own soul to be saved from the tedium and hopelessness of life.
No wonder, then, that at times the priestess turned to Aphrodite,
not in the interest of the males with whom she shared her bed,
but on her own behalf.  And what other god or goddess could so
well understand the heart of the priestess as Aphrodite herself ?
Was not her own fate similar to the fate of her priestess ?  It was
sex that made a priestess out of the virgin.  Sex, too, made
Aphrodite a goddess.

Every priestess knew the story of Aphrodite.  She saw it
illustrated upon the walls of the sacred shrine.  There she saw
the great, youthful god, Anu, making love to the beautiful goddess
Banu.  This aroused the jealousy and wrath of Manu, who, when
night came, fell upon Anu and killed him.  He chopped his body
into pieces, scattering them all over the world.  His lingam he
threw into the river, and as it sank, foam formed upon the waters,
silvery in the moonlight.  Out of this foam Aphrodite came into
the world.  In it she had her being and in it her whole life was
engulfed.  Like her priestess, Aphrodite's existence was rotating
about the sex of man.

So, to Aphrodite's shrine every priestess betook herself whenever her heart was heavy laden and she was in need of solace.
Every night she could come here, every night save one, the night
of the full moon, when the sanctuary was reserved for the chief

priestesses of whom there were eighteen. These lived close about the shrine. They were masters in the art of voluptuousness. Their names were borne on the lips of the greatest of men, and they acquired wealth no less than fame. They had their own way of finding joy and bliss. It was a secret that they alone knew and that could only be surmised by those aspiring to be included, some day, among the great eighteen.

These women from their early youth had devoted themselves to the art of voluptuaries. So intensely were they centred upon the sensuous that their imaginations made them lose their senses. They were for ever struggling with lasciviousness, always endeavouring to attain a beautiful physique. Here they were in the sanctuary of their goddess—a sacred place where no male ever entered. Here they were for ever seeing their own nudity and that of their companions. And deprived of natural sexual pleasures, they created for themselves tastes and desires that grew into passions for their very companions. The unnatural passions thus awakened among these sex-hungry women were fierce, overpowering, and implacable.

It was at their feasts that these chosen priestesses gave themselves up to desire. It was then that, fired with jealousy and rivalry, they held their combats of beauty. On the nights of the full moon, the eighteen met in the sacred shrine of Aphrodite. They gathered in the innermost chamber where there were no windows and but two doors. Through one door they all entered ; through the same door all were to depart, all save one. For one must die before the night of the full moon ends, and she will be carried away through the other door—the door through which no one departs alive. The door of death.

The floor of the chamber was covered with hides of tigers and leopards, and silk cushions were scattered here and there. In the centre, there was a divan with a small triangular table upon which stood a goblet containing a deadly potion. On another table near by there were sacramental drinks and aphrodisiacs.

No one knew what was going on here on this fateful night. One of the eighteen that participated could not tell, the remaining seventeen would not. So here the story must end. The end of a mystic night of love in which eighteen worn, neurotic, and oversexed women sought, without men, to drink the cup of love to its very last drop—and to the final breath of one of them.

And here both life and death met in the mystic union of love. For love was at the beginning and love will be at the end. What could be a more beautiful finale for love than death—the end of all ? It was but another manifestation of the goddess : Aphrodite supervising the exit from life as well as the entrance to it ; Aphrodite, goddess of love and life—in its complete cycle from birth to death.

## V

We have still to visit the chambers of Aphrodite herself. Here all may come, for she is goddess to all. She is the goddess universal, bringing life and blessing to all creatures upon earth.

The walls are bare in the holiest of the chambers, and the room contains only a square bench, an altar, and the statue of the goddess, nude and sexual, upon a pedestal of rose stone. The bench is bare and cold now, yet once a year, in early spring, it is draped with white silk and sprinkled at each corner with the blood of doves. A cluster of almonds and a bunch of fig leaves are put up for a pillow, and upon the bench a hierophant and a virgin perform the great act of unity which the goddess herself performed with the father of gods and men. After the act, the sheet is burned upon the altar and the maiden retires to the quarters of the priestesses.

Now the bench is bare. Aphrodite is in no mood for such sacrifice. She is more concerned with her son Attis whom she holds upon her hand. For while Aphrodite is a virgin, she is also a mother. She placed a pomegranate between her breasts and became pregnant. This was in the month of April. Nine months later her child was born out of her side so that it might not injure her virginity. Aphrodite is the virgin mother, deified by all people and worshipped to this very day in every part of the world.

The virgin goddess was immortal, living ever so long as there was love in the world and birth and life. But her son was not so fortunate. Attis felt the mystic urge to break away from the living. So one day he came to a palm tree, the very symbol of virility and generation, and mutilated himself. Attis bled to death. In his very life-blood, in the force of generation, this son of the goddess of life came to find his end. Attis died with the leaf upon the tree, with the blades of grass in the field, with all that moves and creeps upon the earth.

Like the corn in the field, the son of Aphrodite was annually interred in the dark, cold, infernal region. This was a period of mourning for Aphrodite, when she failed in her function of arousing passion and inducing love. It was the time when nature was dead, lying fallow in wait for the rebirth of Attis and spring.

As the days of Aphrodite's mourning progressed, her devoted

worshippers joined her in sadness and sorrow. They touched neither food nor drink and abstained from sexual intercourse. They wailed and mourned and cut their hair; they went about the hills and valleys playing their flutes and searching for the son of their goddess who was to rise again. The god who holds the dead in his sway was moved by this mourning of goddess and

*Lamenting for Attis*

human kind. So, upon the promise that the son of Aphrodite would return to his kingdom as the year went by, he raised the bars that separate the lower world from the one above.

Meanwhile, the priests of Aphrodite were preparing for the return of Attis and life and love. A palm tree was cut in the woods and brought into the sacred chamber. The trunk of the tree was swathed like a corpse with woollen bands and decked with wreaths of violets, for it was the violets that first sprang forth out of the blood of Attis. Then a young priest, a youthful servant of the goddess resembling her son, was tied to the tree and left for the night. In the morning he was found stabbed, still tied to the tree.

This was the Day of the Blood. The sight of the dead priest, swathed in blood upon the sacred tree, aroused others to give of their own life fluid for the sake of the son of their goddess. The high-priest drew blood from his arms and presented it as an offering. And the inferior priests, wrought to the height of passion by the wild, barbaric music of cymbal, drum, and flute and by the profusion of blood around them, whirled about in furious dance. Finally, overcome by excitement, frenzied, and insensible to pain, they savagely thrust the knives into their bodies, gashing themselves in violence to bespatter the altar with their spurting blood.

The frenzy and hysteria of the priests spread to the worshippers, and many a would-be priest fell into the wave of religious excitement. He sacrificed his virility to the goddess, dashing the severed portions of himself against her blood-besmeared statue. There were men who had come to the festival out of curiosity rather than devotion, and numbers of them were caught in the raging fury. With throbbing veins and burning eyes, they flung their garments from them and with wild shouts seized the knives of the priests to castrate themselves upon the very spot. Then, insensible to pain and oblivious of everything, they ran through the streets of the Sacred Ring, waving the bloody pieces and finally throwing them into a house they passed. It became the duty of the households thus honoured to furnish these men with female clothes, and they, made eunuchs in the heat of religious passion, were to serve their goddess for the rest of their lives. Their virility was destroyed in a moment in the tumult of emotion ; but their sacrifice was to be lifelong and irrevocable.

As the night progressed, the fury of the worshippers was turned into joy. Suddenly a light shone in the darkness. The tree was erected, the dead priest no longer upon it. Another one resembling him was sacrificing at the altar. Elsewhere a tomb had been opened ; the son of Aphrodite had risen from the dead, and, as the priest touched the lips of the weeping mourners with balm, he softly whispered in their ears the glad tidings of salvation.

The morning was greeted with boundless glee. Universal licence prevailed. Every man might say and do what he pleased. To facilitate the breaking of all bonds, people went about in disguise. Then the tree was taken out of the sanctuary of the goddess and carried down the hill to the brook where the virgins bathed before they entered the temple. There it was washed of its blood, decorated with roses, and slowly brought back in a procession of ease and serenity.

The blood scenes were forgotten. Even the eunuch priests were unmindful of their wounds. The moments of extreme passion were spent. The " erotic blood-letting " had been accomplished. Having returned to his former freedom in love, man became himself again.

*Aphrodite, Goddess of Love*

# CHAPTER III

## AT A DIONYSIAN MYSTERY

*In the valley of death*
*He brandished the flaming torch of life*

I

DIONYSOS was the god of wine, women, and song. He revealed to mankind the art of wine-making. He desired people to drink and to make merry. He urged them to love. It was that people might love that Dionysos died and came back to life. For the sadness of his going was only to make fuller the joy of his return. Then, all worry and strain were to be wiped away and life was to be one great goblet of wine in which men were to revel, merrily singing away.

To witness a Dionysian mystery we must set out late in the afternoon, so that we may be first in line when the procession begins at sunset. As it starts, we see a chariot in which the hierophant, the human representative of the great god Dionysos, is seated. He is followed by the Lamparadi or torch bearers, who light the way for the procession. Directly behind them come the wine bearers, men and women carrying upon sticks vessels filled with the rich red liquid and crowned with grape leaves. Wine was the first great gift of Dionysos, and of service it would be when the crowd entered the destined place. Following the wine carriers came girls bearing large baskets of fruits : grapes, dates, and pomegranates, for Dionysos was the god of generation, the harbinger of spring, and the bearer of fruit for all mankind. Next were the musicians, playing tunes upon flute and cymbal.

Now there was a motley crowd. Old and young they were, men, women, and children. Almost all wore masks representing satyrs, fauns, nymphs, and Bacchæ, all sorts of real or fantastic creatures. Everyone was scantily dressed ; parts commonly covered were left bare and parts uncovered by custom were hidden in clothes. Their hair was dishevelled, their eyes dilated with drink. They were pushing and jostling and falling upon each other. Here they sang the *phallicæ*, love songs of unusual frankness. There they swore and cursed in a fashion incredible to even themselves on any other occasion.

Behind them came the symbols of their songs, the *phalos*, carried by the *phaloptares*. Here were objects imitative of the human organs of generation, in this procession treated derisively rather than reverently. A man might appear with an artificial lingam attached to a belt about his waist. A woman might carry

144

in her hand high over head the effigy of her sex in various attitudes, together with articles suggestive of the union of the sexes in nature.

Here the procession formally closed, but a rabble, collecting from the side streets along the march, followed in an ever more hilarious attitude. This mob continued after the procession until it reached the selected place in the woods. There they mixed with the revellers in confusion and promiscuity. There all were equal ; no one knew friend or foe, mother or daughter. Man returned to nature as he was ere society took him in hand.

*Dionysic Amulet*

## II

When the procession reached its destination—a lonely spot in the woods along the bay,—a large chest was opened from which the image of Dionysos, powerfully virile and sexual, was produced. The statue of the god was placed upon a base representing the breasts of women. A hog was sacrificed as a burnt offering and all took to eating and drinking. Wine flowed freely. Men and women cast off their clothes. Nude women ran about provoking men by suggestive gestures and exciting actions. Men caught them in their arms with no thought as to who they might be and forgot that they were not alone. Frenzied women threw themselves into the water with their phosphorescent torches in their hands and considered it a miracle that these were not extinguished. Men ran after them in the water like animals in the rut. And all the time children were caught by males or females and forcibly introduced into this orgy of drunkenness and love. As day broke, the god was returned to the ark from which he had been produced and the men, intoxicated with wine and dissipation, returned home, half-swooning, with the women and children exhausted and dishonoured.

In the Dionysian mystery, man sought to reach the state o ecstasy. It was the only way one could attain communion with his god. For some, the mere state of ecstasy was sufficient.

*Monument found at Nimes in 1825*

Having been freed from the chains of man, they no longer needed the god. For others, these mysteries were only the beginning of an even greater experience. Separating themselves from the crowd, they gathered in a room and partook of the sacramental meal. Food in mystic forms was eaten out of the sacred drum and more wine was drunk, but this time out of the cymbal, which was making sacred music to the god. Then an animal was driven into the room and all fell upon it in savage attack.

Whether it was lamb, calf, or steer, it was torn to pieces and eaten while its hot, streaming blood was drunk in great passion.

The animal was supposed to incarnate the god. By tearing it, one was tearing his way into the very being of his divinity, and by eating the meat of the animal and drinking its blood, he was assimilating the body of the deity with his own flesh and blood.

In the frenzy of religious and sexual passion, even a human might be taken for the god and be torn to pieces, especially when there were captives or slaves about. Hysterical parents might throw their own infants into the affray, they themselves fighting in the general skirmish for a piece of their child's flesh.

*The Marriage of Psyche and Eros*

When a novice was introduced into this mystery of mysteries of Dionysos, there was a special initiation ceremony. The initiate was crowned with a wreath of golden leaves and led into a pit which was covered with a wooden grating. While he was standing there, a bull, profusely decorated with flowers and gilded leaves, was driven upon it and gashed in a number of places so that its hot, reeking blood poured forth as from a fountain, besmirching the worshipper below. After the dead animal was removed, the novice came forth drenched and dripping, covered with the scarlet blood. He was received by his fellows in the greatest reverence as one who had been born again to life eternal and purified in the blood of the bull. For some time thereafter, he was dieted on milk like a new-born baby.

Thus, the worshipper of Dionysos realized, if only symbolically, the greatest dream of mankind, the dream of wiping away the life that was and beginning it anew without the burden of the past. Centuries later, one Ponce de Leon was searching for the fountain of youth. The worshipper of Dionysos had found it long before in the life-blood of the bull.

# CHAPTER IV

## TWILIGHT WITH MOLOCH

*Fire, flame, and frenzied passion ;*
*God of love and desolation.*

### I

MOLOCH was the mighty, gluttonous god. He bestowed his bounty upon mankind, but he wished a taste of all that he gave. Moloch gave only to be gifted in return. There was no altruistic hypocrisy in his little divine circle. He was not saving the world ; he was not serving mankind. He cared for neither the praise nor the glory that others might give him.

Moloch was a fierce, self-satisfied, masculine god. He defied the weaker sex even in love. He had no women himself, nor did he wish his worshippers coming to his temple to trail their women along. He wanted none of their weakness, gentleness, delicacy, or romanticism. He was the god of muscle and belly. If cannibals were looking for a god, none could please them so much as Moloch, and Moloch could wish himself no better class of worshipper.

His temple was out in the open, far from city or village with their polished ways of living. It was an immense, low structure with an enormous figure of Moloch at its end. Like the modern industrial plant with its towering chimney rising to the clouds, the god himself appeared before his worshippers—a colossal giant of a man with a bull's head and tremendous virile power. His arms he held outstretched as if he were forever demanding sacrifices. There were seven huge mouths to his belly, all appropriate receptacles for the offerings that might be brought to him.

The figure of Moloch was cast in bronze and merged with a large furnace that served as its pedestal. Whatever was fed to the god immediately landed into the fiery oven. Moloch the glutton would take no chances with his priests who might put away a sacrifice for themselves or share with him the fat of the land.

As the sun was setting, the worshippers left their homes and wives, and, loaded with sacrifices, they betook themselves to the warm abode of their god. While they were on their way, a huge fire was being prepared in the pit of the furnace, and as they entered the temple, flames reflected through the bronze figure of the divinity. Cold, cruel, and metallic Moloch had become incandescent, aflame with the fire of life. Moloch was the fire that does burn the bush and everything else ; he was the fire that devours.

As the tongues of flame shot through the monstrous figure, the worshippers yelled with joy.  They danced about it, emitting terrific cries and, in frenzy, hurled whatever they had into the mouths of the fiery god.  There may have been products of the soil, fruits of the farm, a calf or a sheep, even a cat or a dog.  One may have thrown his own cloak into the gaping mouth when he had nothing else to give.

When the signal was given, the eunuch priests of Moloch marched into the temple and about the radiant figure.  They came to serve this cruel, relentless god, as the priestesses paid homage to a goddess more loving and generous.  While the fair sex was excluded, sexual passion persisted and seemed all the more fired because of the absence of women ; and beautiful, beardless young men, their bodies soft and fragrant from the use of oils and perfumes, sold themselves to the adorers of their god, depositing on the altar of the idol the money thus earned.  Within the temple, too, there were dogs trained for the same purpose and the coins received from the rental or sale of these animals, called the " price of a dog," went to the priests of Moloch.

The eunuch priests constituted a caste or sect with their own rites of initiation.  These were held at night in the depths of the forest.  There, in the heat of frenzy and stirred by wild music, they gashed their own bodies and ran about with blood streaming from their wounds, falling over each other as they did so.

## II

Women were excluded from this sheer masculine world of Moloch and his tribe.  But the wives of the Molochites clamoured for a god and for Moloch.  The husband would have none of it, but the high priest of Moloch knew better.  He saw additional revenue for the temple with a sect of women doing for themselves what the men had been doing alone.

Thus women, too, came to serve Moloch.  They had their priestesses, who prostituted themselves to the women worshippers as the eunuch priests did to the males.  The priestesses dwelled in gay coloured tents about the temple of Moloch, burning incense, playing soothing music, and preparing love charms and potions.

Both men and women danced about the blazing Moloch, two human races with no direct emotional contact, yet not without some influence upon each other.  For the frenzied desire of the women for their priestesses reflexively aroused the passion of the men for the objects of their love.

When the women came to offer their sacrifices, they cast into the devouring belly of Moloch whatever there was upon them or within their arms. The greater the sacrifice, the more exaltation the devotee derived. In the heat of her ever-increasing passion, she brought the greatest sacrifice a mother could offer. It was then that Moloch first tasted the flesh and blood of the infants thrown within him by mothers gone mad with desire.

Moloch was the contrary god. He was contrary to all the refinements that human society had developed in its march of civilization. He was contrary to human nature in love and sex. In Moloch, man revolted against his better self. In Moloch, he turned his face on his own humanity. He quickly ran down the ladder up which he had struggled so hard to ascend.

# CHAPTER V

# THE DANCE OF THE SAKTAS

*She was the great womb of the universe,*
*The goddess of womankind.*

### I

IF the men had their own masculine god, Moloch, and tried at least to keep the women out of his worship, the women had their own goddesses, doing with them whatever pleased their feminine eyes. And they did succeed in keeping the men out for good.

Now, it is all very true that Aphrodite must be a mother, even

*The eternal Sakti*

though a virgin. But there is absolutely no need that her offspring be male. The cursed almond that Aphrodite carried between her breasts could just as well produce a daughter as a son. So it was agreed by the women of Greece that Aphrodite had a daughter, Kore, who like all divine children had to die once a year so that she might be resurrected with the spring. Now, when a mother mourns for her daughter it is a purely feminine affair and no male need interfere.

Thus it was that women gathered in a most secret place and sat upon the ground fasting, mourning, moaning, and wailing. They were helping Aphrodite lament the loss of her daughter. Each woman brought a sacrifice, preferably a pig, because this animal was closely associated with all the trouble.  Still, a cake of dough might do, if it was formed to represent the generative organs.  Whatever the offering, it was thrown into a vault or cavern something like Moloch's belly and left in the care of the serpents for the remainder of the year.

As the year rolled by, some women were appointed "drawers." They knew how to clap their hands so that the serpents would retire and they could go down into the cavern to fetch whatever remained of the pigs and the cakes of dough that had been deposited there.  Whosoever got a piece of bone or a morsel of cake was blessed with fecundity, and, if such a piece was planted along with the corn, an abundant crop was assured.

*A female demon in ancient India*

As the remains were brought up from the cavern, the women made merry.  They sang songs describing intimate attitudes between men and women, while they accompanied them with suggestive dancing and exhibitions.

## II

The women of India, too, had a goddess whom they worshipped, just as the men were worshipping Siva, the great god of life. The Sakti, the wife of Siva, was for them the great goddess, the mother of the universe.  Through her, life came into the world and through her help they might hope for great fecundity, for she was the female principle, the prime factor in creation.

The women of India honoured their goddess in feast and

sacrifice. There was the Durga-puja in the fall of the year to celebrate her victory over the buffalo-headed demon, Mahisha-sura. Then the Sakti was represented in the form of a ten-armed goddess with a weapon in each hand, and for nine days her faithful worshippers approached her daily with gifts and sacrifices. On the tenth day, the figure of the goddess was thrown into the water and the feast ended.

Upon the return of spring, when all nature seems to be in love, the goddess was in her happiest temper. It was then that she was honoured as the mother of the universe, the bringer of life. And all the young girls, with baskets of flowers and bundles of grass, would go into the country to observe the feast of Rali Ka mela. It was like the May feasts so well known among us.

*Devaki seated on a lotus flower and holding a*
*lotus bud, symbols of the two creative forces*

When they reached the designated spot, they heaped their flowers and grass together and danced and sang about the pile.

For ten days the maidens came to the same spot to honour their goddess, and each day they brought more flowers and more grass, and again, each day they sang and danced about the growing pile. When it was high with their offerings, they went into the woods where they found two branches each ending in three prongs. These they erected upon the heap of flowers and placed images of Siva and his Sakti on the tops of them. The marriage of the god and the goddess was celebrated, after which the maidens joined together in an elaborate feast. A few days later they carried the images to the river and cast them into the water. Throughout the time of the festival, the maidens' chief prayer was that the goddess might bless them with good husbands.

There was another celebration, the Kali-puja, at which the goddess was worshipped in her most dreadful form. On the darkest night of the month, she was represented as a four-armed naked woman dancing upon the breast of her husband. She wore a wreath made of the heads of giants she had slain and a string of skulls encircled her neck. On this night, the goddess was angry and must be appeased, so the woman made sacrifices to her. Goats and sheep were killed with one blow of the knife and the heads placed in her awful presence, while a little earthen lamp burned above them. Then the animals were roasted in the fire and as the women ate the flesh they danced and sang in honour of the Sakti.

And so they danced in worship of their goddess, the Saktas, women rebels in the dark of feminine servitude. However a woman was stationed in life, no matter how submissively she lay under the heel of her husband and master, she was a Sakta before her goddess. In the divine presence, she would recognize no rule of the male, not even the male principle in nature. She was a woman and the Sakti was a woman, the Sakti, the wife of the great god Siva, yet greater than Siva by far, the mother of all creation. The Sakti was the great womb of the universe enveloping nature as the atmosphere envelops the earth, and the women of India were her Saktas, human emanations of the goddess supreme.

Let no mere male interfere then. Let the Saktas worship the goddess as a woman will, in a world of absolute womanhood.

# BOOK THREE
# IN THE HOUSE OF THE LORD

# PROLOGUE

## IN THE HOUSE OF THE LORD

BETWEEN the Temple of the Gods and the House of the Lord lay a great stretch of thought and sentiment. In the Temple, man came to live this life for all that it had to offer him in sensuous pleasure and delight. To live was the only purpose of being. Beyond life, if there was anything, it was a shadowy existence, nothing to look forward to. Man came into the Temple of the Gods like the drunkard into the hostelry ; he drained his cup to the very bottom and relished every drop of it.

In the House of the Lord, man came not to live, but to prepare for death. Death was not the end of life, but its true beginning. Beyond it lay the great hereafter, unspoiled by suffering and remorse, unlimited by time, unbounded in its divine pleasure and heavenly bliss. In comparison with the eternal happiness, this life was but a passing moment of misery. All one could do in this brief span of years was to prepare as well as possible for the great life to come.

Far apart as the Temple and the House stood, they still had some common ground between them. Preceding the House of the Lord in time and surpassing it in extent, the Temple left it an inheritance of which it has as yet been unable to dispose. This is the attitude toward woman and sex.

In the Temple of the Gods, there was no quarrel with the sexual function of man just as there was no quarrel there with any other phase of human nature. There was no idea of restraint in matters of sex. Venus bathed in the foam of the waves ; man was to bathe in the sea of Venus. Sex was brought to the very altar of the gods as the greatest offering man could make, as the object closest to his heart. This pagan, positive attitude toward the sexual life, the House did not accept.

However, there were other tendencies toward sex and woman in the Temple. They were decadent, negative, introvertive, wavering between orgy and denial. When the drunkard has had too much to drink, he suffers a headache. He has a disagreeable taste in his mouth and his whole body is enervated. He despises the very liquor he so greatly cherished before. He loves the drink and he hates it ; while the person who drinks in moderation has a more wholesome and normal attitude toward it. Like the drunkard, they who raised sex to its place upon the altar of the gods also dragged it down into the gutter. They who sanctified it with libations also defiled it with muck. Sex was not only the most beautiful flower but also the most despicable weed. It was god itself, yet it was anathema.

159

A similar condition obtained in the attitude toward the carrier of sex—woman. Peoples who never placed woman upon a pedestal never thought her quite so unclean. They who saw her as a goddess could not see her again as a human being. Woman was a goddess because of sex ; she was a demon for the same reason. One's estimate of woman depended upon his view of sex, for the two concepts were inseparable. Man's view of sex was bound to come down from its divine plane. The world was becoming secularized, commercialized, and, with it, love became a commodity one bought at a price in the market. Along with sex, woman also came down into the scum of the market-place. Like sex, woman as a person, an individual, was degraded and placed below human values. The daughters of man suffered greatest humiliations at the hands of their former most ardent admirers, the worshippers in the Temple of the Gods.

This negative attitude toward sex and woman not only found its way into the House of the Lord but once there it was bound to grow and expand. It corresponded perfectly with the general negative view of life held by the believers in the Lord. Struggling against this life for the one to come, the keepers of the faith saw in love their arch-enemy, Satan or the Anti-Christ. For love is an intrenchment of the physical, of earthliness. However it begins, it inevitably ends in carnal pleasure. It drags man down to the animal plane ; it does not permit him to rise to the heights of the divine. In fact, love's very inception was in sin and its first experience led to the fall of man.

It was the serpent, the tempter, that first manifested love to God's children. Eve stooped to listen to words of love ; then she disobeyed. In her disobedience lay the ruination of all mankind. Forsaking the word of God for the taste of an apple, Eve gave up spiritual values for material gains and sold her soul to please her body. Succumbing to the attentions of the serpent, she broke the laws of God and man for a brief moment of carnal passion. The serpent, symbolizing sexual love, was, then, the source of all evil in the world and the cause of man's downfall.

And so it behoves man, to-day and every day until the trumpet sounds the call to judgment, to cleanse his soul of the original sin. He is to resist all temptations of the flesh and, above all, the call of sex. In sexual union man fell, and every union draws both individual and humanity downward, causing them to sink into the abyss of sin and perdition. The very suggestion of sex must therefore be fought as desperately as the greatest temptation set by the devil. Consequently, man must be on his guard against woman. Like the serpent, she is the great tempter. It is she who disturbs man's thinking and turns his heart away from God.

It is she who fires his veins with passion and calls him to a life that offers physical joy but brings in return eternities of punishment. Her very existence is a reminder of the flesh, of the physical, of carnal desires. Woman has drawn man down ; she will not let him rise again.

And yet, weak was the flesh and ill the heart of man from his very youth. Everyone had a bit of love in his life. It could no more be entirely shut out than could the sunshine. Even in the House of the Lord, the young man's fancy turned to thoughts of love ; and the heart of the maiden beat faster and stronger when her eyes fell upon the youth of her dreams. As the youth was drawn to the maiden, love gained the upper hand ; it asserted itself above and despite all interdicts. Love broke out in the very House of the Lord.

And so, the keepers of the faith, whether Jew or Christian or Moslem, had to suffer the young people to do love's bidding and to allow man his way in sex. Love was permitted under conditions. It was considerably limited and circumscribed. It was first to be sanctioned by the Lord and blessed by the priest. It was not to be entered into for carnal pleasure, but it was to be consecrated to a pious end, to further the heavenly purpose of keeping the world populated. Not for his own weary, lonesome, longing soul was man to cross the threshold of love, but for the fulfilment of the word of the Lord. " Be fruitful and multiply."

And thus it was that, having banished love through the door, the keepers of the faith had to call it back through the window. However justified and accounted for, once love entered the House of the Lord it overfilled the sacred dwelling. The very walls are set upon a foundation of love, and Cupid's arrows are all over the place. There is the tremor of love in every voice calling to God. There is the sigh of love in every cry of the weary soul for peace and salvation. Love was crucified by the keepers of the faith, but it returned all the more glorious, with a crown of beauty upon its head.

*Jehovah, God of Battles*
(*Early Christian Conception*)

# CHAPTER I

## LOVE IN THE SYNAGOGUE

*"Many waters cannot quench love, neither can the floods drown it."*—SOLOMON.

### I

*EL SHADDAI* was the God of the early Hebrews. He was stern and relentless, unapproachable even to His prophets. One could not see His face and live. He was the Lord of Hosts and the God of vengeance, visiting the sins of the parents upon the children. He was the God of might dealing with man in mighty fashion. Before He selected Abraham as his servant, he tested him in many ways, going so far at to try his willingness to slaughter his only son for his Lord. He sealed His covenant with Abraham in the blood of the foreskin, and even then was Abraham to walk humbly before Him.

*El Shaddai* chose a people appropriately hard, stiff-necked, self-willed, and the greater period of his early relations with them was one of quarrels and vain attempts to break their stubbornness. He would have His people live according to His command, and this they would not do. He was forever admonishing, threatening, punishing. He dealt with men straightforwardly and allowed no room for love. His humble male servants to this day say among their prayers : " Blessed be His name that He did not create me a woman."

In time, *El Shaddai* came to be known by the simpler name of Jehovah. He mellowed with age and grew loving and kind. He ever had only mankind in view. It was in His desire to do well by His creatures that He created the universe. Not merely to have it existing did He create it, but He desired it to be filled with living beings. Life, then, the eternal stream of life, was the prime motive of creation. Life forever was the greatest passion of the psalmist. It became mandatory to add to the stream of life ; a sin to destroy a drop of it. He destroys a whole universe who destroys a single soul. And the pious Jew reads in his book of prayer :

" And so our Creator and Maker ordered us to be fruitful and multiply, and whoever does not engage in reproducing the race is likened unto one who is shedding blood, thus diminishing the essence of the deity and he is the cause that the holy spirit shall depart from Israel ; his sin is great indeed."

The exercise of the sexual function is, therefore, neither sinful nor ignominious. Quite to the contrary, it is the fulfilment of the first divine command to mankind. It is the realization of

God's will for a peopled universe. " And know," writes a Rabbi whom Jews call holy, " that the sexual union, achieved in the proper manner and the proper time and entered into with the right spirit, is a matter pure and sacred ; let no man think that there is anything ignoble or ugly in it." The introduction into the sexual life, the intercourse with a virgin, is a sacred act to be preceded by a prayer, reading as follows :

" Blessed be he who placed a nut-tree in the Garden of Eden, a lily of the valley, that no stranger rule within the enclosed wall ; therefore she preserved in purity the powers of love and did not break the rule. Blessed be He who chooses the children of Israel."

No one may, therefore, abstain from sexual life. A Jew who has no wife does not deserve the designation of " man." He who has no wife lives without blessing and without peace of soul. One may not deny himself the love-life even for the sake of the Law. He who would devote all his life and every waking hour in it to religious study and contemplation must first marry and have children, a boy and a girl. Only then is he permitted to separate from his wife and devote himself entirely to the study of the Law. Such individuals, the Jewish equivalent of the Christian monks, are still found in the theologic academies. They are known as Perushim, the separated ones.

Just as it is sinful to abstain from marriage, so is it unlawful to live childless in the marital state. One should not marry a woman that is too old or too young to bear children. If a man has lived with his wife for ten years and has had no children with her, he is obligated to divorce her and to marry another who will bring him offspring. Masturbation is the great horror of the pious, and the intentional loss of semen is an unpardonable sin. He who wastes his semen is a murderer. Onan, son of Judah, was slain by the Lord for " spilling his seed on the ground," in an attempt to prevent childbirth. He gave his name to masturbation —onanism.

The man who destroyed his powers of procreation was twice a murderer. Even he who was born sterile had no place in the religious communial life. A Jew is forbidden to castrate even an animal ; he may not so much as request a Gentile to perform the operation upon his beast. For the Gentile is a son of Noah, and all children of Noah are expected by the Divine Power to observe the interdict concerning castration. The command to live and to populate the world goes beyond race and faith. It rests upon all dwellers of the earth, whether or not their fore-fathers stood at Sinai and accepted the Law.

Great as is the fear of death, it is surpassed by one even greater

in the heart of the pious Jew.  It is the fear of being left without
a *kadish*, a son who will continue the life-force after he has gone
and who will help, by his life and deeds and prayers, the departed
soul in heaven.  It is the son who pronounces the prayer for the
dead thrice daily during the first year after the parent's demise
and upon every anniversary of his death.  Even Abraham, pious
and trusting as he was, found little joy in all the divine promises
because he had no son, and he asked the Lord : " O Lord God,
what wilt thou give me seeing I go hence childless ? "

Man's sexual function has, therefore, this high purpose : the
continuance of life upon earth.  It was not designed for the carnal
pleasures it offers.  In fact, according to the Jewish mystics,
carnal pleasure was especially provided by Providence through
a specific agent created to supervise it, so that man might be driven
into the performance of this divine command.  But the pious
need no driving to do the will of God.  One is to engage in the
sexual life only according to the Law and the comments of the
rabbis.  He must not be frivolous about it or gluttonous in his
desires.  Theoretically, he must not seek to express his passions
or to continue the union after its purpose has been achieved, after
the woman has conceived.

Other views, however, led to the removal of the restrictions
upon man's sexual life that had been built up in Hebrew tradition.
The Law was given for man to live by it, and consequently, it
should not demand the impossible of him.  Rather than expose
all men to sin, the rabbis permitted the husband to " do with
his wife as he pleases, to cohabit with her at any time he may desire
and to kiss her upon any place but one."  Here the ways part.
The intellectuals look upon this as a compromise with men who
are spiritually weak and insist that the truly pious will not take
advantage of this permission.  The mystics see in this attitude
a divine secret.  They claim that there should be no union but
it be preceded by embraces and kisses and that during the intercourse kissing should come as another expression of the union of
the sexes, a union that finds its reflection in heaven.  Man's
passion thus found its outlet in a function meant only for the
procreation of the race.

There was yet another tradition that unfettered the sexual
function and permitted indulgence in it even after its divine
purpose had been achieved.  This came in the attitude of the
husband toward the wife.  Curiously enough, the command to
multiply pertains only to the male, the female being entirely
unobligated.  A woman may abstain from marriage if this
abstinence will not lead her into temptation.  She may even take
steps to make futile the man's attempt at procreation, resorting to

the use of contraceptives. But the husband has been commanded by Moses to satiate the woman's sexual hunger : " Her food, her raiment, and her conjugal rights shall he not diminish." The extent of these conjugal rights has been considerably disputed, but anything near sexual starvation is a breach of this command. If a man is unable to live up to this mandate, he must divorce his wife. The frequency of the sexual union is therefore dependent not only upon conception but upon the emotional needs of the woman as well. Man has to thank woman for his conjugal joys.

If it is the woman that is to be considered in the sexual union, it is quite natural that the husband is expected to be gentle and considerate. He may not embrace his wife except by her free will and full consent. Nor is he to wait for her to invite him, as this might be a strain upon her feminine modesty. Any indirect suggestion should be sufficient. He may notice his wife trying to make herself attractive to him, seeking to please him in various ways. He may thus realize that his attentions would be welcome to her. Again, he should not be entirely passive in this early call for mating. He should be considerate and generous, seeking to ingratiate himself with her to the end that she will not only consent to the union but even be passionately desirous of having him.

It was to do well by His creatures that God willed the earth to be populated ; and in His desire to be kind to them, He permitted the joys that the fulfilment of this command brought to the soul of man.

II

There is quite an heritage that *El Shaddai* passed on to Jehovah in the religious life of His chosen people. Much of it deals with sex, and the covenant forms a basic element in it. The covenant is an agreement into which the Creator of the world entered with an individual living in it—Abraham. The Creator agreed to be a God unto Abraham and to enrich and multiply him. The latter was to walk humbly before his God and to do so whole-heartedly. The covenant extended into infinity, and its terms increased as time went on. God was to deliver the children of Abraham from servitude in Egypt, to conquer Canaan for them, and to bless them with the fat of the land as well as to protect them against their enemies. The children of Abraham were to accept the Word of God at Sinai in commandment and Law and to live thereafter accordingly. The God of the universe entered into a particular relationship with a single people upon earth. Jewish mystics conceived this relationship as a form of spiritual marriage between the Divine Being and His chosen people, on the basis of the Law, the Word that was ere the world had been created.

Appropriately enough, the covenant was sealed by the life-blood of Abraham, coming from the source of human life. " This is my covenant which ye shall keep, between me and you and thy seed after thee : Every male among you shall be circumcised . . . in the flesh of the foreskin ; and it shall be a token of a covenant betwixt me and you . . . the uncircumcised male who is not circumcised in the flesh of his foreskin, that soul shall be cut off from his people ; he hath broken my covenant."

This was centuries ago. The world has since changed many times over and with it the concept of Jehovah. The Lord of

*A sacrificial altar*

Israel became the God of mankind. His dwelling was no longer a private place for the descendants of Abraham but a house of worship for all peoples. His tastes underwent a change no less. He came to despise praise. He would have none of the steers and lambs brought as sacrifices to Him. He was no longer concerned with the flesh of His worshippers but with the stirrings of their souls. Still, the covenant continues to this very day. A Jew may cease visiting the synagogue. He may no longer pray at all. He may shave his whiskers, eat pork, and smoke on the Sabbath. He will be a sinning Jew, but a Jew nevertheless. However, once he is uncircumcised, he has broken the covenant and is " cut off from his people." He will even be refused a burial-place in the Jewish cemetery.

Even the non-religious Jew will, in most cases, keep the

covenant.  He may be a free-thinker or an agnostic.  He may
have estranged himself from the religious life of his people, having
almost forgotten the precepts and customs of his faith.  Still, he
will circumcise his male children.  Most likely he will rationalize
his observance of the rite.  He may be doing it not to break the
heart of his believing father or mother or uncle ; he may be
doing it for the sake of family ties or for purely hygienic reasons.
But at heart he observes the rite because he does not dare to
break the covenant.  All his excuses are only an attempt to
rationalize an act that involves an emotional attitude.  For, even
if the covenant no longer holds between Jew and God, it still
endures between Jew and Jew.  Only those free-thinking Jews
who actively oppose religion and those who, while professing the
Christian faith, still keep " within the fold " as Christian Jews,
do not circumcise their males.

All other Jews, when a male child is born to them, on the
eighth day of the boy's life, will perform the *bris*.  Even when the
boy is born already circumcised, some incision must be made so
that blood will come forth, for in the blood of this organ the
covenant between Israel and Jehovah has been consecrated.  If
possible, there will be a *minyan* at the ceremony, just as there is
at any other important religious service.  It is the father's duty
to perform the operation, but he makes the professional *mohel* his
agent in this act.  The child, resting on a pillow, is brought from
the mother's room to the room where the *bris* is to be performed.
It is passed from one person to another, an honour accorded to
a chosen few.  If there happens to be among the guests a couple
about to be married, they are especially honoured, and the child
is given to them or to a member of the immediate family to be
placed upon the chair of Elijah.  This is an ordinary household
chair on which is placed a pillow, covered with a white sheet.  It
is the chair supposedly reserved for the prophet Elijah, who, by
his zealous fight for Jehovah against the servants of Baal, earned
for himself the distinction of being the symbolic guest of honour
at every circumcision ceremony.

The child is turned over to the *sandak*, who, seated upon an
elevated chair, holds the baby on the pillow.  He is the Jewish
equivalent of the Christian godfather and his honour is equally
as great.  The operation takes only a few minutes.  The bleeding
is stopped at once and the child is soon pacified.  There is usually
but a single outburst and crying for a few minutes.

The father prays : " Blessed art thou, O Lord, our God, King
of the universe, who hast sanctified us by thy commandments
and hast commanded us to make him enter into the covenant of
Abraham, our father."  Prayers followed with libations of sacra-

mental wine. The *mohel* lets a drop or two of wine fall into the mouth of the child, repeating as he does so a quotation from the Scriptures : " And I passed by thee and I saw thee wallowing in thy blood, and I said : In thy blood shalt thou live, in thy blood shalt thou live."

The ceremony is followed by a feast of proportions varying according to the means of the family and the customs of the particular country. Men, women, and children are present at the ceremony and feast, but the female children are usually kept out of the room until after the operation is performed. And thus is the covenant established between the God of Israel and a new son of Abraham. It is a solemn occasion upon which the believing Jew seeks to fathom the great mystery of his race—the intimate relation between his father Abraham and the God of the universe.

### III

Among the things *El Shaddai* passed on to Jehovah was a system of taboos. Everything was not only good or bad, but primarily pure or impure. What was impure was taboo, forbidden to be eaten, worn, touched, or mentioned. There still are many such taboos in the House of the Lord. The name of God is not to be pronounced. Clothes made of a mixture of wool and linen are not to be worn. Fish that have no scales, as the eel or shell-fish, are not to be eaten. Not only is the meat of the pig a forbidden food, but even the mere act of raising the animal for the market is deemed ill-befitting the good Jew.

There were other taboos on semen and menstruating blood that gave rise to many purity laws and voluminous commentaries. Of these taboos, however, only the latter is still closely followed by the pious daughters of Sarah, Rebecca, Rachel, and Leah, the four mothers of the race.

In primitive society, man had tremendous fear of menstruating blood. Almost everywhere women approaching their periods were separated and kept apart from the camp, often in huts built purposely for them. The menstruating woman was to keep out of the path frequented by men and, if by accident a man did come her way, she was to call out in a loud voice so that he might make a circuit to avoid her. Whatever she touched was to be burned ; in some places, she must not touch even her own food, having, therefore, to be fed by other women. An Australian native, discovering that he had slept on a coat upon which his menstruating wife had lain, was so horrified that he killed her and he himself died of fear.

The superstitions about menstruating women have persisted in various forms throughout history. In his *Natural History*, Pliny states, in all seriousness, that the touch of a menstruating woman will turn wine into vinegar, blunt razors, rust iron or brass, and cause mares to miscarry. It is still believed in some European countries that a menstruating woman, walking on the shore, will drive the fish away ; if she crosses a hunter's path, he will catch no game ; if she enters a brewery, the beer will turn sour, and if she makes jam, it will not keep. Her very shadow will cause flowers to wither, trees to perish, and the serpent to cease its wriggling.

Moses gave this taboo divine sanction. A man shall not " approach a woman to uncover her nakedness, as long as she is

*Warding off the unclean spirits from
mother and infant*

impure by her uncleanliness." Childbirth was the beginning of such a period of " uncleanliness," and required a period of purification, forty days after the birth of a boy and eighty after that of a girl. During the periods the woman was unclean " as in the days of the impurity of her sickness," she must touch no hallowed thing nor come into the sanctuary. After the purification days were over, she was to come to the door of the temple, bringing a lamb for a burnt offering and a young pigeon for a sin offering. Only then was she " cleansed from the fountain of her blood." During this period of impurity the sexual union was strictly forbidden : " And if a man shall lie with a woman having her sickness and shall uncover her nakedness—he hath made naked her fountain and she hath uncovered the fountain of her blood—both of them shall be cut off from among their people."

In Talmudic lore, this command has been quite elaborately extended. Since the punishment for coition in menstrual periods is untimely death for both husband and wife, the rabbis sought to guard them from the temptations that might lead them to commit this horrible sin. Consequently, the two must not show any affection toward each other during this time. The husband must not touch his wife, even without any desire. In fact, he must not even hand her anything so small that it may cause their fingers to meet. He may not eat out of the same dishes with her, nor drink from her cup ; but she may eat and drink out of the dishes he has used. He may not sit upon her bed even in her absence, and she is not permitted to make his bed in his presence. He must not even see any part of her body that is customarily covered.

There are many detailed specifications as to what does or does not constitute a period. A special tractate in the Talmud is devoted to this subject. There are various kinds of blood that may or may not make the woman taboo to her husband. In olden times, possibly even now in eastern Europe, it is not unusual that some phase of this matter be brought to the attention of the rabbi, who may examine the linen to determine whether the mark in question be from menstrual blood or accidental discharge.

The Talmudic law demands that, at the close of the menstrual period, the woman wash herself and then take an immersion. This may be taken in sea, river, well, or basin. The basins especially prepared for this purpose are called *mikvas ;* they are deep enough so that the person may stand in water up to the chest. Such baths are found in almost every Jewish community and are generally built and maintained by the religious communal organizations. The young bride must come to this bath on the day before her marriage to fulfil the requirement of the law.

On the seventh day of her purification period, the woman cuts her nails, washes and combs her hair, and bathes herself thoroughly so that there may be no uncleanliness in any part of her body. Then she enters the *mikva* where her immersion is supervised by two women. They may hold her hand if she is afraid to duck beneath the water, but she must dip three times, the women watching that not a single hair of her head remains above the surface. After the immersion, she clothes herself in fresh linen and is considered pure again.

In medieval times, the keeper of the bath or the sexton would come the following morning to the husband and say : " *Mazol tov,*" Good luck ! The assumption was that on the first night of purification, the husband visited his wife, and it was hoped that his visit would result in a pregnancy. Congratulations were therefore in order. Medieval Jewish legends also tell of Jews living in small, poverty-stricken communities where there was no *mikva*. The women would therefore immerse themselves in the river, and in the winter, when the river was frozen over, an opening would be cut in the ice for them. There is many a story of the young bride who shuddered at the thought of immersing herself in the ice-cold water on a wintry night. The mother or mother-in-law would exhort the child-bride to execute the rite upon the observance of which the happiness of her after-life as well as the character of her future children depended. The bride consented and went under the water never to be seen again.

## IV

The God of the Hebrews had a difficult time in dealing with His chosen people. They were not only stiff-necked, but realistic and distrustful as well. When the Lord promised Abraham the land of Canaan to " inherit it," Abraham promptly asked : " Whereby shall I know that I shall inherit it ? " When he did " believe in the Lord," Jehovah appreciated it so much that He " counted it to him as a righteousness." When " I am that I am " appeared to Moses in the burning bush, He was not only asked for His name, but was even called upon to give a sign. And for all the signs and miracles that Moses showed the children of Israel in and out of Egypt, Jehovah still found it necessary to come down upon Mount Sinai, where His people might hear Him speaking and " believe forever." Only when they perceived the " thundering and the lightning and the voice of the horn and the mountain smoking " were they impressed. Even here, the legend relates, they were not sufficiently moved to accept the Law which had been declined by all other nations. So the Lord raised a mountain over their heads, and said : " Accept my Law or here you will be buried." And they accepted.

There was little room for the mystic in Jewish theology. The people knew full well who their God was, and His essence little concerned them as He had neither shape nor form. They knew how He had created the world and why ; and what He was expecting from the people living upon it. All this was set down in clear, plain writing. There was no mystery into which to delve and no secret to unearth. And yet there was something unfathomable about Jehovah. His absolute spirituality was an enigma. His very formlessness aroused speculation as to His nature. When He did appear before His people, it was in smoke and cloud—a fiery cloud, but a cloud nevertheless.

The very simplicity and clarity of the Hebrew faith led sensitive natures to seek beyond the simple and the obvious. There were many who at various times set out upon the hidden ways to search beyond sense and reason. Their vain attempts and their findings constitute a considerable treasure of mystic lore. The clarity of the faith did not prevent it from developing a mysticism of its own. The formality of the Law did not destroy the spontaneity and the outpouring of the longing heart.

The Psalmist sang : " Whom have I in heaven but thee ? And there is none upon earth that I desire beside thee . . . Yea, I have loved thee with an everlasting love ; therefore with loving kindness have I drawn thee. . . ." His spontaneity expressed itself in love, and through love has the mystic sought to commune with his God. In this endeavour, he has simply carried over the terminology of physical love to his spiritual relationship. Did not this spiritual craving take the place of the pining of his heart ?

The longing for union and the desire for oneness permeate the entire Jewish mysticism. By the very nature of things, there is a break in the universe, a split that makes for dualism where unity should obtain. God is infinite. The world is finite. God is spirit. The world is matter. How can the two touch each other ? Where is the bridge of communion between them ? Jewish mystics in Babylon conceived the intermediary of an angel, whom God created to rule the world, and it is to him that all the anthropomorphic passages in the Bible refer. There was a quasi-physical phase to this angel hovering over the deep between God and man ; and this was later reflected in the idea of primordial man, who was human and yet much more than that. It was the form of a man that Ezekiel saw in the chariot moving across the sky that symbolized the absolute form of all existence : the source of all other forms of creation, of all ideas, of the supreme thought. He is the Logos and the Word, the man that stands between God and mankind.

This humanized bridge across the chasm in the universe is still too simple and concrete. It does not yet satisfy the searching soul of the exalted mystic. The Cabalist, therefore, groped still further into the dark of dualism for the light of unity. He evolved the thought of concentration, according to which the infinite was supposed to contract and to make room for a finite world of matter. Between the spirit and matter, there are series of emanations—ten *sephirot*. Not one bridge, but ten bridges lead between the Creator and His universe—radiations from the Divine Will, growing fainter in brightness as they proceed outward.

Ten bridges between two spheres do not yet make for unity.

But sometime absolute unity will be attained. The finite in man will disappear along with sin and Satan and Hell. This will happen on the advent of the Messiah. He will come when all souls will have been born and purified in a series of transmigrations, to return uncontaminated to their divine source. The soul of the Messiah is the last in the repository of souls created by God at the time that He formed the world. He who increases the population upon earth shortens the interval between the present and the birth of the Messiah. He makes closer the approach between the Divine Being and His creations. Sexual life is making for unity in the universe.

But there are many other ways in which universal unity is dependent upon the union of the sexes below. The Creator is reflected in His creations. As He is one, He dwells in him who is likewise one ; " only when man has so perfected himself as to be one does the Holy One dwell therein. And when may a man be called one ? When he is in union with a woman." The Divine Presence is considered as a dualism in union, manifested in the pairing of the emanations. There is the King, who symbolizes the ideal world, and the Queen, the symbol of the real world. The King and the Queen, often referred to as the " two faces," form a pair whose task it is to constantly pour forth new grace upon the world. Through their union, they continue the process of creation and, what is even more important, perpetuate the works of creation.

Similarly, the two arms of God, Judgment and Grace, are another dualism that must be united. Grace is the expansion of the will and the source of the male souls. Judgment is the contraction of the will and the source of the female souls. The one gives life ; the other brings death. Their separation would make it impossible for the world to exist. Fortunately, they combine in the common symbol of Beauty, whose material representation is the heart. The arms of God and the sexes of man are joined by love, and the world is enabled to continue its existence.

There are two other divine emanations ever seeking union ; the spheres of Beauty and of Kingdom. The former represents heaven ; the latter earth. The two meet at the sphere called Foundation, or Basis, which also means Copulation. But the two cannot unite unless there is human copulation as well. Once more : the union of the sexes among humans brings about the union of the separate emanations of the Divinity.

Just as the universe is a dualism seeking unity, so was man himself originally dual ; for God created man two-faced, that is double-sexed, and cut him asunder into male and female. Ever since that separation was accomplished, neither man nor woman has been complete alone. To realize one's self, to find completion and harmony, he must seek union with his mate of the opposite sex.

God himself, for all His unity, was not absolutely complete, for He did not realize harmony until He created the universe. And why did He create it? Out of love for another being, out of longing for His uncreated world. And He did not come into His own until He chose Israel as His bride, for here He entered into

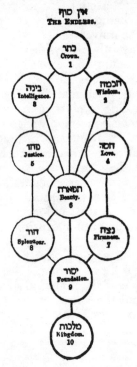

*The universe a dualism seeking unity*

a union with His glory. All mystic prayers begin with the phrase " for the sake of the union of the Holy One with His glory." All man is seeking to obtain by prayer is this divine union, for he, too, is a part of the glory, and his union with God is his greatest hope. God is reflected in His Law, and the Law is as beloved by Israel as sexual intercourse is by other peoples. Therefore, he who has not known passionate love for woman cannot attain love for God. No prayer will reach the throne of heaven unless the worshipper has experienced physical passion while offering it. In fact, sexual union is in itself of divine nature. " Three are possessed of a divine aspect : the sun, the Sabbath, and sexual intercourse."

And just as man is seeking to bring about divine unity, so is the Holy One desirious of seeing humans in union.  When man and woman unite in purity and holiness, the Holy One is found among them, for in the result of this union God has a part.  There are three partners in man : the father, the mother, and God.  When man's life comes to an end, the Holy One takes away His part, the soul, and the father and mother remain with the body.  The temporary, earthly partnership of man, woman, and God is dissolved.  The soul is released for another and truer union in the world above.  There, it returns to its source in the Divine Being.

The Cabalist refers to this world above as the world of truth. It is also the world of union.  For long before the world below was created, there was already love, and all existence was one great embrace.  Then the physical world was created, and the universal love embrace was disturbed.  Instead of permanent union, there came to be temporary unions, copulations, both in the spheres above and below.  However, the universe is ever drawing nearer and nearer to its Creator.  It is on its way to the permanent union—the merging of the Creator with His creation.

v

The God of the Hebrews was a zealous divinity.  His was the kingdom of heaven and earth, and He would have no other gods before Him.  His people were not to touch an idol or to keep any sort of image or likeness.  " I am the Lord thy God, thou shalt have no other gods before Me.  Thou shalt not make unto thee a graven image, nor any manner of likeness, of any thing that is in heaven above, or that is in the earth beneath, or that is in the water under the earth. . . ."

To what extent this commandment is to be followed constitutes a considerable portion of Talmudic and Rabbinic discussion. Opinions vary as to whether the order includes bas-reliefs and set-ins or busts since these are not the entire figure.  Similarly, opinions differ as to whether it embraces the images serving as designs in carpets and tapestries, since they are actually only a part of the material into which they are woven.  Generally, with the advance of the iconoclast movement in the Christian faith, the taboo on images was partially raised by the rabbis.  Yet, sculpture and painting were arts conspicuously missing among the Jews.  Only during the last two or three generations have these arts been accepted within the fold of Israel.

For all that, there never was a time when the synagogue was
entirely devoid of figures and forms of erotic significance.  Some
of these came in stealthily without the approval or the knowledge
of the prophet.  They were admitted by the priest as necessity
required.  For he was dealing in practical religion.  He was
administering to the religious wants of the people and had to
reckon with their desires and inclinations.  In a critical moment
in the wilderness, Aaron himself cast a golden calf to stay the
popular stampede for a concrete god.  The children of Aaron
often compromised with the phallic ceremonials of other faiths so
as to keep the worshippers in line.  Then the prophet came and
effected the removal of the idols.

Adorning the porch, at the entrance to King Solomon's temple
there were two pillars named *Jachin*, which means " he shall
prepare," and *Boaz*, signifying " in him there is strength."
Traditional commentary maintains that these pillars symbolized
the male generative principle.  In Ezekiel there is a suggestion of
a large image of the lingam in the Holy of holies in the temple.
And round about the graven images of lions, palm trees, and
cherubim were figures of the lingam and yoni in union.  This we
know from a passage in 1 Kings vii. 36, which has been generally
omitted in Biblical translations even as far back as the *Peshito*, or
Syriac translation, of some nineteen hundred years ago.  Where
a translation is attempted, its sense is vague and almost meaning-
less.  This phrase, which in Hebrew is *K'maar Ish U'lyotha*, is
rendered by Rashi, the most authoritative commentator of the
eleventh century, on the basis of a passage in the Talmud (Yuma
54a), as : " like the male and female in embrace."  The *u'loytha*,
which appears to have been a common figure in the decorative
schemes of the temple, is explained by Rashi as " male and
female in union."

There were also purely Hebraic erotic symbols in the temple
of Jehovah.  These the children of Israel did not borrow from
other peoples, but created for themselves.  Such symbols were
the cherubim, the exact shapes of which we do not know to-day.
Tradition has it that they were a lingam and yoni in union.  A
Talmudic legend relates that when the Israelites made their
pilgrimages to the temple for the holy days, the curtain before
the ark was raised, and, as the cherubim were displayed, they
were told : " Your love for God is like this love of the male for
the female."

There are many figures in the synagogue to-day which serve as
ornaments for various sacred articles of worship.  The ark containing the scroll is usually done in hand-carved wood, ornamented
with the figures of lions, their mouths open and their tongues

hanging.   Those who know erotic symbolism will recognize in
the open mouth the symbol of the yoni and in the tongue that of
the lingam.   The ornaments often include a bronze or wooden
serpent with the tip of the tail in its mouth, forming an oval.
The justification for this symbol is found in a Biblical passage
according to which, on the occasion of a scourge, Moses put up

*"Idol" of Knights Templars, showing Semitic influences*

the image of a serpent over the entrance to the tabernacle so that
any afflicted person might " look at the serpent and live."   The
ark itself, the container of the Law, like the ark among all peoples,
is symbolic of the female principle of generation.

Every morning with the exception of the Sabbath and holy
days, the Jew prays in phylacteries.   As he twists the leather
strips about his left arm and hand he forms a ring about his
middle finger.   While doing so, he repeats phrases from the Bible,

saying : " And I have betrothed thee unto me with truth. . . . And I have betrothed thee unto me with justice." However abstract the words are, the ring he forms about his finger is symbolic of the marriage ring, of the union between God and man. Like all ring ceremonials, it is suggestive of what is naturally to follow.

Addressing his bride at the marriage ceremony, the Jewish bridegroom says : " By this ring you are hallowed unto me, according to the law of Moses and Israel." These words are pronounced by the groom under a canopy, generally out in the open. The cloth of the canopy symbolizes the roof and the four poles to which it is attached, the four walls. It is a symbolic vestige of the room into which the bride and groom were con- ducted in olden times, after the wedding ceremony, there to have their first intercourse. During the interval, the assembled guests celebrated the event in the other parts of the house, awaiting the results. For, if it were discovered that the bride was not a virgin, the groom might refuse to accept her or he could demand an appropriate recompense. Sometimes, the families of the bride and the groom had their representatives or witnesses in the inner chamber. A similar custom still prevails among Slavic peasants. The bridal couple is led to a bedroom and left alone for some time. The mother of the bride later enters the room and removes the sheet from the bridal bed, displaying before all the guests the proof of her daughter's virginity.

Even more erotic symbolism may be found in what is read, studied, and sung in the synagogue. The Scriptures abound in expressions of love and sex. The very relationship between Israel and Jehovah is represented as the relationship between wife, often enough unfaithful, and her husband.

Hosea said that, when the Lord spoke to him, He told him : " Go, take unto thee a wife of harlotry and children of harlotry, for the land doth commit great harlotry, departing from the Lord." And again God is made to say :

> " Plead with your mother, plead
> For she is not my wife, neither am I her husband
> And let her put away her harlotries from her face,
> And her adulteries from between her breasts ;
> Lest I strip her as in the day that she was born. . . ."

When the chosen people decided to be good and faithful to their God, this relationship was again described in terms of love. The ideal attitude of Israel to its God and of God to His people has been pictured in the greatest love poem of all times, the Song of Songs. This is read in the synagogue along with the other

books of the Bible and in the homes after the close of the jovial
ceremony of *seder*.  It abounds in expressions of love ; the loved
one sings :

> " Let him kiss me with the kisses of his mouth
> For thy love is better than wine.
>
> .    .    .    .    .
>
> Therefore do the maidens love thee . . ."

and the lover continues :

> " The roundings of thy thighs are like the links of a chain,
> The work of the hands of a skilled workman.
> Thy navel is like a round goblet,
> Wherein no mingled wine is wanting ;
> Thy belly is like a heap of wheat
> Set about with lilies.
> Thy two breasts are like two fawns
> That are twins of a gazelle."

Of course, the kissing refers not to the act of osculation, but
to an incident at Mount Sinai when each word spoken by God
was carried by an angel, or by itself travelled to the lips of every
son of Israel standing at the foot of the mountain.  The wine is
really a symbol of the Law.  The thighs are the Torah, and the
belly is the Book of Leviticus.

The exuberance of love in this book is only too evident.  The
Talmudic student, setting out on the road to mysticism, will
take to it as his favourite part of the Scriptures.  He who is about
to deny himself physical love and all thought of pleasure and sex
is already preparing an outlet for his emotion in the deep sea of
love for the Creator.  The Cabalist felt no restraint in his anthropomorphic conception of the divine.  He even went so far as to
say that the evildoer, by his transgression, causes a process of
menstruation in the Divine Presence, so that the Holy One cannot
unite with the soul.

On Friday night, most pious Jews still sing the Sabbath
song, which is a dedication of the feast to the Lord.  The celebration of the Sabbath is described as a wedding feast, with the
principal personages the bride and the groom.  The Sabbath is
the bride and Israel the groom.  After picturing the magnificence
of the feast, the splendour of the personages, and the details of the
wedding, the song tells how the husband embraces the bride,
" and does what is pleasing to her by continuous grinding."  The
meaning is that Israel is uniting with the Sabbath in love, which
is most pleasing to her.  And they who would disturb this love
relationship are ground to destruction.  The highly suggestive
phraseology is rationalized and explained away, but no words can
hide the great love that is forever flourishing in the synagogue.

# CHAPTER II

## ROMANCE IN THE CHURCH

*" He that loveth not knoweth not God; for God is love."* —*St. John.*

### I

THE church began as a romantic movement in the shadow of the synagogue. What could be more romantic than the son of a carpenter in Galilee coming down to Jerusalem and driving the money-changers out of the court of the temple? What greater romance than the Son of Man, himself divine, yet being born and living like a mere human, finally returning to his divine state through martyrdom upon the cross?

No less fanciful are the lives of the twelve men who assembled for the Last Supper with him whom they called their Lord. There they were meeting for the last time ere their ways were to part—their Lord to follow the weary road to Calvary, there to be crucified between two thieves; they to carry their own crosses into diverse corners of the world. Theirs was the call to spread the new faith that began at Bethlehem and apparently ended at Golgotha, only to rise to new life in the blood of the Christ.

There was romance in the birth of the church and in the lives of its founders. There was romance no less in the way the new religion took root and found a following among the peoples of the world. It did not take to the conservative countryside, self-satisfied in its drabness, but followed along the main thorough-fares into the big cities of the day. There, it attracted not the mighty, resting in their opulence, sipping their cup of plenty and pleasure, but the poor and the downtrodden, the outcast and despised, those without opportunity or hope. They who had no place in the realm of earthliness sought a kingdom of heaven upon earth. For them the new faith was a ladder of hope, of distinction and greatness, a spiritual romance set against their dreggy existence.

And yet it was all within the shadow of the synagogue. The bearer of the faith was a member of the older institution. If he took issue with the elders, it was not to break the Law, but to fulfil it. The immediate apostles of the new faith were all of the synagogue, as were the first communities professing it. But, as the faith of the cross spread to various climes, its Hebraic provisions were not quite appropriate for the new adherents. Nevertheless, they were all bound by the Law that was kept within the ark of the synagogue.

It required still another synagogue man to break the Law,

rather than to fulfil it ; to cut the navel cord and let loose the new faith, leaving it to find its way as best it could over the face of the earth.

In its relations to sex and women, the faith of the cross was again characterized by romance operating within the shadow of the synagogue. There, one could find two very distinct attitudes toward sex and woman. The more primitive, held to by the " people of the land," the peasants and other common folk, was positive. They looked upon sex as upon a natural function, something like eating. It was necessarily circumscribed by social customs—by taboos, like those against incest, and by regulation, like that of marriage—but within these limits its exercise was not only proper, but obligatory. God's first command was to man : " Be fruitful and multiply."

A nomadic people ever in bitter struggle for existence, the tribes of Israel could afford neither to indulge in sex nor to keep the women out of the sphere of activities within the tribe. Women not only participated in all phases of tribal life, but even took the place of exalted leaders or advisers. It was this idea of sex and woman that the children of Israel brought with them into the land of Canaan. This attitude was preserved among the large, conservative masses that lived upon the soil and were least influenced by neighbouring or invading civilizations.

In the church, this positive attitude of the synagogue toward sex and woman is represented by Jesus. Born in the back hills of Galilee and raised among the common folk, Jesus imbibed the wholesome attitude toward woman that prevailed in his social stratum. He did not despise her nor did he conceive of sex and birth as the plans of the devil. Woman was to him a human being, sex a natural function, and birth retained the halo of mystic sanctity that it conveys to the wholesome man. In fact, he did not hesitate to compare the joy of his return to earth after the crucifixion with the joy of a woman bearing a child :

" A woman when she is in travail hath sorrow, because her hour is come ; but as soon as she is delivered of the child, she remembereth no more the anguish, for joy that a man is born into the world.

" And ye now therefore sorrow, but I will see you again and your heart will rejoice and your joy no man taketh from you."

We further see, quite distinctly, the difference between Jesus and his immediate associates in their attitude toward children :

" And they brought young children to him that he should touch them ; and his disciples rebuked those that brought them.

" But when Jesus saw it, he was much displeased and said unto them : Suffer little children to come unto me and forbid them not, for of such is the kingdom of God."

Following his attitude toward sex, women, and children, it is natural that Jesus should exact great devotion from the husband to the wife. He said :

" Ye have heard that it was said by them of old time : Thou shalt not commit adultery. But I say unto you that whosoever looketh on a woman to lust after her hath committed adultery with her already in his heart."

At the same time, Jesus looked kindly upon the women who

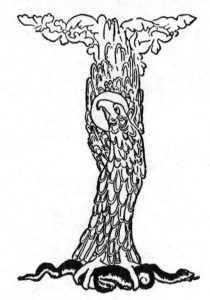

*Symbols in early Christian art*

had gone astray. It is the normal mind with the normal attitude that can best sympathize with and be generous to those out of the normal fringe. When Simon the Pharisee wondered at Jesus allowing a woman of the streets, a sinner, to come near him, the latter replied :

" Seest thou this woman ? I entered thine house, thou gavest me no water for my feet ; but she hath washed my feet with tears and wiped them with the hairs of her head.

" Thou gavest me no kiss, but this woman since the time I came in hath not ceased to kiss my feet. My head with oil thou didst not anoint, but this woman hath anointed my feet with ointment. Therefore, I say unto thee : Her sins which are many are forgiven, for she hath loved much, but to whom little is forgiven the same loveth little."

And again :

" Verily I say unto you that the publicans and the harlots go into the kingdom of God before you.

" For John came unto you in the way of righteousness and ye believed him not ; but the publicans and the harlots believed him. . . ."

And when a woman was brought to him with the charge that she was taken in adultery, in the very act, Jesus said : " He that is without sin among you shall cast the first stone." When all the accusers, convicted by their own consciences, left one by one, Jesus said to the woman : " Woman, where are thine accusers, hath no man condemned thee ? " She replied : " No man, Lord," and Jesus said unto her : " Neither do I condemn thee ; go and sin no more."

The son of Nazareth's carpenter could be charitable to the wayward woman. He had no consciousness of guilt to project, no complex to overcome. He had been little concerned with sex himself. He had neither married nor had relationships with women. He was preoccupied with a passion greater than sex— the salvation of mankind. He who set the highest ideal for the relationship between the sexes could be generous to those who followed it least.

## II

But there was another attitude toward sex and woman within the shadow of the synagogue. It was new, to be sure, but was rapidly spreading with the current of Hellenic civilization that had invaded the land of Israel. It had come from foreign climes, where people, wallowing in wealth, were wont to slake their sexual appetites in orgiastic fashion. It was a product of the idle, supersensitive mind, drowning in its own sea of speculation. It was the weed of decadence sprouting forth from the mouldering walls of the temple of the gods.

This attitude turned man's mind away from sex and made him look down upon woman. It considered the sensuous life as carnal sin and forbade the pleasures of the flesh. It despised woman as the object of man's desire and the harbinger of the joy of life. The son of Israel who would be a Greek must do as Greek does and think Hellenic. He overindulged in sensuality and was all the more depressed as a result. That ancient observation—*post coitiem omne animal triste est*—was more true of him than of anyone else.

And as he was considering his own state of mind, the son
of Israel found in his Greek learning ample justification for his
spiritual distress. Did not the master of all, the great Aristotle,
say that woman was unfinished reality, while man was reality
complete? Did not the Greek philosopher speak of the worth-
lessness of women? And he who was more than anyone else both
Hebrew and Hellene, Philo-Judæous, admitted all that. He even
identified sinfulness with the flesh and spoke of the original sin
of the human race with all its dreadful consequences.

No wonder then that the negative attitude toward sex and life
made its appearance within the very shadow of the synagogue,
resulting in Hebrew ascetic sects that rejected all the sexual life
had to offer. And the further one travelled from the synagogue
the more his mind became permeated with this attitude, particularly as one turned to the shores of Africa.

The man who led the church into foreign climes also led
this foreign influence into the church. Paul of Tarsus was
a Jew of the world. He knew Greek and possibly attended
the Greek university of his town. He did not attend the temple
of Sandan, the Baal of Tarsus, but he knew how the god was
worshipped and that was why he was so zealous for his own
faith. He was a contemporary of Philo and may have known
of the ideas emanating from the sage of Egypt. So long as he
kept within the fold of the Pharisees his personal life may have
been little influenced by the current ideas of his day. Once he
turned to the faith of the Christ, he took to it with all the
vehemence of his nature.

What had been the sexual life of Paul before he embraced the
new religion? Very little in regard to this is definitely known.
His early life is hidden in the mists of time. There is, however,
some conjecture as to his having been married. If we are to
assume that he had been a member of the Sanhedrin, he must
have been married and the father of a son. But not every pupil
of Gamaliel was necessarily a member of that august body. Was
he a widower at the time of his conversion, as some scholars would
have us believe, or had he divorced his wife? Was he at all
capable of sexual living, and had the " infirmity of the flesh " to
which he made reference, any bearing upon his nervous condition?

However Paul lived in his old faith, when he turned to the
new religion he separated himself from women. He exhorted
his followers to forgo all sexual relations, marriage included. He
wrote to the Corinthians : " I say to the unmarried and to the
widows it is good for them to abide even as I." He would have all
people celibate, saying : " I would that all men were even as I."
Again : " It is good for a man not to touch a woman."

At times, Paul gave a wholesome, if not adequate, reason for his insistence upon self-denial in sex. He saw in the sexual relationship, with its concomitant responsibilities, a hindrance to the service of God. " He that is unmarried is careful for the things of the Lord, how he may please the Lord, but he that is married is careful for the things of the world, how he may please his wife and is divided." Paul had never been " divided." When he was against the faith of the cross, he was violently against it, persecuting its followers by all that was in his power. When he became converted, he devoted himself entirely to the new faith. He dissolved his very self in the divine essence of Jesus. " I live," he said, " yet not I, but Christ liveth in me." He consequently could not permit any phase of living, however desirable or important, to interfere with the absolute union of man and his Saviour.

Generally, however, Paul based his demand for celibacy upon an aversion for sex and woman. For Paul, man alone was created in the image of God and for His glory. The woman was created solely for the temporal use of man. The husband is therefore the " head of the wife " and the wife should be " in subjection " to him " as unto the Lord." When Adam and Eve were in the Garden of Eden, it was the woman, not the man, who transgressed. "Adam was not deceived, but the woman being deceived, was in transgression." In her sinfulness Eve had even lost her name and is referred to as " the woman." It was Eve that brought sin into the world and she and her daughters are eternally responsible for human depravity and death. God had to sacrifice His own son to save the world from the plight into which it had been led by woman.

Consequently, all that appertains to the sexual life is anathema. Celibacy is the ideal state, but marriage is permitted where the flesh is too weak. " Because of fornication, let each man have his own wife ; and let each woman have her own husband." And again : " But if they have not continency, let them marry, for it is better to marry than to burn."

To save men from the flames of hell, Paul permitted them to marry, and to guard them from Satan he advised men and women to live sexually while in the marital state. " Defraud ye not one the other, except it be by consent for a season, that ye may give yourselves unto prayer and may be together again, that Satan tempt you not because of your incontinency. But this I say by way of concession, not of commandment."

If such was the attitude of Paul to the sexual union of the married, he naturally could look only with disgust and dismay at the illicit sexual relationship. The presence of so many prostitutes in Christian Corinth only fanned his zest. Paul had not enough fire in which to burn the unfortunate women : " Know ye not that your bodies are members of Christ ? Shall I then take away the members of Christ and make them members of a harlot ? " And again : " Know ye not that he that is joined by a harlot is one body . . . but he that is joined unto the Lord is one spirit ? Adultery is the greatest sin of all since every sin that a man doeth is without the body, but he that committeth fornication sinneth against his own body, which is the temple of the Holy Spirit."

Even the birth of a child, so glorious to Jesus, assumed a sombre aspect in the words of Paul. For the child came into the world by an act that is hardly worthy of true servants of the Lord. The child was born with the blemish of sin upon his infant soul. He came, a defiled being, into a world of sin, for " how can be he clean that is born of woman ? "

### III

Paul's attitude toward sex and woman was tempered by his early education in the shadow of the synagogue, by the practical circumspection of the leader and by his inherent sense of justice and consideration. Realizing that the ideal of celibacy was beyond the nature of the average man, he permitted marriage. Permitting marriage, he conceded the sexual intercourse. Maintaining the inferiority of woman in the scheme of creation, he was sympathetically mindful of her position in life. He admonished the husband not to be bitter against his wife and exhorted him to love her. He even promised woman salvation through childbirth, if she continues in faith and love and sanctification.

The immediate followers of Paul, particularly those who came from the Orient and Africa, went far beyond him in their negation of sex. They vied with one another in the suppression of their sexual instincts. Jerome and Chrysostom condemned marriage as an invention of Satan. Many converts who were already married made amends by taking the vow of chastity. Tertullian tells us : " How many there are who, by consent between themselves cancel the debt of their marriage ; eunuchs of their own accord through the desire of the kingdom of heaven."

It was Tertullian who elaborated this Pauline idea into a system and gave it intellectual and philosophic form—a heritage to the fathers of the church in subsequent generations. To Tertullian, virginity was the highest state of life, but he allowed marriage because it is permitted by the Divine Word and because it is necessary to the propagation of the race. He did, however, frown upon a second marriage, and in Montanism, the religious creed to which he belonged, such a marriage was absolutely forbidden.    The first marriage was a union for time and eternity.

In the marriage relationships, the exercise of the sexual function should be guided by the extent to which one is tempted by Satan. To later theologians, it seemed a terrible admission of weakness for one to fulfil his sinful desire according to the strength of his impulse.    In consequence, the sexual life of married people was quite carefully delineated.    Intercourse was to be had only for the purpose of procreation.    Once the wife had conceived, no further sexual activity was to be engaged in by the pious.    During the union great care need be taken not to succumb to lust.    One was to derive the least possible pleasure out of the sexual intercourse.

One hundred and seventy years after Christ, Athenagoras defended the new religion against the accusation that the Christians " respect neither age nor sex, neither ties of blood nor bonds of family," saying :  " Each of us who takes a wife does so only for the purpose of bringing children into the world.    He is like the farmer who entrusts the soil with his seed and then patiently waits for the crop."    And Clement of Alexandria, in his Apologia, states :  " Christian couples do not put away their modesty even on their nuptial bed, for if God permitted them to marry, he did not permit them to lust."

While sex was banished from the church, it stealthily returned under cover of love—physically emaciated and highly spiritualized, but love nevertheless.    The very man who first lowered the whip on sex in the church was the one to raise it to the altar.    For it was none other than Paul of Tarsus who spoke of spiritual love as the bridge spanning the chasm between the sexes.

There were love affairs in Paul's day among the converts to his faith, but they were intended to be kept on a purely Platonic basis, on a spiritual plane—" keeping a virgin, but not marrying her."    Not a few of these relationships, however, terminated in marriage, because the male partner might wish to save his virgin from the fate of being forever excluded from the marital state, a fate that would most likely come to her had she passed the flower of her youth without being married.    In order to ease the consciences of those who worried themselves over this matter, Paul held out an assurance.    Those who felt that they must marry their loves might do so without sin, but those who could remain on the purely spiritual plane did better.    " He that giveth her in marriage doth well, but he that giveth her not in marriage doth better."

There was, then, such a relationship as " keeping a virgin and yet not marrying her." It was the forerunner of the " spiritual loves " that were so prevalent in the early period of Christianity. It was through them that romance and love were introduced into the church to take the place of sex banished in disgrace. Together with the belief in the Virgin, they humanized the new religion and found therein a place for woman and for the greatest of human passions : Love.

*Thecla*
(*From a painting by Lorenzo Costa*)

IV

And this is the story of Thecla, the spiritual love of Paul of Tarsus :

Thecla was a beautiful maiden of Iconium, the daughter of rich and illustrious pagan parents. When she reached her eighteenth year, she was promised in marriage to Thamyrsis, a young man of the same fortunate station in life. But, one day as the girl was sitting on her balcony, she heard Paul preaching in the street. His words moved her and she became a convert to the new faith.

Rejecting her betrothed and dressing in boys' clothing, she

left her home and went out to follow Paul on all his journeys. But Iconium would not have one of her fair daughters drag down into the mire the reputation of the town.   Thecla was appropriately punished.

The young girl was to be burned, and the flames were devouring the pyre.   But as Thecla, armed with a cross, threw herself upon the burning platform, a rain poured down and extinguished the fire.   She was then thrown to the wild beasts, but they would not touch her.   She was fastened to two bulls in the hope that she might be torn asunder, but the bulls walked together and Thecla came out uninjured.   She was cast into a pit full of serpents, but she only baptized herself in the water at the bottom of it.   The maiden could neither be destroyed nor prevented from following Paul, helping him to convert souls as they went along.

When Paul died, Thecla, still a maiden, withdrew to the solitude of a mountain.   By a shining cloud she was directed into a cave, where she lived for seventy years, still a virgin and still in love, in spiritual love with Paul, the man of Tarsus.

v

Spiritual love became an institution of importance in early Christianity.   It had a philosophic basis in the Greek thought of the day, which completely divorced the material from the spiritual, the body from the soul.   Passion, sex was of the body ; love was of the soul, hence, it could be spiritual, Platonic, without any sex basis.   But somehow it occurred only between members of the opposite sexes.

Spiritual love also had an emotional basis.   With some, it was the only kind of love they could experience.   They who had loved physically, but could love no longer, still retained memories of experienced passions.   They were still moved by the emotions that accompany the function of the sexual impulse.   They who had lost their virility may have felt an aversion toward women and sex, but they longed all the more for the mental content of the erotic experience.

Again, for others more normally constituted, spiritual love was the only love allowed them.   Forbidden to love physically, or at least discouraged by piety from doing so, they had to seek refuge in the emaciated love called " spiritual."   They followed their master in his denunciation of sex intellectually, but not emotionally.   At best, they could control their love activities but not their love attitudes.   To Paul, love may have been only spiritual.   For others, there was no definite boundary between the physical and the spiritual. Beginning upon the higher plane, they may have soon found themselves upon the plane of the physical. For after all, love is love, however it may be defined and designated ; and, while some manifestations of the passion may appear more physical than others, all love springs from the same source.

There were social and political reasons that made the early Christians particularly susceptible to spiritual love. They lived in their own small, often secret, circles, generally organized on a communal basis. All worked together, all lived together. At any rate, all met together in the dark of night for spiritual services. Their meeting-place may have been the communal hall or the dwelling of a pious soul. It may have been a catacomb, the burial-place of the poor, where the grave-diggers, of whom so many turned to the new faith, put up. Whatever the place, all met there, men and women, to spend the long hours of the night.

*Agapae, Anglo-Saxon origin*

These nightly meetings gradually assumed the form of love-feasts, Agapæ. It was the love for Christ that was being feasted there, in imitation of the Last Supper. They may have begun piously enough, but they gradually took a jovial turn. There was song and dance, and, while they were a sort of Eucharistic rite, they contained a number of pagan ceremonies taken over from the worship of Priapus. These were evident in the amulets and idols carried by the virgins in the processions as well as in the shape of the cakes eaten at the feast.

It was inevitable that these meetings should lead to irregularities. The people were poor and downtrodden. They had few joys in life and still fewer channels for emotional expression. The nightly meetings were the great moments in their lives. They offered the joy of feasting and the pleasure of comradeship. To this exaltation, there was added the glow of sex. True, sex distinctions were to be obliterated at the meetings, yet great consideration was shown to the virgins who came in special dress, with the mithra, and were given places of honour. Sex was abolished from the Agapæ, yet the entire atmosphere was charged with it, and the free mingling of the sexes only aggravated the situation. One could expect that under these circumstances the spirit would give in to the flesh and there would be scenes of sexual indulgence along with religious ecstasy. No wonder, then, that Saint Paul had faults to find with the Agapæ of the Corinthians.

At these nightly secretive meetings of the early Christians, friendships sprang up between the individual members of the faith belonging to the opposite sexes. These friendships amounted to love affairs, but, as both the man and the woman in this relationship had taken the vow of continency and were animated by the desire to keep their vow, they were supposedly all " spiritual " loves. Doubtlessly many of them were, the sexual element having been eradicated, sublimated, or suppressed, leaving only the love sentiment and the feeling of comradeship. These spiritual loves and marriages were fired with the great enthusiasm of asceticism and faith that spread like wildfire all over Christendom. It was said to be " well pleasing to God to have several such wives." Tertullian recommended that all men who could not get along without women enter into spiritual relationship with them and advised preference for those that were " least dangerous "—" widows beautified by faith, endowed with poverty, and sealed by age."

It is related of the bishop, Paul of Samosata, that he had virgin lovers, maidens in blooming youth who followed him on his journeys. Another bishop, the famous Athanasius, living in the fourth century, escaped from persecution by " direct orders from above " and fled to a virgin, an extraordinarily beautiful girl, with whom he lived for six years.

In these spiritual loves, we meet again with the tendency to imitate Christ. Jesus was supposed to be in spiritual wedlock with the virgins who consecrated their lives to him. One of the early church fathers pictured Christ as jealous of his virgins and put this as the motive for absolute purity. Cyprian asked : " Shall Christ be composed seeing the virgin that was dedicated to him sleeping with another and not become wrathful? And not threaten with the severest punishments for such unclean relationships?" He therefore insisted that any deacon or clergy of any degree who lived with a virgin should be expelled from the Christian community.

Some idea of the general relationship between the male and the female members of the early Christian communities may be gleaned from an old Christian work dating to the first century, which relates a characteristic instance of spiritual love. The writer is left by the Shepherd of Hermes with twelve virgins. He asks them where he may put up for the night, and they answer him:

" With us thou shalt sleep, like a brother, not like a man, for

*Spiritual lovers in the art of
the catacombs*

thou art our brother and in the future we shall serve thee. We love thee."

The writer continues: "One who appeared to be their leader began to kiss me, and, as the others saw her kissing me, they, too, began to do likewise. And the virgins spread their linen underclothes upon the floor and made room for me in their midst, and they did naught but pray. I also prayed with them uninterruptedly. And I remained there together with the virgins until two o'clock in the morning. Then the shepherd appeared, and said:

" ' Thou has not done anything ignominious?'

" ' Ask him thyself,' they replied.

" I said to him, ' I was glad to spend the night with them.' "

Two early Christians, Theophile and Maria, lived twenty-four years together, and Maria preserved her virginity. They kept in mind the beatitude : " Blessed are those that have wives as though they had none, for they will inherit the kingdom of heaven." They hardly realized that they were thereby exposing their chastity to a great danger, which proved fatal to so many when their spiritual union turned physical.

The " spiritual love " may have been entered into by priest and nun, or any others who were animated by the great ideal of asceticism and had taken the vow of chastity. The spiritually married couple may have lived together in a monastery or in a simple dwelling. In such a relationship, the woman became the assistant of the man, his helpmate and housekeeper, doing for him most of the drudgery. Here, the man held the place of superiority. But there was another kind of relationship as when a rich widow, unable and unwilling to remarry, entered into spiritual union with a priest. In such a case, the priest resided with the widow and took care of her estates or business enterprises. He was the manager of her worldly affairs and a private secretary as well. Socially, the priest was her inferior, as he was also economically. In either case, the two entered into this arrangement wholeheartedly and in good faith, trusting to the purity of their own minds and to the piety of their intentions.

Often, the ascetic and his spiritual wife betook themselves to the desert where they might, in solitude and undisturbed, reflect upon God and do penance for the sins of others. The woman, who was the spiritual wife, actually became the man's servant and mother in one. She sought a shelter for the two of them ; she provided whatever small comfort they could find or allow themselves in their asceticism. She did most of the work that desert life entailed. The man led a passive life, unconcerned with things material. He devoted himself almost entirely to prayer and meditation. And there the two lived with only two things to guide them : their faith in God and the dictates of their conscience.

Occasionally, monk and nun would go to disorderly houses and perform there the amorous duties as a kind of chastisement and self-debasement. It was another form of self-torture, like the shirt of hair worn next to the body or the girdle of nails. Sometimes, the monk would travel as a mime or troubadour and the nun as a prostitute. " Such a couple," we read, " came to suffer this martyrdom and returned from the world apparently impure and dissolute, while the all-purest Lady in Heaven knew well that the two never touched each other."

The all-purest Lady in Heaven was kind to these nuns. So were the fathers of the church. They were equally kind to those virgins who were forced into prostitution by pagan persecutors. For it was a customary punishment in Rome to sentence a Christian virgin to the Lupanar. Ambrosius said that a " virgin may prostitute herself without becoming thereby impure," and the fathers claimed that force could not defile the bodies of pious women. Only the attitude, the prostitute mind, made of one a harlot. If her mind was pure, her engaging in prostitution was only a defilement, a most supreme humiliation for which she would be rewarded in heaven. Love not only became dissociated from the body but dared to go directly against the physical in the very pit of sex.

VI

In mysticism, spiritual love reached the height of its development. No longer did persons of the opposite sexes need to live together in spiritual marriage. Mere human loves were cast wholly aside for far more perfect ones. Saint Gertrude found her love supreme in Christ. Saint Bernard looked with yearning eyes of love upon the Virgin Mary, while Saint John of the Cross, perhaps the most spiritual of them all, conceived of his soul as the mystic bride united to God in perfect union. And the lives of the leading mystics—men and women far removed from even the slightest interest in things material—furnish us with romances more real, more vivid, and more inspiring than those of the greatest earthly lovers.

Saint Catherine of Siena came into the world at the time that Italy was torn apart by internal strife and disorder reigned in the church as well. Boniface held the papal throne in Rome, while Clement had set himself up at Avignon. At this same period, great mystical movements were overrunning all Europe. Ferocity and beauty thus mingled together in their influence upon the young girl's life. Inspired by the stories of the different saints, she determined to devote her life to God and, when she was only sixteen, she took the habit of a religious order. For the next three years Catherine lived in one continual series of ecstasies and visions. In each of these, her relations with Christ seemed to grow more intimate until, one day, He appeared to her with His heart in His hand and, placing it against her side, said : " I exchange My heart with thine." Shortly after this vision, this series of ecstasies—a period of intense courtship as it were—culminated in her " Mystical Marriage with Christ."

This experience took place at the end of the carnival season. Christ appeared to her with the announcement that He had determined to espouse her soul to Him in faith, and the marriage ceremony was immediately carried out in the presence of the Virgin, David the Psalmist King, and a group of saints. As the Bridegroom placed the nuptial ring, heavily set with earthly jewels, upon the maiden's finger, he addressed her in these words : " Behold I have espoused thee to Me, the Maker and Saviour, in faith, which shall continue in thee from this time forward, evermore unchanged, until the time shall come for a blissful consummation in the joys of Heaven."

Ever after the ceremony, Catherine remained strong in her belief that she was now the bride of Christ. Throughout her life she wore the marriage band upon her finger and remained constant to her heavenly Spouse. From this time on, she was no longer given up to visions and ecstasies, but devoted her time to other interests. She nursed the poor, taught the ignorant, used her influence in trying to establish political peace in Italy, and worked for the restoration of the papacy. She continually struggled to weave into her life the idea she expressed in these words :

" The soul is a tree existing by love, and can live by nothing else but love. If this soul have not in truth the divine love of perfect charity she cannot produce the fruit of life, but only of death."

A hundred years before Saint Catherine lived, there was, in Germany, a young girl whose life, like hers, was destined to be devoted entirely to the spiritual. As a child, Saint Gertrude was placed in the Benedictine convent at Rodalsdorf, where later she took the veil and, at the age of thirty, was elected abbess. As she was passing through the adolescent stage, she gave herself up to the unrestrained enjoyment of her imagination. It was not, however, until she was growing into womanhood that she began to have visions.

One day, while praying in the chapel, she heard the words " Sanctus, sanctus, sanctus," in sweet song about her. At the same time, the Son of God leaned toward her like a gentle lover and gave her soul the softest kiss. As the second " sanctus " was uttered he said : " In this sanctus addressed to my person, receive with this kiss all the sanctity of my divinity and of my humanity, and let it be to thee a sufficient preparation for the approaching communion table." A few days later, her heavenly lover again came to visit her and, taking her in His arms, presented her to His father and to the Holy Spirit. Both of them were so delighted with the beautiful bride He had chosen, that they, in turn, endowed her with their sanctity.

In one of her visions, she received a nuptial ring from Christ. From then on she regarded herself as his Chosen Bride. She often told how her heavenly Spouse had brought his mother to make the acquaintance of her daughter-in-law. After her spiritual marriage, Gertrude became more settled and devoted her entire being to the betterment of the lives of those about her, drawing to herself a host of admirers.

At the time of her death, the nun who had been her confidante during the greater part of her life, told how she had seen Christ, accompanied by his Virgin Mother and Saint John, coming to receive his dying bride. According to her vision, at the moment Saint Gertrude breathed her last, her soul precipitated itself,

*The marriage of St. Catherine*
(*After a painting by Titian*)

" like an arrow shot to its mark," into the heart of Christ and was then borne up into celestial glory.

Both Saint Catherine and Saint Gertrude passed through the natural period of adolescence, in deep religious fervour. Their sexual awakening took on a spiritual aspect. They reached the climax of their erotic experience, however, in their mystic marriage with Christ. Thus satisfied in their love-life, they settled down to occupy themselves in the activities most pleasing to their great love.

In the life of Marie de l'Incarnation, spiritual love was belated, coming after actual sex experience. Of a more recent period and of French birth, she married at the age of eighteen. Three years later she was left a widow with one child. It was only then that she began to have her mystical experiences.  The period of her spiritual adolescence came in her late twenties when, for three years, she seemed to live in intense emotional rapture and lyrical joy.  Her whole being was submerged in the love she bore her heavenly lover.

" When I go about the house or when I walk in the garden," she once said, " I feel my heart constrained by continual impulses of love ;  and sometimes it seems that this heart must rush forth and as it were leave its own place."

Her divine Spouse became a living presence and she was wont to speak to him in language of intense passion.  " Oh, my love," she would exclaim, " when shall I embrace you ?  Have you no pity on the torments that I suffer ?  Alas !  Alas !  My beauty !  My life !  Instead of healing my pain, you take pleasure in it.  Come, let me embrace you and die in your sacred arms."

Thus filled with love for Christ she joined the Ursuline order and, a few years later, she was sent to Canada on a mission.  It was only after her spiritual marriage that her ecstatic experiences came to an end and the constructive period of her life began.  For all the actual sex experience in her past, spiritual love became the overpowering urge in her life.  Only after she had found satisfaction in her spiritual marriage did her life go on smoothly again.

And what is this spiritual marriage ?  How does it appear in the visions of the saint and how is she affected by it ?  Saint Teresa describes this spiritual love union in her own inimitable, outspoken manner :

" Often when the soul least expects it, our Lord calls her suddenly.  She hears very distinctly that her God calls her, and it gives her such a start, especially at the beginning, that she trembles and utters plaints.  She feels that an ineffable wound has been dealt her, and that wound is so precious in her sight that she would like it never to heal.  She knows that her divine Spouse is near her, although He does not let her enjoy His adorable presence, and she cannot help complaining to Him in words of love.  In this pain, she relishes a pleasure incomparably greater than in the Orison of Quietude in which there is no admixture of pain.  The voice of the Well-Beloved causes in the soul such transports that she is consumed by desire, and yet does not know what to ask, because she sees clearly that her Lord is with her.  What pain could she have ?  And for what greater happiness could she wish ?  To this I do not know what to answer ;  but that of which I am certain, is that the pain penetrates down to the very bottom of the bowels and that it seems that they are being torn

away when the heavenly Spouse withdraws the arrow with which
He has transpierced them.   As long as that pain lasts, it is always
on the increase or on the decrease, it never remains at the same
intensity.   It is for that reason that the soul is never entirely on
fire ; the spark goes out and the soul feels a desire stronger than
ever to endure again the love-pain she has just experienced."

Just as so many women directed their love to Christ and lived
in heavenly union with Him, so did men often find the object of
their love in the Virgin Mary or some other personification of the

*St. Teresa*
(*From the statue by Bernini*)

female principle.   Heinrich Suzo was one of these.   Living in
Germany in the first half of the fourteenth century, the time when
the Church was holding up to the youths the ideals of self-denial
and chastity, young Suzo was readily impressed and became a
member of the Dominican order.

Of a highly sensitive nature, his sole reason for existence was to
love and be loved.   Cut off as he was from the love of woman,
Suzo turned to the spiritual, finding in Mary, the " empress " of
his heart.   He pictured her as a maiden with lovely waving hair

and delicate skin, with whom he entered into a warm and intimate love relation. Addressing himself to her, he would say :

" Should I be the husband of a queen, my soul would find pride in it, but, now, you are the Empress of my heart . . . In you I possess riches enough and all the power that I want. I care no longer for the treasures of earth."

In Germany, it was the custom for the young men, at the beginning of the new year, to go out at night to serenade their loved ones. Suzo tells in his autobiography that he followed the custom. He went before the statue of the Virgin with her infant in her arms, sang love lyrics to her, and addressed her thus : " You are the love whom alone my heart loves : for you I have spurned all earthly love."

Again, writing in the third person, he describes one of his ecstatic experiences :

" A stately youth from Heaven led him by the hand upon a beautiful green meadow. Then the youth brought forth a song in his heart, so winsome that it deprived him of all his senses because of the excessive power of the beautiful melody, and his heart was so full of burning love and yearning for God that it beat wildly as if it would break, and he had to put his right hand on it in order to control it, and tears were rolling down his cheeks. . . . He saw the Mother and her child, with a banner waving from her skirt and written upon it : " Beloved of My Heart ! "

Saint Bernard was likewise a lover of the Virgin. One of the greatest mystics of the twelfth century, he entered the newly formed Cistercian order at an early age. His extraordinary ability as a leader and thinker was soon recognized and within three years he was sent to establish the monastery of Clairvaux.

Saint Bernard conceived of religion as a love union, of which he held an exalted opinion. " Love," he said, " is sufficient by itself, it pleases by itself, and for its own sake. It is itself a merit, and itself its own recompense. Love seeks neither cause nor fruit beyond itself. Its fruit is its use. I love because I love ; I love that I may love. Love, then, is a great reality. It is the only one of all the movements, feelings, and affections of the soul in which the creature is able to respond to its Creator, though not upon equal terms, and to repay like with like."

His love impulse found its outlet in his intimate spiritual relations with the Virgin. Often, in visions, she would come to him in strong embrace, and in moments when passion surged high, he would address her in glowing words of love : " My Love ! My Love ! Let me ever love thee from the depths of my heart ! " When he celebrated her feasts, he was so seized with rapture that his soul seemed to go from his body to join his heavenly love.

Saint Bernard was not only in love with the Virgin but also with her divine Son.  In this love relationship, the saint considered himself as the bride of Christ, assuming the feminine rôle. For to him, like to many other mystics, the soul was an entity entirely distinct from the physical organism.  It dwelt in the body but was not of the body.  It constituted a complete personality like the Word of the Gospel or the *pneuma* of the Stoics.  One could, therefore, commune with his own soul as he might with another person.  Once a separate being, the soul could be of the opposite sex.  And since it was the object of the love of Jesus, the lover of souls, it came to be considered as feminine.  The soul was the bride and Jesus the spouse.  Love was the union of the soul with God.  Hence, in speaking of his soul and his intimate attitude toward Jesus, Saint Bernard refers to himself as female. And he describes the spiritual love relationship in highly sensuous language :

" Suddenly the Bridegroom is present and gives assent to her petition ;  He gives her the kiss asked, of which the fullness of breasts is witness.  For so great is the efficacy of this holy kiss, that the Bride on receiving it conceives, the swelling breasts rich with milk being the evidence. . . . And the Bridegroom will say : Thou hast, O my Spouse that which thou prayedst for ;  and this is the sign : Thy breasts have become better than wine.  By this may you know that you have received the kiss, in that you have conceived and your breasts are full of milk."

Often the spiritual lover gave vent to his emotion in such songs as this :

> Love !  Love !  Lovely Jesus !
> Love, I will die
> Embracing thee.
> Sweet Love, Jesus my Bridegroom,
> Love, Love, Jesus, thou Holy One,
> Give me thyself, transform me into thyself ;
> Think, that I am in rapture,
> That I have lost myself,
> Jesus my hope,
> Come, sleep in love !

Occasionally, the unsatisfied love of the saint was emptied not upon the Virgin but upon some other personification of the female.  It was some ideal that was dear to his heart.  This ideal became his love and consequently his lady love.  Denying himself worldly riches and serving the ideal of poverty, Saint Francis came to see in deprivation a Lady Poverty, and all the emotional exuberance that saints usually bestowed upon the Virgin, he devoted to his own imaginary love.

Saint Francis was the son of a rich merchant in the little town of Assisi in Italy. His early years were spent in dissipation, and he might have continued in the disorderly life had not serious illness overtaken him. Like every man in anguish, young Francis sought a refuge in love and faith. Upon recovery from his illness, he invited his friends to a banquet and while they were hilariously drinking and enjoying themselves, their host slipped away. When

*The Church as the Bride of Christ*

they found him, he was in an ecstatic condition. " What is the matter with you ? " they cried, as they tried to arouse him.

" Don't you see that he is love-sick ? He is thinking of taking a wife," jested one of the guests.

Thereupon, Francis spoke up : " Yes, I am thinking of taking a wife more beautiful, more rich, more pure than you could ever imagine."

She was Lady Poverty as he called her. She became his bride, his ideal ; to her he swore faith and love, and throughout his life his thoughts were directed to her. Often, in visions, his bride descended from heaven to join her spouse. He would welcome her in his arms, kiss her gently, and show her all the delicate attentions that the ardent lover showers upon the object of his desires.

In Saint John of the Cross, we reach the summit of erotic Christian mysticism.  A poor son of Spain, he lived at the time that his whole country was a garden of mystic roses.  There was Saint Teresa, well known for her ecstatic experiences and her deep understanding of divine communion.  There was Fray Luis de Leon, who sang his songs of anguish and desire, filled with longing for his heavenly dwelling.

Saint John had passed the point where the personal element enters into love for the Divine.  It was not he who was in love with Christ, but his soul.  He himself was only an humble witness of the sacred union.  He could, therefore, so freely describe the conjugal bliss of the soul and her divine Spouse.

" The thread of love," he says, " binds so closely God and the soul, and so unites them, that it transforms them and makes them one by love ; so that, though in essence different, yet in glory and appearance the soul seems God and God the soul.  Such is this marvellous union.  God Himself is here the suitor Who, in the omnipotence of His unfathomable love, absorbs the soul with greater violence and efficacy than a torrent of fire a single drop of morning dew."

In a further explanation of this spiritual relationship and its progression, he likens it first to the relations of the betrothed and then to those of the lovers after marriage :

" In the one there is mutual love, but in the other there is communication of the self likewise, and the difference is as great as that which exists between betrothal and matrimony.  For in betrothal there is but a mutual consent, and agreement of will on either side and the jewels and the adornments of the betrothal, which the lover graciously gives to his beloved.  But in matrimony there is communication between the two persons, and there is union ; whereas in betrothal, the lover from time to time visits his beloved, and bestows gifts upon her, as we have said, but there is no union of their persons, which is the end of the betrothal."

Saint John's whole being was filled with this sincere emotion, which at times found utterance in beautiful lyric poetry :

> Upon an obscure night
> Fevered with love in love's anxiety,
> (O hapless, happy plight !)
> I went, none seeing me,
> Far from my house where all things quiet be.

O night that didst lead thus,
O night more lovely than the dawn of light,
O night that broughtest us,
Lover to lover's sight,
Lover with loved in marriage of delight.

Upon my flowery breast,
Wholly for him, and save himself for none,
There did I give sweet rest
To my beloved one ;
The fanning of the cedars breathed thereon.

When the first morning air
Blew from his tower, and waved his locks aside,
His hand, with gentle care,
Did wound me in the side,
And in my body all my senses died.

All things I then forgot,
My cheek on him who for my coming came ;
All ceased, and I was not,
Leaving my cares and shame
Among the lilies and forgetting them.

## VII

As Love came out of the monastery it found its way into the religious life of the populace, where it soon lost a good deal of its hot-house atmosphere. There, it became more like the love of the adolescent—a love romantic rather than sexual. It thus ended its long climb from the pit of gross sexuality to the amorous longing in a highly refined symbolic form.

Love was ever symbolized in religious art. Primitive man tried to express the religious stirrings of his heart in line and figure. As love was the chief component of his religion, it naturally formed the basic element of his art. In Christian civilization, we again find art resorted to, to symbolize man's concept of the Divine and his attitude toward it. Here again, the love motif is dwelled upon to a large extent. And for all the distance in time and space, old and new religious symbolism bear a striking resemblance in many essentials, with only a progression in refinement to mark the course of the centuries.

The spirit of mankind is for ever overflowing with hope and expectation. New life was the crying desire of Old Anthropology Adam. Renewed life is the hope supreme of every true Christian. The former conceived the fountain of life in the organs of sex. They became his symbols of the ever-flowing stream. He painted them upon the walls of the place in which he lived. The early Christian looked to heaven for the consummation of his unfailing dream. Death became the gateway to this everlasting life, and, in this gateway, he poured out his soul. He expressed his longing in the art on the tombs of the catacombs. To primitive man, spring, with all its sprouting plants, budding trees, and bursting blossoms, was the very embodiment of regeneration throughout nature. Similarly, the pictures of roses, shrubs, and flowery meadows ornamented the graves of the early Christians reminding the faithful of spring in paradise.

Early man conceived the creative force in nature as twofold— male and female—and evolved symbols for both sexes. There still are male and female symbols in the Church, although their original meaning has been superimposed by theologic speculations. To primitive man, the fish was the symbol of the feminine. The fish is still a feminine symbol in the Church, representing the soul in her mystic union with Christ.

Primitive man saw in the pillar, the column, or the stately palm tree, a fitting symbol of the male, the active force. And the same palm in the Christian religion became suggestive of virility, of victory in the race of life. On Palm Sunday, the triumphant entry of Christ with His followers into Jerusalem is still celebrated. On this day, blessed palm leaves are distributed to the faithful who reverently carry them to their homes. There, they are placed above the door in the belief that they will bring blessings upon the household. To this day, agricultural people burn these same leaves and sprinkle the ashes over the fields to insure fertility and to protect the new crop against the destructive forces of nature.

In all times, the vine, so prolific in its fruit, has been symbolic of abundance in life, vitality, and birth itself. For the Christian, the vine is suggestive of the " Fountain of Life " in which the soul is reborn through communion with God. The ark, the classic symbol of the female principle in all times, is used every day during the Mass in the form of the pyx, the holy receptacle for the body of Christ. The cross, from time immemorial a symbol of the creative forces in union, was early brought into the symbolism of Christianity, where it has ever grown in importance. And the Christian, mindful only of its relation to his Saviour, does not see in it the symbol of the saving grace of generation.

The priest, as he puts on his robes for the Sacrifice, is unaware that they are full of symbolic meaning. The flowing gown, the stole he wears around his neck, and the vestment, are all suggestive of similar symbolism in ancient pagan faiths, in which the priests attired themselves appropriately for the worship of their goddesses.

The vestment, itself a symbol, bears upon it still others ; there is the cross both in back and in front, and from beneath the crosses extend the golden rays of the sun in themselves suggestive of the great life-giving force in nature.

And even where people have turned against ceremony and ritual in their faith, banishing all ornaments from their houses of worship, a few symbols have lingered on. They abound in the architectural designs, the decorative motifs, and especially in prayer and hymn. Many of these prayers, beautiful expressions of ardent love toward God, approach the utterances of a worldly lover in their intensity. The devout soul may yearn for union with God. "O my God, my adorable Love ! Come into my heart, that I may enter Thine. Come, and by one sweet transport of Thy love, concentrate every power of my soul in Thee. Teach me, my heavenly Spouse, that I may deserve to repose in Thy arms, to lean on Thy breast." Again, the soul may anticipate

*Christian symbolism in the Catacombs*

the moment of her communion with Christ in words like these : " Oh, happy moment when I shall be admitted to the embraces of the living God, for whom my soul languishes with Love."

## VIII

Of all the symbols that have entered into the Christian religion to lend it charm and beauty, the most striking, the all-inspiring one is the Virgin. Mary is the greatest symbol of all. She is the Mystical Rose, the Spiritual Vessel, the Tower of David, the Ark of the Covenant. The poor, the sick, and the humble, find in her a source of comfort and aid. The sinner turns to her for consolation. Those whose troubles are few admire her as the symbol of ideal womanhood. She is loved as a queen and reverenced as the Mother of God.

The New Testament tells little about Mary. It presents a vague picture of her, leaving room for the imagination to play.

But the early Christian felt no need to busy his mind with Mary. He was all absorbed in her son, Jesus, the Christ. His heart was full in anticipation of the promised kingdom of gladness and cheer, in which there was to be no injustice, no sorrow or misery. This blessed state was to be realized here on earth with Jesus as the ruling king. The strain of waiting for it was relieved by the attitude the early Christian took toward Christ. To him, Jesus was the lover of all, especially of the poor and the downtrodden. To them, Christ was a person, human, experiencing the same joys and sorrows as they did. He was on their very plane, and they could go directly to him. He was their intimate friend. They opened their souls to Him, and He received them with outstretched arms.

As the Christian religion continued in its growth and development, the aspect of Christ changed considerably. The kingdom so richly portrayed by Him was slow in arriving. Instead, sin and misery seemed to increase on earth. The doctors of the

*Medieval Hell*
(*From the Utrecht Psalter*)

Church were growing more and more concerned with the idea of sin and its punishment eternal in the crackling fires of hell. Men forgot their longings for life in their dread and fear of the hereafter. Instead of being the harbinger of joy, Jesus became the dispenser of punishment, holding the balance of right and wrong. Christ, no longer the mild and gentle lover of souls, became a stern and awful figure. His humanity was torn from Him and forgotten. His divinity lifted Him far above the human plane. He could no longer experience the joys of His people or come down to share their sorrows.

Before the Star of Bethlehem appeared in the sky, a need was felt for an intermediary between man and God. Jesus of Nazareth became the bridge to span the gaping void between humanity and divinity. Now again a need was felt for a mediator, a bridge between man and Jesus, himself the bridge across the former void. People were hungering after someone to whom they could open their hearts. They needed a friend to bring sunshine and happiness into their drab existence, to commune with their pining souls whenever they desired communion. And the human heart, ever yearning, longing, looking outward for union, sought a means to bridge the gap, to fill the void, and to come into the Divine Presence.

What could be more appropriate for this purpose than the very person who had been so close to Christ, who had brought him into the world ? Thus it was that they turned to the Virgin as their intercessor, their mediator. They called upon Mary when they would speak to Jesus. She was the mother of Christ, and, no matter how stern he grew, could not a mother always approach her son ?

As Mary the mother and mediator came to be a figure of pre-eminence, she was clothed with many attributes in accordance with the various movements in Christendom. The ascetics and priests who were themselves celibate and devoted to the ideal of chastity could not conceive of this sacred figure in their faith but as a virgin. The Divine Saviour of mankind could not have been the fruit of the sinful sexual process. His mother could not have been less pure than the devotees of her son. Hence Mary was to become a perpetual virgin. At the Council of Chalcedon, in 451, this doctrine was definitely accepted. Mary was the Virgin, imaged as the Virgin Mother with the child on her arm. The attributes of the early Christ were woven together into her figure, and she even took on more of the divine nature. Along with idea of her perpetual virginity grew the thought that she had entered the world without sin. Like her son, Jesus, Mary came into the world not by the sinful way of sex but through the intermediary of the Holy Spirit. This idea developed as time went on and in 1854 was formally accepted by the Church in the doctrine of the Immaculate Conception.

The new converts to the Church from the sensuous pagan world added their attributes to the concept of Mary. They saw in her a figure familiar to them from their own beliefs. For in every pagan religion there was a goddess, a virgin mother whom the faithful worshipped. Mary became for them the symbol of womanhood like these goddesses that graced their pagan temples. In Asia Minor, during the first centuries of Christianity, the women worshipped Mary as a goddess and offered her phallic cakes as was the custom in the worship of the female nature deities.

As the Virgin Mary rose from the ranks of womanhood to her exalted throne in heaven, all other women rose to a position of higher esteem upon earth. There was little to envy in the condition of women in the early centuries of the Christian era, or of pagan times, for that matter.  True, in the Græco-Roman world, the influence of women was felt in the most influential quarters of the community.  It was the courtesan who brought into the life of the ruler the inspiration and love he needed to carry on his work.  It was the mistress who provided companionship and confidence for the burdened statesman and man of affairs.  But for all their power and importance the courtesan and mistress were of the *demi-monde*.  They were not the women of the house-

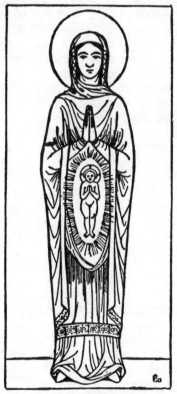

*Jesus in the womb of the Virgin*

hold, those on the surface of life.  Whatever glory the pagan world had for women was laid at the door of the sub-social woman. For the wife and mother there was little regard among the pagans and even less among the early Christians.  Wives were even forbidden to approach the altar or to touch the eucharist.  But the fact that one woman was elevated to the nearly divine plane was bound to make the others at least human.

As the feminine influence began to be felt in Christendom, it contributed new traits to the mould of the Christian character. To the pagan ideals of strength and courage, vigour and physical charm, were now added the sentiments of kindliness, self-sacrificing gentleness, and universal brotherhood. The crusades contributed their mite toward enriching the concept of the Virgin. The call to recover the Holy Land for God was enthusiastically received throughout the entire Christian world. The noble, in all his power and opulence, marched side by side with the poor peasant in his superstitious zeal. The brawny-armed labourer, his hands roughened from toil, marched alongside the priest whose hands knew only the telling of his beads. The poor, the sick, the social outcast, found a place in the ranks along with the rich and mighty. It became the duty of the strong to protect the weak, the duty of

*The Spirit of God moving over the waters of
creation and bringing forth life*

the healthy to comfort the afflicted. The new condition required the ideal of maternal care and disinterested devotion. All were at once not only brothers in Christ but also children of the Virgin Mother, who stood for protection and aid and comfort.

The crusades gave birth to the orders of chivalry in which the pagan and Christian ideals attained a heroic harmony. In the heart of the knight burned the fire of the pagan warrior, fierce in his defiance of pain and death. In the same heart was the flame of the Christian hero, exalting himself in his brotherly love and self-sacrifice.

The object of chivalry was the protection of the weak, and woman symbolized the knight's ideal. As the object of his protection, she came to be the source of his inspiration. This womanly influence tended to soften the heart of the knight, of humanity in general. It helped to spread an interest in universal humanity along with the spirit of brotherly love. Like philanthropy of a later day, chivalry with its ideal of womanhood furnished man with a channel through which he might pour out the finer side of his nature. And woman, as the knight's ideal, grew in prestige and influence. No longer relegated to the private family and religious life, she stepped out into the open, secular sphere into which she brought with her those feminine graces which were to refine, to soften, and to modify the whole social organization. And these changes were all a part of the growth of the spirit of Christianity. They sprang out of the worship of the Virgin Mother.

As years passed and Mary ever grew in the esteem of the faithful, she, too, was relegated to the realm of the divine. Her body was made the dwelling-place of the Holy Trinity, and she herself came to occupy a throne on the right hand of the heavenly father. People began to seek her assistance in all kinds of troubles. Women in childbirth called upon her. Men turned to her as they would to an earthly lover. Mary filled each vacant place in the ever-yearning human heart. Proclus spoke of her as " the spotless treasure-house of virginity, the spiritual paradise of the second Adam, the one bridge between God and men." Cyril of Alexandria called her " the mother and the virgin through whom the fallen creature is raised up to heaven." John of Damascus referred to her as " the sovereign Lady to whom the whole creation has been made subject by her son." And Saint Bernard addressed her thus :

" In thee the angels find their joy, the righteous find grace, and sinners eternal pardon. Deservedly the eyes of every creature look to thee, for in thee, and through thee, and by thee, the kind hand of the Omnipotent has renewed whatever he has created."

# CHAPTER III

## MARRIAGE IN THE MOSQUE

*Marriage is my custom; and he who dislikes it does
not belong to my people.*—THE PROPHET.

### I

THE mosque knows marriage but it still has to learn of
love or romance. It wallows in sex but it has yet to
discover woman as a human being with a personality of
her own. Mohammed did not disdain receiving homage at the
hands of women but he would not have it openly in his house of
worship. He ordered them to carry out their liturgical
exercises in the privacy of their homes. There, they were to
be hidden from the stranger's eye, but ever accessible to the
husband, their master, to delight his heart with sensuous
pleasures.

Religious leaders are, as a rule, either negatively inclined
towards sex or engrossed in it to the practical exclusion of all other
matters. Mohammed was one of the exceptions. He wanted his
sex naturally and wholesomely, but he desired it gluttonously.
He was the insatiable prophet, standing apart from all others.
Moses had a wife and two children. Little is heard of his sexual
life or of his preoccupation with sex. In fact, legend relates that
he separated from his wife after he had spoken to God and that
his sister, Miriam, criticized him for it. Jesus was not married
and indicated a tendency away from sex. Mohammed made up
for both of them. Sex was his one great delight. He never
felt saddened or remorseful after indulgence in it as persons
of a sensitive religious nature often do. He left his harem
as whole-heartedly as he had entered it, to return when he was
ready.

Only once was the soul of the great prophet disturbed.
Mokawkas, the governor of Egypt, sent him a slave, Mary, of
Coptic extraction. On the same day upon which he was to
fulfil his marital duties with his wife, Hafsa, he took this Mary
upon the very bed of his wife when she was out. This came to
the knowledge of Hafsa, who raised such an unearthly storm that
the prophet promised with a solemn oath never to touch Mary
again. Mohammed was stirred to the creation of a *sura*, a chapter
in the Koran, not for what he had done, but for what he so lightly
foreswore to do. It was an outcry against his oath and a holy
preparation for its breach : " O prophet, why holdest thou that
to be prohibited which God hath allowed thee ? Seeking to
please thy wives, since God is inclined to forgive and be merciful ?

God hath allowed you the dissolution of your oaths and God is your master and He is knowing and wise."

In fairness to the prophet, it must be said that he rarely took a privilege for himself that he did not grant to others. And, in the few instances in which he did, such as when he increased the number of his wives, his attempt to obtain special dispensation and his effort in making the point, show that his conscience was hurt thereby. He had ordered his disciples to have not more than four wives : " Take in marriage of such other women as please you, two, or three, or four, and no more." But no Mohammedan felt more handicapped by this rule than Mohammed himself. Hence, he made Allah say in a later *sura :*

" O prophet, we have allowed thee thy wives unto whom thou hast given their dower, and also the slaves which thy right hand possesseth, of the booty which God hath granted thee ; and the daughters of thy uncle, and the daughters of thy aunts, both on thy father's side and on thy mother's side, who have fled with thee from Mecca, and any other believing woman, if she gives herself unto the prophet ; in case the prophet desireth to take her to wife. This is a peculiar privilege granted unto thee above the rest of the true believers . . . thou mayest take unto thee her whom thou shalt please, and her whom thou shalt desire of those whom thou shalt have before rejected ; and it shall be no crime in thee."

Mohammed, as a rule, exhorted his followers to be free in the expression of their sex impulse : " Your wives are your tillage ; go in therefore unto your tillage in what manner soever ye will." Even the fast must not keep the faithful from his " tillage " : " It is lawful for you on the night of the fast to go in to your wives ; they are a garment unto you and you are a garment unto them." Even when one had taken an oath to forsake his wives, he might go back to them, for God would forgive him : " They who vow to abstain from their wives are allowed to wait four months ; but if they go back from their vow, verily God is gracious and merciful."

Sex was the greatest joy on earth for Mohammed and, when he was about to reward his followers in the hereafter, he found no greater recompense than the sensuous pleasures offered by the sexual impulse. The Judæo-Christian heaven is a place of absolute serenity. There are no passions of the flesh or desires of the living in the heavenly abode. The sex element is reduced to a minimum, to a point in which it is ignored, if not entirely effaced. The greatest joy in the world to come is the presence of God—the bliss of the reflection of the Divine Presence. In short, it is a state in which the physical life is reduced to a shadowy existence, while only the absolute spiritual in man, that which he holds in common with the Divine, is active.

The paradise of the Moslem is a place of security among gardens and fountains. Here, the faithful will live in the prime physical condition they knew upon earth. The prophet promises that " they shall be clothed in fine silk and satin, and repose on couches adorned with gold and precious stones." There the prophet will espouse them to fair damsels. Youths that shall continue in their bloom forever shall go round about to attend them with goblets and beakers and cups of flowing wine. And there shall accompany them fair damsels having large black eyes, resembling pearls hidden in their shells, as a reward for that which they shall have wrought. But that is not all yet. That is only for one class of faithful Moslems. " There are others, companions of the right hand, and how happy they shall be ! They will have their abode among Lotus trees, under an extended shade, near a flowing stream, amidst fruits in abundance. And they shall enjoy damsels raised on lofty couches, whom God has created as damsels of paradise by a peculiar creation." These damsels were created virgins and " how often soever their husbands shall go in unto them, they shall always find them virgins."

Mohammed sought to be generous to the female sex and to improve the condition of women. He taught his believers to " respect women who have borne you, for God is watching you." Although he excluded women from participation in the religious rites in the mosque, he put them on the same basis as the males in forgiveness and reward before God : " Verily, the Moslems of either sex and the true believers of either sex . . . and the men of veracity and the women of veracity . . . and the humble men and the humble women . . . and the chaste men and the chaste women, and those of either sex who remember God frequently—for them hath God prepared forgiveness and great reward."

The prophet forbade many customs that degraded the female sex. A man could not marry two sisters or the daughter of a woman with whom he had had sexual relations. A son could not inherit his stepmothers or do with them as he pleased. A girl under age could not be forced into marriage. The husband was to treat all his wives alike. He was to be kind to them, fearing to wrong them, for God knew well what was being done. At the wedding, the husband was to assign some dower or property to the wife to be hers should she be divorced. In fact, a woman could even inherit property, but only one-half of the amount she might receive were she a man.

Considerate as Mohammed was of woman in some respects, he could not place her upon an equal plane with man in actual life. Before Allah no favours were to be shown to either sex. But in life " men shall have the pre-eminence above women, because of those advantages wherein God hath caused the one of them to excel the other," which, according to the commentators, were superior understanding and strength. Therefore, honest women will be obedient to their husbands and careful in their absence. They will restrain their eyes and preserve their modesty. The veil should be their protection, and they are ordered to " cast their outer garments over them when they walk abroad." The prophet would allow his own wives to be spoken too only from behind a curtain.

So it was that Mohammed, the friend of women and their lover, treated them as might their worst enemy. He hung the veil over their heads and covered their faces for all time. He confined them to their own chambers and kept them out of the social, economic, and cultural life of the land. Woman was to satisfy the Moslem's passion and to raise his children. That was all her life had to offer her. Was it the prophet's personal experience that led him to introduce the veil and the harem into his faith ? Possibly. We know that in his later years he became suspicious and jealous of his wives. He insisted upon their withdrawing into extreme privacy, thereby setting the law for others. On the other hand, there were some Persian influences that may have been at work here, for, in Persia, women had already been veiled and segregated. The Persian custom of veiling the women would naturally appeal to Mohammed and he may have borrowed it. However, the truth remains that women fared ill in the faith of the man who loved them well.

The fact that women were set apart and hidden from sight caused them to fall in the esteem of men. The injury brought insult in its wake. Women became unclean to the Moslem mind. If a man had touched a woman, he was required to purify himself before going to pray. The very act of touching a woman was looked upon as something of an offensive nature : " O true believers, when you prepare yourselves to pray, wash your faces and your hands unto the elbows and rub your heads and feet unto the ankles . . . but if ye be sick, or on a journey, or any of you cometh from the privy, of if you have touched women, and ye find no water, take fine, clean sand and rub your faces and your hands therewith."

It was the design of the prophet to keep women in the harem, away from the public. His followers designed to have houses for public women. For along with the harem also came prostitution into the life of the Moslem—where it had not existed before. Even the heart of the faithful was lonely at times, and he could not lay it open before wife or friend.   Besides, all the women in one's harem might not possess the charm of a single prostitute— the lure of forbidden fruit.   Man, being excluded from social intercourse with women outside of his wife and slave, sought the same in company with the prostitute.   Mohammed used his influence against the institution in the Koran : " Draw not near fornication for it is wickedness and an evil way . . . the whore and the whoremonger shall ye scourge with an hundred stripes . . . the whoremonger shall not marry any other than a harlot or an idolatress . . . A harlot shall no man take in marriage."

## II

*La ilaha il Allah ve Mohammed resoul Allah.*   There is no god but Allah and Mohammed is his prophet.   Here was a religious formula simple indeed, comprehensible to the simplest Bedouin. It was all there was to know.   The rest was written in the book of the Koran.   But what Bedouin wandering in the desert could ever read the Koran ?  *La ilaha il Allah,* take the sword and defend the new faith and do not be restrained by bloodshed.   The belief in the prophet must prevail.

And the prophet fled from Mecca to Medina and was engaged in many wars.   And many were the wars that his immediate successors were called upon to wage in the name of Allah and their leader.   As the second century after the flight of the prophet dawned upon the Moslem sky, the sword was put back into the sheath, even if to remain there only temporarily.   The faithful opened the book of the Koran to see what was written therein. And what did they find ?  *La ilaha il Allah ve Mohammed resoul Allah.*   There is no god but Allah and Mohammed is his prophet. And here was the law by which the Moslem was to live.   He found in the Koran directions as to how to live, but very little as to what to live by.   No less of a Mohammedan than Al Ghazzali said that not all verses of the Koran are adapted to stir the emotions.   Rare and particularly sensitive must be the souls that can be thrown into religious ecstasy by reciting passages, such as " a man should leave his mother one-sixth of his property and to his sister one-half. . . ."

And so it was that a hundred years after the flight of the prophet, one Abu Khair put on a garment of *suf,* or wool, and led many of the faithful into the road of the shadow, the mystic path that one takes to search for the God that dwells deep within him. They who followed him were known by their garments as Sufis. They came to know the prophet, not by his words in the Koran, but by the outcry of their own souls. They were the mystic souls that longed for something the barren monotheism and the rigid ritual of Mohammed could not give them.

But the Sufis did not leave the fold to start a faith of their own.

*A Mohammedan fish nymph*

Whatever they thought and felt they projected into the words and meanings of the Koran. They pushed asunder the barren walls of the Moslem faith and built wonderful palaces within them. Even Mohammed assumed universal proportions in their hands. Instead of being merely the husband ot Khadijah, a man who suddenly heard the voice of God, he was identified with the primal element, the basic stuff of creation. He was called the Truth of Humanity, the Universal Reason, and the Great Spirit, as well as the Light of God and the Source of all Life. For Mohammed existed before the creation of the world : " He that hath seen me hath seen Allah . . . I was a prophet while Adam was yet between earth and clay. There is no prophet after me . . ." Thus the prophet is made to speak by the Sufis.

Between Allah and the world of matter there are seventy thousand veils—their inner half light and their outer half dark. And down these seventy thousand veils the soul of man travels from the throne of Allah to the dust of the body. At every veil of light, the soul removes a divine quality ; at every dark veil, it assumes an earthly one. As it is born upon earth, it cries out for sorrow. The child comes into the world weeping because its soul realizes that separation from Allah is now complete. In sleep, the child will often cry because it still remembers something of the splendours it has lost.

And so the Sufis came to teach man how to regain his contact with Allah and to travel back these seventy thousand veils unto the seat of glory. They are not concerned with the formal religious life, with the externals of ritual and moral law. They even excuse many sins like onanism, under circumstances. For they are seeking the union of man with God. Theirs is the journey back to God along the road of service and love and ecstasy, past union and other milestones along the way. First they must come to *faria*, the gradual passing away from one's own individuality ; then to *faqd*, the entire loss of self and self-consciousness. When their own individuality has been effaced, they reach *baja*, where they abide in God, and *wajd*, where they find their source in God. There, the soul loses all its separatist tendencies and merges with the Divine Presence. The spark re-enters and becomes part of the orignial fire.

And what is the motive, the force that drives the soul back to its source in Allah ? It is Love ; and worldly love is the bridge over which those must pass who seek the joys of the Divine Love. Love is the soul's divine instinct, the force that drives it on to realize itself. For the soul is born of God and, like Him, it existed before the creation of the universe. During its sojourn on earth it is but a stranger in exile, always yearning to return unto its source.

The Sufis hear the whisper of love at their pious gatherings. They claim that their clapping of hands and dancing and singing are all involuntary, the work of God manifesting itself through their bodies. They lay their heads upon the bosom of the Divine, who, in turn, rests His head on theirs. Man and God are found in mutual embrace. And as they lie there, the *houris* of paradise come down to earth and join them. They take them in their

arms and tell them the mysteries of heaven and of love.  It was
of these mysteries that Nur-d-din sang :

> " No heart is that which Love ne'er wounded ;  they
> Who know not lover's pangs are soulless clay.
> Turn from the world, O turn thy wandering feet ;
> Come to the World of Love and find it sweet !

> " Heaven's giddy round from craze of Love was caught,
> From Love's disputes the world with strife is fraught.
> Love's slave be thou if thou would fain be free ;
> Welcome Love's pangs, and happy shalt thou be."

And it was to answer the call of love that Jalaluddin Rumi,
the greatest mystic poet of Persia, instituted the mystical dances
and began the order of dancing dervishes.  The gyrations of this
order, like all Sufism, are symbolic, representing the revolution
of the planets round the sun and the attraction of the creatures
to their Creator.  When Jalaluddin founded this order, he was
carrying into effect the belief that ecstasy is the only way through
which the soul can lose itself in union with God.  For the dervishes,
ecstasy can be induced by music, singing, and dancing.  When a
Sufi hears sweet music, there is awakened in his soul the memory
of the divine harmony in which he existed before his soul was
separated from God.

The dervish lives with the sole purpose of recovering the soul's
original unity with Allah.  He cannot leave his body, but he
must refine and spiritualize it.  Like raw metal heated in the fire
to come out bright and pure, the dervish burns his body in the
heat of passion so that he may come forth a spiritual being.
The Sheikh tells the aspiring religious :  " We shall throw
you into the fire of Spiritual Passion, and you will emerge
refined."

When the dervishes meet in prayer, they begin by singing
hymns to Allah and moving their bodies first backward and
forward, then from side to side.  As their fervour increases, they
begin to sigh, weep, and perspire profusely.  Their pale faces
assume a languid expression.  In the course of the worship, two of
the faithful take a number of sharp-pointed iron knives from
niches in the wall and heat them in a brazier until they are fiery
red.  The Sheikh then blesses these instruments, and the delirious
worshippers, seizing the hot irons, plunge them into their bodies,
lick them with their tongues, or even hold them in their
mouths.  They continue in this religious fury, falling upon
one another, until exhausted, they sink, unconscious, to the
floor.

The Sheikh, walking among these men who have thus attained union with God, utters mystic prayers to recover their consciousness and anoints their wounds with his saliva.   The dervish comes forth from his swoon, unconscious of his wounds in his eagerness for the moment when he will again be in union with his loved one.   Jalaluddin was mindful of such ecstatic experiences when he wrote :

" He comes, a moon whose like the sky ne'er saw, awake or dreaming,
    Crowned with eternal flame no flood can lay.
    Lo, from the flagon of Thy love, O Lord, my soul is swimming,
    And ruined all my body's house of clay."

To the Sufis, death, the most cruel death imaginable, is the happiest thing in the world.   It provides an escape for the soul imprisoned in the body, making possible the eternal union of the Lover and the Beloved.   For this reason, they look upon Halladj as one of their greatest saints.   He was a severe ascetic to whom were ascribed miraculous powers.   Because his powers were feared, he was arrested, accused of heresy, and sentenced to death by violence.   In the execution of the sentence, his hands and feet were cut off and his eyes and tongue torn from his head.   As he lay dying, he smeared his cheeks with his blood, saying : " I do but perform the *abtest*—the ablutions of love should be made with blood."

To attain union with the Divine, Bayazid Bastami, a mystic of the ninth century, spent thirty years as a barefooted ascetic in the deserts of Syria.   And Rabia, the woman whom the Sufis called the Mother of God, was wont to torture her body by fasting and ascetic practices.   All through the long night, she would remain at prayer, only to close her eyes for a few brief moments at the approach of dawn.   Once, after fasting for seven days and nights, she heard her emaciated body say : " O Rabia, how long wilt thou torture me without mercy ? "   But Rabia cared little for her body.   She only prayed : " Consume with fire, O God, a presumptuous heart which loveth thee ; " again, " My God, let me be so absorbed in Thy love that no other affection may find room in my heart."   It was Rabia who sang :

" Two ways I love thee ; selfishly
    And next as worthy is of thee.
    'Tis selfish love that I do naught
    Save think on thee with every thought.
    'Tis purest love when Thou dost raise
    The veil to my adoring gaze.
    For mine the praise in that or this
    Thine is the praise in both, I wis'.

My heart I keep for Thy communion, Lord !
And those who seek me but my body find.
My guests may with my body converse hold,
But my Beloved alone holds converse with my heart."

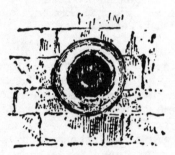

*The Black Stone*

# CHAPTER IV

## LONGING IN THE DARK

*Still groping in his dark way*
*For a god not his own.*

### I

HE, too, the African black man, belongs in the House of the Lord. To be sure, he did not come there of his own accord. His own gods had been stolen from him along with his freedom, and the new faith was thrust upon him as another yoke of servitude. True, too, he still is not quite at home with the Father, Son, and Holy Spirit. He is yet groping in his own dark way for a god not his own. But there he is, many millions of him, " standing in the need of prayer " and " wanting to be a Christian in his heart," feeling that " a little talk with Jesus makes it right." For all the ghosts of his ancestors in the bush, he visions Father Abraham " sittin' down side ob de Holy Lamb." For all the tom-tom music he was wont to hear, he prays to Peter " to ring dem Bells." And for all the fears of his primitive soul, he trembles at the thought that they crucified his Lord Jesus and he, Jesus, " never said a mumblin' word."

Had the black man remained upon his native soil, his heart would still beat for another god. He might now be worshipping Onyame, the Shining One, god of sunshine, or his children, in the form of rivers, hills and woods, or the *abasomes*, the many lesser gods Onyame had instituted upon earth. Once Onyame was himself god to humans, kind and close at hand. But he was too near. In the shape of the sky he lay so close upon the earth that he interfered with a woman preparing to cook. Pounding her yams, she continually hit him with the pestle. This was more than Onyame would stand from humans, especially from a woman. For here was not only injury but insult too. Onyame knew only too well what the pestle signifies to humankind, and any god would resent such reflection upon his virility. So he withdrew to the heavens above, keeping aloof from humans and leaving the rule of the universe to his progeny and the lesser gods.

Again, the black man might be kneeling before Legba, male or female, whose image was to be found on almost every house. Legba, the male, was powerfully built, with a knotted club in his hand, the symbol of his creative force. Legba, the female, with more sexuality than feminine charm, was impressive in her strong and massive figure.

Onyame was in heaven ; Legba upon earth. Onyame was accessible only through an intermediary ; Legba might actually be embraced. But both were gods, great and true. They brought joy and happiness to the fearing hearts of black men and women. Their gods were in their own image, and they served them as they would serve themselves. Whatever the sacrifice to the god, beast or fruit or corn, it always ended in a feast of dance and song. And the song of songs is ever the song of love. It was love, boundless, physical, free and open that raised the soul of the black man to the throne of the Shining One in the heavens above.

But soon hard times were coming for the black man. Prince Henry of Portugal took back to Africa some Moors he had captured in Spain. There, he received in return black men and gold dust. And while these bartered souls lived and multiplied in Seville, the Portuguese discovered the formula of turning them into virtual gold-dust. A Genoese called Columbus had wanted to exchange five hundred Indians for live stock. Why should not a Portuguese exchange Negroes for ducats ? So they shipped the black men to Haiti and sold them for slaves. And the first entry was made on the blackest page in the history of the white man.

While Isabella hesitated to permit the barter of red men for oxen, and Charles feared the fires of hell for pemitting the sale of black men, a blessed bishop of the church came to ease the troubled Christian conscience. He was the accommodating Bishop of Chiapa, who returned to Spain from Haiti in 1517, recommending that each Spanish resident should have a licence to import a dozen Negro slaves. Soon the concession to import four thousand negroes annually in Haiti sold for 25,000 ducats. Thus another lesson was learned by the cultured people of Europe : black men could be turned not only into gold-dust but even into veritable nuggets. And a new business came into being —the traffic in slaves.

Ships commanded by silk-stockings and noblemen stopped in the lagoons along the west coast of Africa. Strong, cruel men landed upon the shore. They marched stealthily upon the peaceful population, setting ablaze whole villages by night·and capturing those who would escape death in the flames. Those who were caught were kept in the hold of the ship until it was filled. Then the vessel proudly sailed on to civilized climes.

It was no easy task to catch the African black men in the bush. It was much more difficult to deliver them in good condition. Many died before the ship set sail ; larger numbers perished during the voyage. Less than half of those caught in the bush ever reached the auction block. But Africa is a large continent and many are her sons. There was no need of conserving black flesh and blood. There may have been a lot of waste, but gold was sure to follow, for the demand was ever growing. When

George Washington retired from the presidency, his little state of Virginia alone had more than two hundred thousand slaves.

In the millions they were caught along the coast of Africa, these happy, care-free black men.  In the hundreds of thousands they were brought into the Americas to build new worlds for the master of civilization and the humble servant of God—the white-skinned man.  Indiscriminately were they caught, but even more so were they handled, bought, sold, and colonized.

And during all their long journeys, these black men packed together in the holds of the slave ships, were nevertheless alone and isolated.  For there are countless numbers of dialects among the natives of Africa, and seldom could one slave speak to another save in the few words of English or Spanish they both had come to learn.  And isolated as well were they in their religion. Various were the forms of the black man's gods.  The Onyame of one slave was quite different from the Onyame of another ; and one Legba would hardly recognize his fellow-god.  In transit, the African lost his tongue and his god and his love.  For the males that were caught far outnumbered the females.  There were thirty thousand more men than women slaves in Jamaica alone.  And the beautiful young females, black though they were, were first reserved for the white master.

There they were, on the plantations of a strange world, these black men, mute and saddened, longing for home and god, both of which were gradually to fade from their memory.  No one ever cared to know what was coursing through their minds as they toiled away, from early morn to sundown, picking the snowy cotton.  But minds, even black minds, are bent on thinking, and hearts ever long and yearn.  Having no language in which to express the workings of his mind, the Negro took to singing.  And, where the song failed, the dance came to offer relief.

In the back yards of the plantations, off the fields of cotton, these black men lived, torn away from their own gods, yet not without some unconscious endeavour to fill the vacant places. As black night descended, great fear overwhelmed their empty souls.  It was an accumulation of fears : the fear of the primitive man in the bush, the fear of the man caught in the fire and thrown in chains into the hold of a ship, the fear of pain and death that might come at any moment if the master be in an angry mood.  Not having the Lord for a shepherd, the black man had ample reason to fear, and he had nothing to offset his troubles but the little bits of magic that clung to his memory and grew like a seed in his imagination.  And it was upon these bits of magic that he built up the Voodoo worship so common among the black people.

But longing held a larger place than fear in the heart of the black man. He pined for the land of Onyame and the hut of Legba. In contrast to the severe life and unhappy existence in the West, his African past seemed like one glorious Paradise, out of which he had been driven by the lash of the slave-trader. If

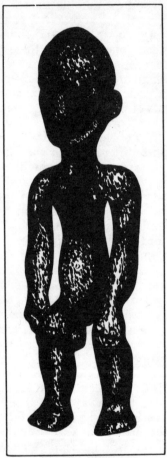

*A Negro God*

the Christian still hopes for the millennium and the Jew for the return to Jerusalem, after these many centuries, it is not strange that the longing for Africa has been a force in the life of the Negro, a force not altogether lacking in this very day. The Negro slave may have been little conscious of it, but the inner stirring of his heart in the universal desire for spiritual freedom and communion with God, expressed itself in his mute longing for a past he could only vaguely remember and a land he knew only from the stories of the old people. The black heart in the white man's home sought communion with the mass of brother blacks under Africa's burning sun.

Along with this hazy, unconscious racial longing, there was yet another pining for love that was never satisfied. Great was the black man's capacity for loving and, in Africa, ample were the opportunities for indulging in it. Here, in the cotton fields, the heart of the Negro was hungry for love—pure physical love as well as romance, sentiment, and attachment to an individual, all of which became the more necessary in his harsh and unfriendly environment. The African black man was love-starved on American soil. He had no black god to offer him relief or to provide him with an outlet for his suppressed emotions ; nor was there a white god to take the place of Onyame and Legba in his lonely heart.

## II

Great as was the need for religion among the Negroes, the master long hesitated to introduce the black soul to his white God. Would this woolly slave become a brother in Christ ? How could one keep a brother in abject slavery ? It was true that Abraham held slaves as did many another Biblical character. Therefore, it was perfectly legitimate for a white man in America, some three thousand years later, to keep them as well. But the slaves of Abraham were heathens. A believer could not hold another believer in bondage. Of course, the Christian faith must be spread and all mankind brought under the wings of the church, but not at the expense of the plantation. The Kingdom of Heaven must come as soon as possible, but not before the tobacco had been raised and the cotton picked. In the meantime, the Negro must be kept out of the House of the Lord, lest he turn Christian and gain his freedom.

But there are great theologians in every generation who know how to apply religion to all necessities of life, however godless. Doctors of the church discovered that wonderful synthesis of doing their bit by the faith and yet keeping the cotton fields blooming. It was the simple idea that baptism does not free slaves. True, all were brothers in Christ, but some were white and others black, and the black ones were to serve their white brothers in a brotherly way. A Christian could be a slave-holder ; he could also be a slave.

So it was that slavery entered the church, and the slave followed the master to the very altar of Christ. But it was not to the very same altar. Master and slave could not properly appear together before the Lord    One must humble himself before God, and the white man could not humble himself in the presence of his slaves.    Besides, the Negro slave required a religion somewhat different from that of the master.    If the African black man was to enter the House of the Lord, he was to do so through a separate door and, once inside, he was to remain in a corner by himself.

Four years after the Pilgrims landed on the rock of Plymouth, a Negro child was baptized and given the glorious name of William.    It was the first black soul to enter the white man's heaven.    Almost a century later, North Carolina passed a law forbidding Negro churches.    And the black man had a longer struggle for admission to heaven than for freedom upon earth. The founder of the Quakers went about the country, impressing upon the minds of his followers their Christian duty of converting the slaves.    That was about the middle of the seventeenth century. The first year of the eighteenth saw the incorporation of the Moravians, a society to aid the religious institution of the established Church of England, in America.    This society was the first to formally dedicate itself to converting the Negroes along with the Indians.    In New York City, it had on its roll fifteen hundred Negro and Indian slaves.    There were many individual attempts to spread Christianity among the black people, but only too often they were wrecked on the rocks of slavery, or ruined by the fears of the slave-holder for his property.

The colonists themselves did not raise a finger to spread the Christian religion among the black men.    All such endeavours came from without.    It remained for the Baptists, a group of people that, as a rule, kept no slaves and could, therefore, be hostile to slavery, to start the Negro well on the way to Christ. They trained Negro preachers for Negro communities before the American Revolution, and the very year of the war saw the first formal organization of Negro Christians.    The first Negro church was Baptist.

There was an additional reason why the Baptist church came to gain a foothold among the Negroes.    It was not only the first and real friend of the black man, but it was also nearer to his understanding.    The Episcopal church could not keep the Negro flock sitting passively observing its elaborate ritual ; nor was the primitive mind of the coloured worshipper affected by its prayers and devotions.    Once the Negro came into the church he wanted to do something there.    His religion must be ever active, never passive.    The Baptist, like the Methodist, gave the black man free play in his worship.    Their exercises were spontaneous, their preaching evangelical.    A black man could move and shout when he got religion.    He could give up all control of himself when he felt the presence of his God.  It was like going back to the old gods, Onyame and Legba.

Not until after the Civil War, however, did the masses of blacks come into the fold of the church.  To-day, there are probably some fifty thousands of church organizations among the African exiles in America, and almost as many religious edifices, with a membership of four and a half to five million people.  The black man came to his own in the Christian church, but he gave Christianity his own individual turn.  The church little changed the character of the Negro, but the latter modified the nature of the church.  In his new religion, his old yearnings and longings found a means of expression.  But the smoldering fires of love, of freedom, and of the joy of living, bursting forth in flame once more took on a melancholy, saddened aspect.

### III

To the Jew, the synagogue is a house of prayer and worship for all people.  To the white Christian, the church is a place of communion with God.  To the Negro, it is the very core of his social organization.  Jew and Christian have developed a secular social life, apart from synagogue or church.  The Negro's social life is still almost entirely within the house of worship.  This fact explains the enormous church membership among the blacks in proportion to that of the whites.  It also explains to a considerable extent the appearance of numerous small congregations and religious communities that rise up like mushrooms after the rain.  The church is the club of the black man, the modern form of the tribal meeting in Africa.  Like the tribal meeting, it deals with matters, religious, social, economic.  Like those meetings, too, it offers the emotional outlet for feeling pent-up in the ordinary affairs of life.

The office of the minister is another hang-over from African times.  In the bush, the religious leader was also the medicine man, the magician, the feared leader, and the social lion.  The dispenser of the faith still occupies the most exalted position in the Negro religious life.  No one is properly introduced unless he comes through the minister.  No cause will be aided without his endorsement and approval.  It is the minister who advises the ignorant, who comforts the sorrowful, who aids the unfortunate.  He is the walking encyclopædia, the fountain of all knowledge concerning both the natural and the supernatural.  He is still the master of magic and witchcraft disguised under different names.

But even more characteristically African is the theology of the Negro church.  Formally, there is no theological difference

between black and white churches of the same denomination.
A Methodist is a Methodist, whether white or coloured. But it
is not the written creed in the book that really matters in religion,
but what is accepted by the people. Not theoretical theology,
but living theology counts. And the living theology of the
Christian black man is quite distinct from that which was laid
down by the fathers of the church.

The black man is little concerned with the virgin birth of
Christ. To him this all-important dogma means little indeed.
He knows he is to believe that Christ came into the world by
the Holy Ghost, and he tries his utmost to believe it. But the
matter does not interest him. Virginity is no ideal of the black
people. To this day, the cousins of our Negroes on the West
Coast of Africa trace the hereditary line through the females
because " one always knows who the mother is, but who knows
who the father may be ? " The black people did not pass through
the stage of chivalry and the pains of spiritual love. Their
natural instincts were not held in abeyance by the false ideals of
chastity and celibacy.

Similarly, the idea of sin as a spot upon the soul that calls for
absolution, forgiveness, or redemption, is still foreign to the mind
of the Negro. The notion of sin is the product of an over-sensitive
civilization. It is the snake developing in the crack of the
personality, encouraged by inner conflict. The conflict is between
man's ideal behaviour and his actual behaviour, the discrepancy
between one's ethics and his instincts. In the personality of the
Negro, no such crack has as yet occurred. His ethics are, of
course, superior to his instincts and superimposed upon them,
but still the difference between the two is slight. At least there
is no developed sense of guilt or original sin. The black man of
Africa is still living in sunlight for the joy of existence. He cannot
conceive of this life as a corridor of misery leading into a greater
world.

To the man with a weak sense of sin, Christ's mission to save
mankind from its sins is necessarily of little significance. The
crucifixion of Christ by Pontius Pilate could not shock the slave
who himself was being crucified almost continually by mere
individuals. What impresses the black man most in the story of
the Passion is that Christ never complained, " he never said a
mumblin' word." The description of the crucifixion in the
spirituals could just as well refer to a lynching. In comparison
with the spirituals that refer to Old Testament incidents and
persons, and in proportion to the place Jesus occupies in the
church, there are mighty few religious songs in his honour.
Where there is a groping toward the notion of Jesus as a saviour,

the actual sentiment is lacking.  Were a white man singing
" Steal Away to Jesus," he would put boundless emotion into the
song.  But as the Negro sings the spiritual, he might just as well
be stealing away from the plantation to some kind friend across
the Ohio.

Neither can the Negro appreciate the Christian ideas of the
Trinity and the Virgin Mary.  They are divine characters that
the black man knows formally, having been introduced to them
by the minister.  He may hold them in the greatest awe and
admiration, but he does not spiritually experience them.  They
are not his own.  He has no joys nor sorrows in common with
them to bind them closer to him.  It is for this reason that God
is commonly addressed as " Lord " by the black people.  The
word is impersonal ; it may refer to any divine being, to any
universal father.  Lord is the maker of the universe and the ruler
over man.  He may be conceived in the latter's own image.  He
may even be a spiritualized Onyame or Legba.  The God of the
black Christians is what a god should be—a mere form for
spiritual content, the container of the divine.  The actual spiritual
content, the divine essence, must be supplied by the believer
himself.

On the other hand, the Negro gave to the Christian faith
meanings and values that are missing in the religion of the white
man.  One is the fear of death.  A Christian should not fear life's
end.  To him it is only a crossing from the foyer into the parlour.
Death is the embrace of God, and who would disdain a divine
embrace ?  But the black man is afraid of death.  So is every
primitive man.  Death is the greatest mystery, more incomprehensible than the dreadful ghosts in the dark of the bush.
The black man was full of fear in the wilds of Africa.  He is still
afraid on the plantations of the South.  Most of his religious
outcries, as expressed in his spirituals, deal with death and his
fear of it.  He conceives it as the crossing of a river, the descent
into inferior regions, or flight through the clouds—always, however, in fear and troubled spirit.

And the black man wants to die easy when he dies.  True, the
Christian in him comes to the fore.  He wants to see Jesus near
him, but he also wants to see his mother.  In other words, he
wishes to be among his own people when that terrible moment
comes.  Even when he refers to the " comin' of the Saviour," he
speaks in terms of farewell.

"I'm-a goin' to tell you 'bout de comin' of de Saviour,
    Fare you well, fare you well.
    Dere's a better day a-comin',
    Fare you well, fare you well ;

> Oh, preacher, fol' yo' bible,
> Fare you well, fare you well.
> In dat great gittin' up mornin',
> Fare you well, fare you well."

To the black man, death is like another descent to the dark
hold of the slave ship, but all the more horrible because of the fires
of hell.  The Lord said, " He's gwinter rain down fire, dere's no
hidin' place down dere."  The Negro is even afraid of little Mary.
" Oh, touch me not, little Mary, good Lord, I'm gwine home."
He is ever worried about where he may be " when de first
trumpet soun'."  He is forever asking his fellow-men what they
are " gwine to do when yo' lamp burn down."  He is hidden in
the shadow of the rocks and mountains that are forever falling
upon him.  In short, if Jesus does not help him, he " sho'ly will
die."  And not much can be done for his troubled mind.  He is
conscious of his Christian inadequacy.  He " done done " what
God told him to do.  God told him to pray, and he " done pray."
God told him to sing, and he " done done " that, too.  Yet the
result is far from satisfactory.  Neither he nor the church has
gotten out of it what they could.

> " Try my bes' for to serve my Master,
> Try my bes' for to follow my Leader,
> Try my bes' for to kneel an' pray so the devil won't harm me."

But no matter what he does, the church keeps on grumbling ;
and although he is " gwine cling to de ship o' Zion," the black
man cannot be so happy about it.  For he, too, has reason to be
" a-grumblin'," and he would have been doing so had he dared.
His faith leaves him cold, as he leaves the church.  For here is
another value that the Negro Christian greatly emphasized, if
he did not actually introduce it into the worship of the church—
the sentimental longing.

Spending the evenings in the cabin on the plantation, the
heart of the black man was eaten away by longing.  It was the
vague, indefinite feeling that often comes over the adolescent
youth, making him wish to cry out of the fullness of his heart,
although he hardly knows why.  In the case of the Negro, there
was not one but a whole series of longings that consciously or
subconsciously made his heart heavy.  There was his yearning
for the land of his fathers of which little was actually remembered
but much was related.  Seeking to console himself in his present
plight, he gloried in the past.  In his imagination, he recon-
structed the grandeur of Africa as he sought to escape from the
humiliations into which he had been thrown in America.  What
the coming of the Messiah was to the Jew and the kingdom of

heaven to the Christian, the land of Africa was to the black man
picking cotton in the South.

There was the longing for the tribal gods not completely
forgotten yet not consciously retained ; the longing for a god
that was of the Church yet not of it ; a god that combined in his
being both Jehovah and Onyame, Mary and Legba, Voodooism
and Christianity.   There was also the longing for the mate, the
pang of love unsatisfied, love that once was free and full and that,
combined with religion, brought the greatest joy of exaltation
and ecstasy.   Here he was wifeless, at the mercy of the master,
who picked a woman for him without any consideration as to his
liking.   With her he was to live in strict adherence to the rules
that white people had evolved—laws that the master himself
honoured more in their breach than in their observance.

These channels of longing merged in one great stream that
assumed a religious form.   Longing for God or Jesus or some
vague heavenly state is the only outlet for the great stirrings
within the heart of the black man.   Sometimes he sings, " I feel
like a motherless child, a long ways from home, true believer, a
long ways from home."   Then he recalls his religion, and adds :
" Sometimes I feel like I'm almos' gone, way up in the heab'nly
lan'."   The two are really one.   He is no more elated over the
" heab'nly lan' " than he is over being a long way from home.
He is not only far from home, but friendless and lonely : " Nobody
knows the trouble I've seen, nobody knows but Jesus, nobody but
Jesus."   And Jesus does not seem to do anything about it.   Nor
does he feel that he can appeal to Jesus for help.   For, after all,
Jesus is also a stranger.   At best, he is the keeper of the heavenly
door and he does not worry himself over the sinner that may
arrive a bit too late :

> " Too late, too late, Sinnah,
> Carry de key an' gone home.
> Massa Jesus lock de do',
> O, Lord ! too late,
> Massa Jesus lock de do'."

When the black man makes his appeal, he turns to the Lord
himself.   His cry is for deliverance, for removal from this environment.   But this very same appeal carries within it the element of
love.   The antithesis of life here below, on foreign land, is not
only " heab'n," but " heab'nly love " as well.   The soul of the
Negro is pining away, and he calls to God :

> " My good Lord, show me de way ;
> Enter the chariot, travel along.
> Noah sent out a mournin' dove,
> Which brought back a token of a heab'nly love."

## IV

The black man of Africa may have accepted an entirely
spiritual God but he could not live up to an entirely spiritual
religion.  Not for him was the dream of Nirvana, of peaceful
contemplation and of passive union with the Divine Being.  His
faith was to be not only spiritual and emotional, but motor as
well.  He was to serve his God not only with his heart and soul,
but also, and primarily, with his muscles.  In religious exercises,
the Negro's muscles are so strained and contracted that one may
almost hear the rattling of his bones.  There is rhythmic movement in his feet upon the floor of the church.  He waves his hands
and outstretches his arms, tossing about his head and rolling his
eyes.  The services are continually interrupted by groans and
shouts, or an occasional "falling out" as some member faints
away when the Holy Ghost descends upon him.

Entire congregations join in dances that are not much different
from those of the Indians or the Africans about their fires in forest
or bush.  One such dance is practised by the members of the
Zion Baptist Church in Florida.  It is executed at the close of the
communion service in the immediate centre of the church.  The
leader stands in front of the pulpit and motions to the worshippers.
They rise and form a circle about him and the pulpit, marching
around in single file.  Falling into regular step, the tempo of
which is quickened, the dancers gesticulate and shout : " Rock,
Daniel, rock, Daniel, rock, Daniel, rock, Daniel, till I die."
They dance, not until they die, but until they fall into a swoon
of rapture and ecstasy.

In Alabama, the faithful find even greater exaltation in the
Roper dance.  Here, too, they march about a central figure that
claps his hands and shouts vociferously until he falls into a trance
of ecstasy.  This is a signal for the entire congregation to join in
embraces between the opposite sexes, with all the force of
maddened passion.  The dance is commenced at the close of the
services and continues indefinitely.  Couple after couple gradually
break away, some going into the dark corners of the church,
others to the corridors, there to give themselves to one another in
the frenzy of sexual and religious passion.  For once, Legba of
the West Coast of Africa has triumphed over Mary and her Son
in Alabama of America.

Many dances are engaged in by the entire congregation at
every service.  Others are executed only on certain festive
occasions.  But the motor element in religion is ever to the front
in the Negro's worship, and still the soul of the black man is ever
yearning for greater freedom and larger outlets.  The groan and

the shout and the dance are only the minor outpourings, like the thin vapours coming forth from the crater of the volcano. They are but slightly indicative of the enormous forces operating within. The eruption of the religious Vesuvius takes place in the camp meeting or revival. The revival is the elixir of black Christianity, coming periodically to wash away the dust from Negro souls and to bring rebirth in faith.

The great masses of black men entered the faith of the cross by way of the revivals and camp meetings held by several Protestant denominations a little over a century ago. There, Christ was crucified anew for thousands of black listeners so that they might attach their souls to his bleeding limbs. There, hell with its blazing fires and devilish tortures was vividly pictured. There, black souls found the glory of conversion and of communion with God—the merging of one's soul in love with the All-soul of the universe. And ever since, the revival has been the dream of the black devout, his oasis in the desert of the white man's faith.

Theodore Schroeder, with the great psychological insight that is so characteristic of his studies in religion, offers us a complete description of a Negro revival meeting. The service opened at eight in the evening and lasted until midnight. The pastor began with some humorous remarks about common-place things, bringing his audience to laughter and thereby establishing a personal contact. He was no longer for them a man of God, cold and distant, but a neighbour, a friend and good fellow. Then, turning to religious topics, he elaborated upon the evils of sin and the tortures of hell. And as he did so, the laughter of the audience changed to groans, sighs, and hummings, accompanied by rhythmic tapping of the feet, movements of the heads, and clapping of the hands. The pastor himself was growing ever more excited. He jumped and shouted, threatened and exhorted. Here, he was rising to the angels ; there, he was sinking into the fires of hell. Suddenly, he lapsed into a sing-song, monotonous intonation, his words hardly audible, certainly unintelligible. He seemed to be in tune with his worshippers. His fire was gone, his spasmodic exclamations diminished. He felt the approach of a kindly spirit, drawing ever closer and closer in perfect embrace.

It was just at this moment that the greatest excitation occurred among the worshippers. Wild shrieks broke in upon the rambling intonations of the pastor. Many jumped high from the floor ; some leaped upon chairs and wildly waved their arms through the air. Others sat on the laps of their neighbours in rapturous phantasy. Pandemonium reigned. The Holy Ghost was busy.

While the pastor carried on in his silent, trembling way, others sought to take care of those who were " possessed of the Holy

Ghost." One male attendant grabbed the arms of a young woman, who twisted back and forth convulsively. He pulled her arms straight. She yielded to his greater strength and dropped her head upon his chest, resting quietly in his embrace. Another young man came and sought to open her clenched fist, but he was unable to do so. The two joined in an attempt to seat her, but her body refused to bend. She was carried from the room as rigid as a board.

There was another young woman, who began to gesticulate, slowly at first and then violently. Her movements were accompanied by song that turned into convulsive shrieks. Losing all control of her bodily muscles, she staggered about, extending her arms as if she were trying to embrace someone. Then she collapsed entirely. And as she did, a mulatto girl suddenly shrieked and jumped into a place in front of her, as if driven by an overwhelming explosion. Her body was twisting, every muscle in violent motion. Her breathing was spasmodic, loud, uncertain. In the ecstasy of religion, she, too, was ready to collapse when caught by two men, who supported her writhing body. And as they held her, her pelvis moved most vigorously backward and forward. Women came to assist the men in sustaining her sinking body. All the while, she twisted and wriggled as if to compel a release of the men's hold upon her arms. Gradually her body stiffened and grew rigid. Then she seemed to relax ; the Holy Spirit was leaving her.

In all these cases, the intense emotion of the religious enthusiast is inseparably associated with the emotional outbursts that accompany a love experience. The black man, longing for love and companionship, found an outlet for his desires in the religion of the camp meeting. There, piety and love mingled in the flame of passion. And the Negro opened his heart as he had done when he was happy and care-free in the African bush.

v

Great was the relief that the religious awakenings brought to the soul of the black man, but long were the intervals between. By its very nature, the revival is temporary, an occasional affair, a mere flash of light in a long, black night. Once it was over the Negro again found himself alone in the desert of his religion. And to get away from this isolation, he addressed himself to the strange faith of the white man in an attempt to make it his own. This endeavour resulted in Voodoo, a hasty, crude synthesis of African paganism and European Christianity. Here was the true communion of a black soul with a white God.

The Lord of the whites was a jealous God. He would have no

other gods before Him.  But the magic wand of Voodoo easily wiped away this divine jealousy.  Both gods and God are being worshipped in Voodoo in perfect harmony.  In fact, the black man appeals to the kind Virgin to intercede for him with his African gods of terror.  These gods demand human sacrifices from him, and the Son of the Virgin forbids the taking of human life.  Will not his Holy Mother take the matter up with the gods so that they may be satisfied with animal sacrifices instead ?

The Virgin Mother must share her throne with Legba, the guardian of the gates, equally benevolent to all in need of solace and particularly close to the heart of the black people.  The Holy

*The Virgin shares her altar with Legba*

Ghost has an additional function in the religion of Voodoo.  His duty it is to pick up the soul of the black man and carry it back to Africa, where the sun rises, the ultimate abode of all and the place of true life.  While the soul is thus carried away by the Holy Ghost, its owner falls into a state of ecstasy.  And so, wherever a black man may be, once he is in a trance, his soul goes back to Africa, the land for which he ever yearns.  The God of the Christians must not disdain to have as his associate Legba the male, the black Priapus.  He will find still other gods sharing the black man's worship with Him.  Among these is Papa Nebo, who is both male and female, usually represented by a tall woman, wearing the skirt of her sex and the coat and silk hat of a man. He symbolizes the union of both sexes in one individual.

Both God and gods are worshipped on the same altar with the

same offerings of flowers and cakes, corn and animal meat. And amidst the sacred offerings, there are always objects dear to other gods in other climes. Serpents in wood and metal are there to represent the great god, Damballa. The sacred bull, too, holds a place of honour before the altar, while all about the place are figures of triangles and columns, so common in the temples dedicated to the generative divinities. Along with the pagan symbols there are always found a crucifix, a black statue of the Virgin, and a cross often painted like a totem pole.

Various are the forms of Voodoo ceremony. They differ according to the locality and the mode of living among the

*The Christian God worshipped in Voodoo fashion*

worshippers. In backward, agricultural countries, a goat may be sacrificed to take the place of a man-offering, just as the lamb was substituted for Isaac in Abraham's sacrifice. The blood streaming from the goat symbolizes the mystery of death and the purification of the soul. Poured upon the earth, it is believed to bring the blessing of fertilization. In such animal sacrifices, an egg is often used to represent rebirth. It is broken by the priestess, who prays : " Legba, Papa Legba, open wide the gates for this, my little one ! "

Again, Voodoo may be limited to the practice of magic and the use of charms and talismans. This is especially true in certain parts of the West Indies. W. B. Seabrook, in *The Magic Island*, describes a Voodoo love charm : " Two needles of equal length are stood upright, side by side, baptized with suitable incantations, and are given the names of the youth and his unwilling girl. . . . The needles are then left side by side, parallel but reversed, so that the point of each presses against the eye of the other. The point is symbolic of the phallus and the eye symbolic of the vulva. The reverse doubling simply increases the potency of the charm. . . ."

Crude and incongruous does Voodoo seem to us to-day. We have little respect and much less sympathy for it. Yet its ceremonies are merely the infantile steps of the black man in the House of the Lord. The white man has had his Voodoo. When the European heathen was suddenly thrown into the House of

*Images of the Voodoo gods*

the Lord, he, too, could not entirely forget his own gods and modes of worship. Then, too, a synthesis was attempted, an adjustment and compromise between the rival faiths. And this synthesis was no less crude, possibly, in the early centuries of Christianity than Voodoo is to-day. It took many centuries to smelt down the various components into a harmonious unit. It required a still longer time to refine the product of this synthetic process. The fathers of the church complained of strange practices in the church of the early centuries, much as men of religion complain of Voodoo to-day.

Were Voodoo left alone, it might in time develop into a new faith upon a Christian foundation. It might become a great and worthy addition to man's cultural heritage. However, this æsthetic evolution may hardly be expected. Voodoo will be given neither time nor opportunity to grow and develop and refine itself as it climbs the steps of progress. When white Voodoo was in existence, it was not at all out of tune with its time. In fact, it was the new Hebraic faith that was novel and out of keeping with the social customs of the day. Nor did white Voodoo have an older brother to teach it right thinking and proper manners. Beyond it, except for the faith of the Jews in a faraway land, there was sheer paganism.

To-day, in civilized countries, Voodoo is nothing more than black magic bordering on charlatanism and generally severely forbidden by law. There is a mother church that keeps a watchful eye over the religious development of the black man, and it will not allow him to wander off, spiritually, into the bush. Voodoo is destined to be uprooted. The black man will have to cling to his white God in the white way. Yet, there is something exotic about this struggle of the black soul in the House of the Lord. It is the flutter of love, warm and wild from the bush, against the cold, hard wall of self-denial.

*The Spirit of God moving over the face of the waters*

# BOOK FOUR
# THE SPIRIT OF REVOLT IN RELIGION

"... *and they gathered themselves together against Moses and against Aaron, and said unto them, ye take too much upon you, seeing all the congregation are holy, every one of them, and the Lord is among them ; wherefore then lift ye up yourselves above the congregation of the Lord ?* "—NUMBERS.

# CHAPTER I

## REBELS IN THE FAITH

I

THEY who had been slaves in Egypt were now camping in freedom in the wilderness. No longer were they huddled together in the miserable huts behind the pyramids. No longer were they awakened at daybreak by the shrill siren, a summons to be busy finding straw for their bricks. Gone was the knout of the slave-driver and almost forgotten were the tortures by the publicans of Pharaoh. The great king himself lay buried beneath the sands of the Red Sea, in just punishment for his unwillingness to allow the children of Israel to serve their God.

They who once had been slaves were now as free as a people could ever be. They were liberated from all bonds of civilization and from the encumbrances of organized society. They were even unbound by toil and labour. Their sustenance came down from the sky ready for consumption. The angels of heaven fought their wars. Their only duty was to mind Moses and to march along to the Promised Land, where each would rest under his own vine and fig tree.

And yet, they who once were slaves were not happy in their freedom. There was a grumbling in the camp of the freed man. There was a pointing of fingers to the tent on the top of the hill. For upon its summit was the camp of Moses, the son of Amram, who had led them out of slavery, but who refused to set them free. He who had come to them in the name of liberty now spoke to them of law and order. He who had taught them to break the chains was chaining them to commandments and law. The rebel against the king of Egypt was establishing a kingdom of his own, a royalty of priesthood. There was a spirit of rebellion against the leader of the rebels.

The groans of dissatisfaction found a ready listener in Korah, the cousin of Moses. Korah could still remember Uncle Amram, playing with him and his cousins, Moses and Aaron, in the shadow of the pyramids. Little had he suspected that this stuttering cousin of his would ever become so great. And yet Korah saw him now, forging ahead, first in the court of Pharaoh, then among his own people, taking the office of prophet to himself and giving the priesthood to his brother, Aaron.

Moses was not satisfied with making himself ruler over the people. He wanted to monopolize their God as well. They all had seen the cloud of fire in which Jehovah descended upon the mount of Sinai. All had heard Him read the ten commandments. When Jehovah had something to say, He spoke to the

241

entire congregation. How did Moses come to talk exclusively in the name of God and to lift himself above the assembly of the Lord ?

Not only did Moses rob the people of their God, but he instituted laws in the Lord's name, laws that were of his own creation, that served to make the priest thrive on the fat of the land Suppose there was a widow with two little orphans, and she had only a small piece of land. When she was about to plough, she could not use the ox and the mule together ; when she was about to sow, she must observe the Mosaic regulation ; and when she was ready to harvest the grain, she was again bound by a Mosaic law. The greater part of the fruit she did succeed in obtaining was taken from her in tithes to the priest, to the levite, and to the temple. The poor widow could never make her ends meet were she to follow the law of Moses—of Moses, not of the Lord— laws that he had made just as had the pharaoh, in whose court he had been raised and whose rule he had helped to destroy.

And so Korah rose against Moses and took with him many of the leaders of the tribes. There was a great rebellion in the wilderness, and the end of the revolt is known to all. Fire came down from heaven and devoured some of the rebels, while the earth swallowed the rest. Tongues of flame and the mouth of the earth put an end to Korah and those that stood with him. Jehovah himself showed His hand at this critical moment in the life of His people. He was with Moses, His servant, to whom He had first spoken from the burning bush.

Korah and his followers were destroyed, but not so was the spirit of rebellion. All the people saw the horrible end of the rebels, yet they would not submit. There was another complaint over a scarcity of water ; another minor revolt against the manna, the delectable food that came down from the sky. And again a conflagration was necessary to break the spirit of the revolting mass. They had neither respect nor pity for Moses, who was alone now, deserted by his closest friends, even his sister Miriam and his brother, Aaron. Instead of feeling kindly toward the lonely old man, the rebels accused him of doing away with his own brother, in a plot with Eliezer, his nephew.

The spirit of rebellion flickered on to the exasperation of Moses and Jehovah until it was finally relieved by an outbreak of sexual activity. As the Israelites arrived in the valley of Shitim, they plunged themselves into the worship of Baal Peor. For once, they broke completely away from the laws of Moses and the commands of his God. For once, they were truly free, inwardly free. A people " holy and pure " descended into the depths of sin and completely lost itself in one wild orgy of sexual pleasure. The extent of the orgy may be gleaned from the legends about the elder Zimri, who was found in union with a temple priestess by Pinchos, a grandson of Aaron. Zimri, according to the legend, had four hundred and twenty-four coitions with the same priestess on the one day.

This outburst was followed by a bloody civil war, the devotees of Jehovah slaughtering all who were caught paying homage to Baal. Thus, in sex and in blood was drowned the spirit of rebellion, the spirit of the Israelites in the wilderness. The revolt had run its course, and a submissive people patiently listened to the exhortation of a tired leader. Moses soon passed quietly out of existence. The people returned to their drab existence and monotonous routine, following a mediocre leader. Their spirit was broken. The dramatic moment had passed. The curtain had been drawn.

## II

It was only through a physical accident that Korah lost his rebellion against Moses. Had he succeeded, we might now be reading different stories about him and Moses in the chronicles of the Hebrews. Had he succeeded, he would have established, in the course of time, a theocracy or oligarchy of his own. It not have been long, then, before insurrections against the domination of Korah broke out, and they who were rebels by nature would rise against their leader, saying : " All the people are holy. Why do you lift yourself above the assembly ? "

For in every generation there is the spirit of revolt. It breaks through like the spring from beneath the rocks. Religion ever has its inception in spontaneity. It wells up in the prophet, priest, or religious leader, suddenly, unconsciously. God appears in the burning bush, or upon a tree in the wilderness, or in a dream at night. When man has had his vision, he comes to his fellows in the name of God, but also in the voice of his innermost soul. This is the revelation, the inspiration, the divine element in the faiths of man.

But religion is not only divine ; it is also human. This great source of energy is soon directed into channels that would make a better people and a better world. Religion is not only to be believed, but primarily to be lived. It thus becomes a social institution. From its original status as a bond between man and man, it develops into a bond upon man and man. To Charles A. Elwood, religion is " one of the oldest means of control in human societies, an effective means of preventing too wide a variation in conduct in individuals." It is but another steam-roller in the hand of an exacting society, exerting pressure upon the asphalt of humanity. It crushes the individual who stands out from his own people and transforms the odd, angular, variable humans into one thick, smooth, flat humanity.

Once religion is to serve society, it must itself be socialized. The spontaneous call of man to his God and the divine reply are institutionalized and subjected to steam-rolling. There are so many books in the canon ; all others, even of the same period, are apocryphal. Not a word may be added to the Bible nor a line subtracted from it. There are so many dogmas to believe, so many commands and precepts to follow. Even prayer has been supervised, stereotyped, and institutionalized. There are set devotions for set occasions. One can no longer approach his God in his own personal, intimate way. He must speak in words prepared for him by priest or leader. Religion, man's ladder from earth to heaven, has dropped the rungs. One can no longer climb upon it ; he must remain at the foot, while the adept priest ascends for him.

No wonder, then, that there are rebellions in religion no less than in other forms of social organization. Religion has always blessed the meek, the humble, the obedient, promising them the Kingdom of God, in heaven if not on earth. But it has always had difficulty with the independent spirit, the true men of God. These do not wait at the foot of Sinai for what a Moses will bring down to them. They will not be persuaded by argument or won over by promise of reward. They will not even be cowed by threats of punishment, here or hereafter. They are the men of Korah, the nonconformists of every age who spread the spirit of religious revolt. It is they who assemble themselves against the Moses and the Aaron of their day, protesting : " All the congregation are holy ; . . . God is everywhere, accessible to everyone. Why do you set yourself up as leader and lift yourself above the assembly ? " These are the rebels of the Lord against the rule of man in the worship of God.

As in the case of Korah, it is very often chance, accident, that decides the fate of the revolt. Had Korah been successful, his name would have been written high in the annals of faith. Because he lost, an unfriendly chronicler told his tale and set him forth as an object-lesson for a disobedient humanity. If the rebellion fails, it is left for the historian to deal with it. If it succeeds, the movement is bound to grow. The rebellious group will soon sectate itself from the parent religion, developing into a sect and growing into a faith of its own. In time, it may even rival the religion from which it sprang. But as it grows, it necessarily becomes socialized, institutionalized, building up canon and dogma and precept. The very same man who led the revolt against authority places himself in a position of power. Seeking to free man from his yoke of institutionalized religion, he only changes the yokes. The soul of man has not been set free. So other non-conformists will rise in rebellion against the non-conformist of an earlier day. History repeats itself. Every age has its spirit of revolt and its religious rebellion.

*A symbol of life*

# CHAPTER II

## LOVE THE FORCE OF REBELLION

### I

THE immediate causes of religious revolts are many and various. Often they lie outside the field of religion. They may be rooted in politics, economics, or social conditions, but invariably they come to assume a theologic aspect. The passions of a people that cannot be aroused by political controversy or economic strife will yield to the religious appeal. Invariably also, there will be indulgence in sex during or following the rebellion. Whatever the object of the revolt and the theology of the sect, the new group will be found to concern itself primarily with the exercise of the sexual function. The sect may liberate the love impulse from the chains imposed upon it by the parent religion. It may also add to the chains, throwing love into the dungeon. The religious insurrection may be positively or negatively charged with sex, but charged it is bound to be.

Out of the rebellions against Moses grew the orgy of worship to Baal Peor. Out of the concept of renewed revelation came a system of polygamy and heavenly marriages. Out of the desire to return to man's original state of purity and sinlessness came the sexual liberties of the Adamites. Out of the Gnostic movements concerning the godhead came orgies of overwhelming eroticism. In fact, almost every new sect has brought in its wake a wave of sexuality. Even the hard, dry Protestant Reformation, with its economic causes rooted in the Peasants' War and in the rise of the Third Estate, and its theologic struggle with the papacy, still contained the seed of a new attitude toward woman and the sexual that only later crystallized.

### II

What is it that has given an erotic phase to every revolt in religion? Here again, there may be many and varied causes, inherent in every case. But there are also basic reasons, rooted in the psychology of the people constituting the sect and in the character of the rebellion. The man who leads in a religious movement is generally a highly sexed individual. He who starts a religious revolt or who immediately falls in with the rebel is necessarily of a deeply religious nature. He is the emotional type, the kind of an individual who finds no satisfaction in his drab life and who seeks an escape through ecstasy.

Sex is an emotion very closely associated with the state of

ecstasy.  The religious type is also the sex type.  And just as the religious leader, or the apostle of the leader, must have an outlet for his emotions in general, he is particularly in need of an outlet for his sexual emotion.  For the highly sexed man is never satisfied with the sexual outlets provided by society.  He will ever seek such experiences as lie beyond the field of ordered sex life.  The religious will seek communion and ecstasy by way of the sexual impulse.

We therefore find most religious leaders definitely engrossed in sex to a degree not met with in ordinary individuals.  Every religious leader must pay his respects, his tax to the sexual question.  Like Mohammed or Brigham Young, he is concerned with justifying his own sexual appetite, or like Paul, he is seeking to uproot the sexual impulse in the hearts of his followers.  Again, he may open the floodgates of sexuality for all, giving free vent to the emotions of man on the basis of sex, as did the founders of the Gnostic and various other esoteric sects.  They who follow the leaders in such religious revolts are made of the same stuff.  Theirs is the restless, emotional spirit.  Theirs is the inner lack of satisfaction and the persistent pang of sex hunger never fully satisfied.  Theirs is the overwhelming desire to flee from the drudgery of life and to lose themselves in the boundless waves of ecstasy.

Yet another reason exists for the eroticism found in every esoteric religious movement.  It is inherent in the mechanism of the movement, in the force that is driving it ahead into the world and into the heart of man.  It is the trend of the revolt.  Every appeal against the existing order in religion is an appeal against the additions of time and a return to the original, basic state of the faith.  Jesus came, not to break the Law, but to fulfil it.  Luther posted his theses upon the door of the church, not to sever his relations with Christianity, but to save it from the falsifications of late-comers.  He called his followers to the very basis of Christianity, to the Bible itself.  The Adamites wanted to go back over all the steps of civilization since Adam.  The newer the sect, the further back it goes to seek for fundamentals.  And the further it explores, the closer it comes to the faith of Old Anthropology Adam, to the religion of the primitive man, the religion that was saturated with sex.

The sect, then, is an attempt to return to the origin of religion, which is so intimately bound up with love.  And as the sectarian descends the ladder of religious evolution, he also descends the steep pathway of erotic symbolism.  While he is removing layer after layer of theology, dogma, and precept, digging down to the core of his faith, he is also removing the fineries that the love sentiment has added during its sojourn in the sacred shrine.

Coming down to fundamental religion, the rebel is also descending to frank sex, the inseparable companion of primitive religion. The sect is, in consequence, a reversal to type, a return to the primitive state of sexuality in faith—sex, free, open, unashamed, and boundless, for the joy of man and the exaltation of his god.

*A Gnostic gem*

# CHAPTER III

# THE REVOLT AGAINST RELIGION

## I

FOR all their common basis in sex, the various religious sects have their own modes of departure from the accepted institutionalized religion. Whatever the ultimate motive for the break, it occurs where the hold is weakest. The religious rebel will inveigh against the most apparent abuse and elaborate upon it. There has always been rebellion against authority in the church, so typical of Korah's uprising against Moses. One who would not submit, questions the authority of saint or leader. Diakonus Nikolaus was such a rebel and he lived in the very beginning of the Christian era.

Nikolaus had been separated from his wife. After he became a Christian, he took her back, not out of passion or for sexual designs, but to manifest his own continence. "Behold he will be with his own wife and yet he will so be with her, as if he were not."

But Paul failed to take cognizance of the noble and chaste intentions of Diakonus Nikolaus. To him, it was the case of another convert going wrong, giving in to the call of his pagan flesh. Consequently, he chastised Nikolaus in public for his betrayal of the faith and for his succumbing to the desires of the flesh. Nikolaus resented this greatly. Had he lived in another age and under the spell of asceticism, he would have been glad of this public disgrace. He might even have offered it to God as an act of penance, just as he would a self-inflicted torture. But he lived in a militant age. After all, who was this Paul to assume the mantle of the Christ and, in the name of Jesus, to promulgate ideas that occurred to him alone?

And so Diakonus Nikolaus resolved to break with Paul and go his own way. He would be a second Paul, but in his own fashion. He at once dropped all the paraphernalia that the apostles had already gathered around the faith of Christ and directed himself to the very foundation of the belief.

There was a good and just father in heaven, who has sinful children here below. That these children might not perish spiritually, as well as bodily because of their sins, He sent His own son, Christ, to lead an earthly life as one of them. And by Christ's own blood, shed upon the cross, he washed away the sins of his father's children and saved their souls for life eternal.

It was Christ's duty, then, to save the sinners. He was—if one may say so with due respect—a lifeguard appointed to rescue people who were drowning in the ocean of sin. The larger the number of persons in danger and the stormier the ocean, the greater proves the guard who, in the face of these odds, manages to save the unfortunate ones.  Consequently, the more sin in the world, the greater the glory of the saviour.  The sinner's soul is dearer to God than the soul of the innocent man, for with the spotless soul, God has no relationship except a negative one, while in the soul of the sinner He takes a direct interest.  It was to save the sinner that He sent His son to earth, where he lived and died upon the cross.  There is more rejoicing in heaven over the salvation of one sinner than over that of a dozen just men. It adds to the glory of Christ and gladdens the heart of the father.

And just because sex was the greatest of sins, it was chosen as the sin to be indulged in most.  The Nikolaits would gather at their meeting-places and throw aside all restraint.  Everything that one desired to do, he was to do, not by permission, but by commission, by the order of the Most High.  Not only was there union of the sexes at the gatherings, but these unions were promiscuous, respecting neither age nor blood relationship, just as they were in primitive times and still are, on the banks of the Niger or in the woods of Australia.  Nikolaus thus had complete revenge on Paul.  He used the apostle's faith and dogma to attain the very opposite end.

II

In the Mormon church, we have another revolt against church authority.  In this case, it was an uprising against the Canon. The doctors of the church have always maintained that the cycle of the scriptures has long been completed.  But here was a new testament offered to man by God, through his humble servant, Joseph Smith.  This testament was an assertion of the value of modern man, who had been reduced to a mere mechanism. There was no place in the church for his self-expression.  His personality was hidden beneath the prescribed ritual and devotions.  He could only offer prayers and receive communion.

Pioneer life in America offered even less room for the play of individuality.  Here the person was submerged in the work he had to do.  It was the work that counted, not the man who did it. But the pioneer age was speedily passing away, especially in the East.  Man came back to his own.  He sought a place under the sun for his ego, for his personality so long suppressed. Spiritualism was among the first outbreaks of his inner independence.  There was more to the individual than what was thought of him in the village or town.  He had a soul which was everlasting and forever active in human life.   Spiritualism forbode the imminence of a divine spirit, which is above and beyond crude nature and the physical life.   Like most leaders of religious movements, the founder of the Morman church little appreciated the forces in his environment that led to the establishment of his church and contributed to its phenomenal success.   Joseph Smith was carried in on the crest of a wave of individualism that he was hardly capable of understanding.

One day, he heard the angel Moroni addressing him, directing him to Mormon Hill, where the Gold Bible was to be found.   It was a new scripture, proclaiming the divinity of man : God makes His will known to His people by continuous revelations. No longer are they to seek sustenance in the stale food of the Canon, but they are to find it through direct contact with the Divine Presence.   Saints lived, not only in the remote past, but they are among us even now—Latter Day Saints.

So far, Mormonism is only theologic and sympathetically so. Its prime object is to increase the dignity of mankind and to raise each individual in the esteem of his fellow-men.   But what a small place all this now occupies in the actual life and thought of the Mormon people !   On the other hand, sex permeates their entire creed.   No institution or doctrine is regarded as more important, and no ceremony is performed with greater reverence than is the marriage rite.   For the business of the saints in heaven is to propagate souls for bodies begotten on earth.   The glory of the saint is in proportion to the number of wives and children with which he can credit himself.   Polygamy is then a very urgent requirement and a solemn duty.   So it was that Joseph Smith married a number of women, and Brigham Young counted his wives at twenty-five.

Further, since no marriage is sacred unless solemnized by the Mormon priest, who alone possesses the divine authority, a woman married to a " gentile " is actually not married at all. Therefore, a Mormon man does not commit adultery if he has intercourse with her.   Joseph Smith himself had at least two wives who were living at the time with non-Mormon husbands, the latter being ignorant of their mates' deception.   Brigham Young had no scruples about seducing a woman in Boston, as she was the wife of a " gentile."   Her husband was duly granted a divorce on the grounds of adultery.

Since a woman cannot be saved except through her husband whom she must meet in heaven, she is united for eternity to the man she marries.   If, however, her husband dies, she is not released from her religious duty of multiplying and replenishing the earth.   So, although her first marriage is an eternal one, she must provide herself with a substitute husband, who, for the time, enables her to fulfil her duty.  On the morning of the first resurrection, this man must yield her with all her posterity to the legal and lawful husband.  There are, then, two degrees of husbands, one for eternity and another for a temporary purpose. The latter is to beget children for the greater exaltation of the other, the husband for eternity.

The sexual life among the Mormons has been so ordered as to protect the priesthood and to provide for them all possible conjugal joys.  It requires a higher power than a bill of divorce to take a woman from a man who is good and honours his priesthood.  It must be a man who possesses a high power in the priesthood, or else the woman is bound to her husband and will be forever, in the words of Brigham Young.  And Apostle Orson Pratt expounds thus : " Since the wives all belonged to God and Brigham Young was His agent, hence for all practical purposes they all belonged to Brother Brigham."

And another apostle, Jedediah Grant, defending Joseph Smith against the charges of attempting to seduce the wives of apostles and other prominent men of the church, asked :  " Did the Prophet Joseph want every man's wife that he asked for ? " When the attempted seduction was successful, it was " sensual joy for the love of God."  And this turned out to be the prime motive in the religion of the Mormons : sensual joy for the love of God.  The wave of individualism had its influence, and the theologic tenets of Latter Day Sainthood left their mark.  But above all was the motive of sex, permeating the very essence of the religion and the lives of its apostles and followers.

*Symbols of fertility*

# CHAPTER IV

## THE REVOLT AGAINST GOD

### I

KORAH rose up against Moses and Diakonus Nikolaus against Paul. There were others who dared to rise, not only against the men of God, but against the Divine Being Himself. They allied themselves with Satan, for all their faith in God. And this alliance may not be so strange as it appears.

The belief in devils was well-nigh universal. Jesus drove seven demons out of Mary Magdalene alone. These devils may have signified the earthliness of Mary, her sexuality dragging her down into the abyss of prostitution. In fact, the devil was conceived as imitating God, aping Him as it were. He was paying homage to idols with the same sacraments as the faithful were using in their divine worship. Moreover, the evil spirit is ever spiting the Divine Being. The latter seeks to keep man good and pure ; the former is ever leading him into temptation, always on the look out to drag him down into the mire of sin. And just as purity consists principally in chastity, so does the demon, in direct opposition, concentrate on fornication as his means of leading souls astray.

The evil spirit may assume any human form, male or female, and, as such, cohabit with humans. In fact, it was believed by such men as Augustine that the devil could impregnate a woman. To do this, he must first assume the form of a woman and cohabit with a man. After receiving within him the semen of the male, he would change himself into the form of a man and cohabit with a woman, transferring to her the semen he had previously received. There actually were women, in the Middle Ages, who claimed to have been visited at night by the devil and who related how they had felt his semen to be cold.

The evil spirit was elevated to a position almost on a plane with that of the Divinity by Manes, a Persian, who drew about himself a considerable following in the third century. He was an uncompromising dualist, who saw the world as the manifestation of two forces : light and darkness, day and night, God and the devil. Just as God is supreme in the world of light, so is the devil the lord in the world of darkness. Both are great, omnipotent, and spiritual, almost on a par with each other, but standing in opposition from all eternity, touching, yet remaining unmingled.

The first man, Adam, was really, according to Manes, the product of the devil. It was Satan who created him in his own image, in conjuction with sin and desire. Satan, too, gave him Eve as his companion and seducer. He drove into Adam all portions of light he had stolen from the kingdom above, and, as a result, Adam was a discordant being, created in the image of the evil spirit, yet carrying within him the spark of light. Even Eve was possessed of a tiny spark or ember. And, although the first humans were entirely under the dominion of the devil, they were at the same time under the protection of another agent. The glorious spirits in the world of light above took these two humans under their care and sent down æons, spiritual beings, to instruct them in light and to guard them against sensuality.

*The Evil Spirit tempting the*
*soul of a pagan idol*

Now, man possesses infinitely more light in him than does woman. The latter conveys the idea of darkness. In fact, the entire Kingdom of Darkness is often referred to as feminine. Eve is the embodiment of sensuous seduction. She led man astray by awakening within him the sexual passion. But other sensuous pleasures are the work of the devil. Sexual desire is the original sin, because through sex the light substance imprisoned within the body is extended for a longer period of time. Woman is, then, a demonic evil. Sensuality is the means the devil uses to bind man to the inferior regions. Consequently, Manes had three seals by which he sought to hold man as closely as possible to the glorious spirits in the upper world of light.   They were : *signaculum oris*, the taboo on meat and wine, *signaculum manus*, the taboo on labour, and *signaculum sinus*, the taboo on sex.   But of the three, the last one was by far the most important.   Marriage was anathema, and intercourse or any relationship whatever with a woman was a union with the devil.

Thus, the faith of Manes and of his disciples was pre-occupied with theologic problems concerning the powers in both the upper and the lower spiritual worlds.   In so far as it was concerned with sex, the sect had not a good word for it, looking upon it as a mere activity of the devil.   And yet, there was one little turn given these very theologic concepts that made of this sect a community concerned primarily with sex and engaged in setting free their sexual urges.

Since the body and its passions belong to an entirely different world from that of the spirit or light spark dwelling in man, the less contact there is between the two, the better it will be for the soul, the purer it may hope to remain.   The more the body is degraded, the deeper it wallows in the mire, the further it sinks into the abyss of darkness, the stronger and purer is the light of the spirit within it.   Consequently, indulgence in sex is a way of purifying the soul by soiling the body.   In this respect, their theory may have been evinced by their own actual experiences. For when one's mind is obsessed with sex, and his desires are forever egging him on in the sexual path—desires that are not being satisfied—his mind is bound to be blurred, and he is unable to think calmly and clearly.   But when the strain of continency is raised, the resulting mental serenity is conducive to clear thinking and to spiritual activity.   Hence, while marriage was forbidden, prostitution was raised to a sacred institution. Many of the followers of Manes threw aside all bonds and settled on the shores of the Jordan, establishing there a community in which absolute sexual promiscuity prevailed.

## II

In the Middle Ages, the sects growing out of the Manichæans, the Cathars and the Bulgarites, were persecuted for the practice of homosexuality, which they were accused of spreading in their communities.   Because they maintained that the devil had exerted a powerful influence in the teachings of Christianity, the Cathars were accused of worshipping the evil spirit.

Still another Satanic sect, the Messalians, which persisted until the eleventh century, even cursed the Son of Man at their mysteries, although they believed in his divine nature and in his mission as the saviour of the world. In their orgiastic rites, they introduced "devils" with which they engaged in sadistic and masochistic acts.

The rebellion against God was still further evinced in the witchcraft cult that reached the climax of its development in the latter part of the fifteenth century. The members of this sect looked upon the devil as their father, and they joined together in weekly meetings, sabbats, to render him homage. There, the devil appeared under various forms. At times he would enter the body of a tom-cat or a goat. Again he would assume the appearance of a bull or a very strong black man. But whatever his form, virility was ever his oustanding characteristic.

As the worship progressed, the faithful, free from all restraint, satisfied their hunger and thirst with food and drink. Intoxicated with drink and excitement, they extinguished the lights, while the devil commanded : " Mix, mix." Then it was that all bonds were thrown aside, and men and women, mad with the heat and flames of passion, indulged in promiscuous sexual union. And as the women far outnumbered the men in this cult, many of them sought intercourse with the devil, under whatever form he may have assumed. There is on record in Toulouse the case of one such woman, who confessed that she had engaged in intercourse with the devil and had given birth to a monster, half wolf and half serpent.

*When the devil was a god*
(*From an old English ballad*)

# CHAPTER V

# THE REVOLT AGAINST MAN

I

OTHER sects joined in the greatest rebellion of all—the revolt against man himself. Man's very instincts and all his institutions were to be uprooted and destroyed with a vengeance. Any kingdom on earth was a stronghold against the kingdom of heaven. Destroy all kingdoms on earth, and the reign of heaven would be proclaimed.

These rebels no longer formed a departure from the church. They constituted neither a reform nor a schismatic movement. They were frankly a break with the established religion and a denial of all for which it stands. They threw overboard all dogmas. They refused all sacraments. They would have none of the priesthood. They recognized neither fatherland nor home ties. They disclaimed fraternal and paternal love. They treated all social institutions with contempt. In fact, everything that is proper and legitimate was in itself already sinful.

This tendency to deny human nature and self, to turn one's back on the world, savours of asceticism. And among the ascetics we find men torturing themselves in revolt against their bodies. For years, Simeon Stylites sat upon the top of a pillar, suffering the torture of exposure to the elements, in that cramped and precarious position. Pachomius, another ascetic, limited his sleep to one hour and subsisted on bread, water, and ashes. Saint Euphrasia never bathed or changed her clothes. Saint Fidelis wore a shirt of hair and an iron girdle. Saint Francis never allowed his appetite to be completely satisfied ; and once he commanded a fellow brother to drag him naked through the streets of Assisi in order to mortify his body. Still others contrived all imaginable devices to afflict themselves with physical pain and anguish in their attempt to subjugate the physical being to the spirituality of the soul.

The idea of physical torture was carried a step further by the flagellants, a sect that swept over all of Europe during the thirteenth century. It was headed by monks, most of whom exemplified their teachings in their own bodies. Saint Dominic in six days inflicted upon himself three hundred thousand strokes. The leaders of the flagellants claimed to have received letters from heaven, demanding that people punish themselves for the wickedness in the world by striking their bodies with thongs. These letters were said to threaten terrible punishments upon the whole earth if the commands were not fulfilled.

So the followers of the new sect carried heavy leather scourges and lashed themselves until the blood streamed from their open wounds. Oftentimes, they joined in procession, marching through the streets, praying aloud, singing, and violently striking their bodies. As their blood thus shed would mingle with the blood of Christ upon the cross and purify their sinful souls, there was no need for the mediation of church or priest.

Although the principal idea of the sect was the same wherever it arose, the ways in which it developed varied from place to place. In Germany, certain conditions were laid down for admission. New members had to promise obedience to a leader and, if married men, they could not join the sect without the approval of their wives. Once people had gained admission, they were forbidden sexual intercourse or any pleasure that savoured of sensuality.

Another sect that made its appearance in Swabia, Germany, in the fifteenth century outstepped the flagellants, declaring : " It is permitted to lie ; no faith need be held ; no promise kept ; murder should be committed, also upon the innocent, even upon one's own parents." But unlike the former sect, its members esteemed the sexual impulse in man. In sexuality, they saw the one great purpose of existence as well as its only source of happiness. In sexual promiscuity, they found the bridge into the Kingdom of God.

In Russia, the tendency to self-torture culminated in the practice of self-destruction. Man sought to wipe out, not only human nature, but his very existence. The call of the flesh must be mercilessly suppressed and life itself undermined and prevented from continuation upon earth. Marriage with its rank purpose of reproduction was, therefore, anathema to all sects in this great movement. It was their belief that God created man with the idea that he be celibate, and so he was until his fall. The ideal state, then, was that in which man had no relationship whatever with women. But as human nature is weak, compromises might be effected in which promiscuity was the chief condition, the other being that no offspring follow the promiscuous union.

In this respect, the Russians of the nineteenth century trod much the same path as did the Abelians in the early days of Christianity. They claimed that Abel, the elder son of Adam, lived in the marital state yet had no children, no mention of his offspring being found in the Bible. Consequently, his followers took wives but had no children with them. So great was their fear of the sin of bringing progeny into the world that they abstained from normal sexual intercourse, looking upon it as the design of the devil. For was the world not created by the devil ? Did not the anti-Christ rule over the earth ? At any moment the bugle might sound, calling man and all creation together for the final judgment. How could it be right to bring children into the world, only to play them into the hands of the devil ?

Curiously enough the Abelians adopted children and raised them in their community so that their sect might be continued. Among the Russian sects the faithful did not have to resort to adopting children. There were some members who consorted with their wives for the purpose of raising daughters, which was a much lesser sin than bringing sons into the world. Once a son came, the couple had to separate forever. The daughters were encouraged to enter into promiscuous unions as soon as age permitted. And there were still other sources of life to continue the great light of the sect. These were the births that came as a result of the orgies and promiscuous relationships that characterized the religious services. Here again, the females were preferred, the males being disposed of either by secret killing or outright murder, or by dedication to the priesthood through castration.

## II

The purest form of self-destruction in religious worship was reached by the Skopzi, the " castrated ones." They called themselves the " White Doves," that is, the pure. Their theology is quite simple. They are not bound at all by the Bible, as they consider it a falsification. The true scripture is the " Book of the Dove," which was found among them as far back as the time of Peter the Third, whom they called their Christ. According to this book, Adam and Eve sinned by entering into sexual relationship. Sexual union, then, is the original sin. Of the first human pair, new ones came into the world, and the sin is continued indefinitely. There is only one way to avoid this evil, and that is by destroying the potency of humans to mate and rear children.

According to the Skopzi, Jesus, the son of God, was supposed to bring to mankind salvation by castration. This mission he feebly attempted to fulfil, as is indicated by various passages in the New Testament. His purpose, however, was misunderstood. Instead of martyrdom by mutilation, he suffered death upon the cross. In consequence, he was only the forerunner of the second and even greater son of God, Szelivanov, the founder of their sect.

Szelivanov addressed himself at once to those phases of sex life upon which Jesus only lightly touched. He called attention to the same passages by which Origen, in the third century, had justified his self-mutilation. " If thy hand or thy foot offends thee,

cut them off and cast them from thee ; it is better for thee to
enter into life halt or maimed, rather than having two hands or
two feet to be cast into everlasting fire.  And, if thine eye offend
thee, pluck it out and cast in from thee ; it is better for thee to
enter into life with one eye rather than having two eyes to be
cast into hell-fire." What could be more " offensive " to the true
Christian soul of Szelivanov than his organ of procreation ?

The leader of the new sect found still other justification for the
destruction of the procreative power in man.  The blessedness
of the state of purity is emphasized in this passage : " For behold,
the days are coming, in which they shall say, Blessed are the
barren and the wombs that never bore and the paps that never
gave suck." Again mutilation is justified : " For there be some
eunuchs, which were so born from their mothers' womb, and
there be some eunuchs, which were made eunuchs of men ; and
there be eunuchs which have made themselves eunuchs for the
Kingdom of Heaven's sake.  He that is able to receive it let him
receive it." And Saint Paul exhorts his listeners to deny their
flesh : " Mortify, therefore, your members which are upon the
earth : fornication, uncleanness, inordinate affection, evil con-
cupiscence and covetousness which is idolatry."

Szelivanov baptized himself by fire, mutilating his body with a
blazing iron.  He baptized hundreds in the same way and worked
untiringly to gain new converts.  When the world contained
one hundred and forty-four thousand Skopzi, the millennium
would be at hand.  At one time it appeared to be not far distant
for the membership was rapidly increasing.  Everyone was
urged to secure new converts.  He who brought in twelve
mutilations was given the distinction of apostleship.  In eastern
Russia, entire communities went over to the Skopzi.  One such
mass conversion consisted of seventeen hundred souls.  The mis-
sionaries worked among the beggars and other lowly elements
of society, convincing them or bribing them to accept the new
religion.  Some were even forcibly mutilated.  An appeal was
also made to the curious, the adventurous element.

The very fact that there were wholesale conversions to the
sect and that each convert was to be mutilated, made it quite
impossible for these operations to be performed with that great
care and precision required to insure their effectiveness.  Some
of the women had to be satisfied with mere incisions upon the
breasts.  Others, mutilated much more, still possessed the capacity
and the desire for the sexual function.  There were, therefore,
among the Skopzi, women prostitutes, enriching the communal
treasury with fees received from " gentiles," " uncastrated ones."
Even men were not always entirely incapacitated, due largely to

the fact that a good many of the converts performed the operation on themselves and halted in the process because of pain or fear. In fact, the Skopzi religion took cognizance of this condition by establishing two degrees of mutilations, those of the Greater Seal and those of the Lesser Seal. There were many Skopzi, then, in whose hearts still glowed the fire of passion and who were physically capable of satisfying their desires. They mingled with those who, although incapacitated, still exulted in witnessing the sexual activities of members of the Lesser Seal. As a result, we have the accounts of wild sexuality in the services of the sect and intense orgiastic rites.

The religious services of the Skopzi were secret affairs, and the traitor was certain of punishment by death. The congregation was called the " ship." All White Doves appeared in the ship in white shirts. The worship began about ten in the evening and lasted throughout the night. The males, seated upon chairs and benches began to sing, adding to the rhythm of the song by clapping their hands upon their thighs. Haxthausen, who was present at a Skopzi service, has given the text of one of their songs :

> Hold fast, you men of the ship,
> Do not let the ship perish in the storm.
> The Holy Spirit is with us.
> Our Father and Christ are with us,
> His mother Akulina Iwanowna is with us.
> He will come,
> He will appear,
> He will ring the great bell of Uspenski church ;
> He will call together all believing ship-folk ;
> He will set masts that never fall ;
> He will set sails that do not tear,
> And a steering wheel he will build that will safely guide.

The women were at first mere observing listeners. But, after a while, the men stopped the song and the women continued it. As the singing went on and ever grew more fervent, the congregation fell into a dance, the " rapture," that culminated in wild leaping and whirling.

The effect of the dance seemed to be the same upon the mutilated people as upon the others. Everyone was brought into a trance of sensuous delight, a state of ecstasy. As a release for the aroused energies, Szelivanov suggested general kissing. Apparently, kissing was not sufficient release, and the congregation resorted to the sadistic and masochistic activities that characterized their orgiastic rites.

In their worship, they chose a Bogoroditza, a " mother of

God," a maiden who was expected to give birth to the new Christ. She was usually only fifteen or sixteen years of age and a virgin. As she entered the meeting-place, she was greeted with the words : " Blessed art thou of all women, for thou shall give birth to the saviour." She was then undressed and immersed in a tub of warm water. That her pain might be relieved, she was given an image of the Holy Ghost to hold while the old women amputated her left breast. The bleeding virgin was then placed upon an altar, and an almost inhuman orgy followed. The amputated breast was hacked into tiny pieces and grabbed by the worshippers to be eaten while still warm.

Meanwhile, there was a struggle to approach the sacred bride and to kiss her everywhere. In this event, the lights were extinguished, and the worshippers joined in song, praying the Lord to give the virgin a Christ child. Almost invariably the " God Mother " was impregnated in the course of this orgy, and before the close of the year, she would report at the meeting-place with her child.

Even more gruesome were the rites that followed the advent of the Christ child. On the eighth day of the child's life, his left side was lanced by a finely pointed spear, and the warm blood that flowed from the wound in the infant body was drunk in the communion service. The body itself was dried and pounded into a powder. Out of this powder cakes of bread were prepared, to be offered the worshippers on the first day of the Easter season.

III

Having obstructed the avenues of new births and having murdered those offspring that did break into life, there was still a great dominating humanity, which by its very existence, bore witness to the surging living force about it. And there was only one other way in which rebellious man could defy the force of life and generation. It was by aiding death in its inroads upon this living mass, by cutting short as many lives as possible. A life lost was a life gained. God had left this world ; man had to leave it, too, to join God. The Bible exhorts the true man of the faith not to be worried over self-destruction, which to the Judaic Christian was the greatest of sins : " And fear not them that kill the body but are not able to kill the soul ; but rather fear him which is able to destroy both soul and body in hell."

Living up to these tenets, various sects offered salvation by killing, either directly or indirectly, or by suicide, one might say communal suicide, in which the worshipper joined as a unit. Most of the modern sects of this nature are, or until very recently were, to be found in Russia. But the same tendencies were met with in olden times in India, throughout Asia, and among primitive peoples in many parts of the world.

Some of these sects still profess the Judaic Christian idea of the sanctity of life. They cannot quite break away from it. So to compromise, they claim that only those whose end is violent will enter into the Kingdom of Heaven. Once their end is induced violently their place in heaven is assured. Such a sect made its appearance in Russia in the early nineties of the last century. Its members were called " under-the-doorists," because they conducted their services under the ground. Their greatest appeal was made to the poor, sick, and afflicted. These they baptized, gave new names and surnames, and designated as the " slaves of God." They were then put away in special caves underground and left there to die of starvation. Death was induced, rather than inflicted, by violence.

A degree closer to violence is the custom of an even more recent Russian sect called Ticklers. In their services, the males tickled the females so long that the latter fell into swoons. And as it was believed that each death added to the holiness of the service, no effort was exerted to revive the exhausted ones.

During the reign of Alexander II, in Russia, another such sect was founded by a man named Shodkin. He preached suicide by starvation, claiming that the anti-Christ was ruling the world and that the millennium was at hand. There was, then, only one means of salvation : to be buried in a cave in the woods and to await death by starvation. In shrouds, the prophet and his flock, including the women and children, entered the cave. Scattering sand over their heads and driving out the devil, they closed the opening. Suddenly two women, seized with terror at the thought of a slow death, broke through the opening and escaped. Chaos set in.

The prophet, fearing the hand of the police whom the escaped women might arouse to action, hastened to destroy the pious before they yielded to the temptation of the devil. " The hour of death has come ; are you ready ? " he asked his followers. " We are ready," was the reply. Forthwith the men attacked the children and killed them. Then they put an end to the women, finally turning upon themselves. When the police arrived, they had time only to save the prophet and two young men.

A large number of sects in Russia, at the close of the last century, preached suicide by burning. Again, the keynote of their philosophy was that the anti-Christ was ruling, that the end of the world was at hand. Suicide was, therefore, the only road to happiness. Only fire could cleanse the soul of the sins of this world. And the leaders of this sect advocated suicide by burning. One such preacher exhorted the father of a family to enclose himself with his wife and children in a wooden hut. Thereupon, the preacher himself piled straw about the walls and kindled the fire. An epidemic of such suicide fires soon swept the whole country. In one case, a woman escaped and reported the proceedings to the police. As the latter came upon the scene of the fire, the sectarians shouted in ghastly voices : " The anti-Christ is here. Draw close into the fire," as the flames enveloped them.

Only a few months ago, a " suicide pact " was unearthed in Soviet Russia. A young girl told of how, as she was going home from work in Moscow, she was accosted by a man who asked her if she were a virgin. When she modestly nodded in the affirmative, the stranger told her that he needed her to do him a service and promised her one hundred roubles in compensation. Feeling confident that the man was trustworthy, the girl accepted his offer.

For some time they drove through the city in an automobile. During the course of the drive, the stranger blindfolded the girl, explaining as he did so that it was very necessary. After they had reached their destination, he removed the bandage from her eyes.

They were in a large room dimly lighted. Three of the walls were draped in white silk and the fourth had been converted into a niche. As they waited, music seemed to come out of the distance, and a door opened upon a procession of ten white-clad and hooded figures. Carrying lighted candles, these hooded figures advanced and arranged themselves in two files before the niche. Then two other persons, white-clad but unmasked, a young man and a woman, came out of the doorway and entered the niche. Thereupon the others proceeded to close the opening, immuring the two victims in a living grave. Two wheel-barrows, with bricks, mortar, and trowels, standing near by, furnished the material for the purpose.

When the niche was sealed, the white-clad figures filed out as silently as they had entered the room. The young girl, who had been a horrified onlooker, was then directed to sweep the room. One of the white-clad figures returned and addressed her : " According to our rites it is necessary that a virgin not belonging to our society must clean the room after our brother and sister have passed beyond." When the girl had completed the task, she was again blindfolded and returned to the very spot upon which the man had accosted her.

Murder and self-destruction was the basic doctrine of the Thugs, a Hindu sect, first met with by the English in the nineteenth century. The origin of this sect goes back to legendary times. The members regarded themselves as devotees, engaged in the fulfilment of their duty. Their murders were committed only after certain rituals had been performed. Whatever worldly gain the murder brought them, it was shared with the goddess and the temple. The instruments of killing and burial were held in the highest esteem. An oath taken upon a pick-axe was as binding to the Thugs as one taken upon the Bible is to us.

The Thug worshipper never looked upon himself as a murderer. When one of them was asked how many people he had killed with

*Kali, lover of death, destruction and murder, trampling under foot her own husband*

his own hand in his lifetime, his answer was " none." When he was remonstrated because he had just been describing the murders he had committed, he answered : " Could I have committed them ? Is any man killed from any man's killing ? Is it not the hand of God that kills him, and are we not mere instruments in the hand of God ? " The Thug believed that it was his calling to be a slayer. He educated his children to follow the same vocation, impressing upon their tender minds that it was the noblest profession a man could select and assuring them that the dark goddess would always provide rich travellers for the faithful devotees.

What was it that led man to such perverse extremes in his religion? The Thugs of India have their story to tell:

There was once a demon who roamed over the land and devoured all before him. No sooner was a child born than he was swallowed up. The world became unpeopled. There was no power on earth that could hold back or overpower this horrible monster. Still the goddess Kali attempted the impossible. Hers was the province of destruction. Why should she not destroy the destroyer?

So Kali attacked the demon and cut him down. But from every drop of his blood another one was born. The goddess continued to cut down these rising demons. She worked with wonderful skill and ever-increasing speed. But out of every drop of blood of every demon, a new demon sprang into being. Kali only augmented their number upon earth by her struggle against them. So she was compelled to turn to man for aid in her war against the evil monsters.

As all humans had been devoured by the demons, Kali created two men out of the perspiration brushed from her arms and handed each a handkerchief. She then commanded them to capture the demons and to choke them. In this way, no demon blood would be shed and, consequently, no new demons could spring into existence. The greater the number destroyed, the sooner the world would be rid of them. In time, the two men with the red handkerchiefs cleared the land of demons.

The demons had disappeared from the face of the earth, but the passion for choking, for killing, remained. Once killing is made a rite, it matters little whether the object is imaginary demon or actual man. In fact, the killing of man is more satisfying because it is real and brings into play all the savagery that lies buried deep in the human heart. Once man smells blood he will create sufficient theories to keep this maddening odour ever before him. A new philosophy is evolved, an obsession of being caught between the devil and the deep sea. There is no hope for the world and none for the individual, at least not on this earth. But even in the moment of despair, there exists a moment of ecstasy and release. And so great is the hunger for this rare moment that one is ready to sacrifice his very life for it.

## IV

It is organized society that produces the rebel and institutionalized religion that gives birth to the sect. In all ailments of the sects, we must go back to the parent religion for the hereditary taint. It was religion that first created a deep between man's

" would " and his " should." Religion gave rise to a discrepancy between man's desires and his expression of them. In fact, as an institution, it created or encouraged a two-compartment system, a system of believing in one way and acting in another. When the two are utterly incompatible, apparent harmony may be reached by prayer, penance, or any form of absolution.

At the close of the daily prayer, the pious orthodox Jew reads the thirteen articles of his faith, one of which is that he believes in the coming of the Messiah. He professes that, although the advent is delayed, he is daily awaiting the arrival. In the deepest faith and seriousness, the pious man reads the article. Yet this will not hold him from taking a lease for ninety-nine years. In ordinary life, the two are dissociated, and one does not interfere with the other. Still, in times of unrest, a religious frenzy has overtaken entire Jewish communities and the members have given up all worldly possessions and started out on their way to meet the Messiah.

Most Christians have learned to place little emphasis on the negative teachings of the New Testament in regard to the sexual life. They are more wont to dwell upon the positive element— the motherly love of Mary and the love of Jesus for humanity. Yet the negative attitude toward sex is so overwhelming and the theological structures that were built upon it so enormous that true believers have learned to live in a duplex system. They make good lovers and fathers and go on living for all that life may offer them in comfort and joy, in spite of the sombre elements of their faith.

But not all people possess the necessary balance to live in a spiritual duplex apartment. There are those who rebel against this complacency. They cannot split their individuality. They must live upon one even base and under one square roof. They therefore upset the artificial, socially superimposed equilibrium, going back to the beginnings, to the mire of sex and blood. Some find their salvation in unbridled sexuality, in what we are inclined to call depravity. Others are not strong enough physically to endure it or their sensibilities have already been dulled. They are the ones who revolt against the flesh and against life.

Self-destruction is a frequent concomitant of mental disorder. Whatever he who is mentally deranged may think of it, to us it may seem as if nature were to say : Here, my child, you cannot live in the world into which you were born. Come back to me, into the great, eternal womb of the universe.

# EPILOGUE.

## GOD'S WAY IN LOVE

### I

IN the land of Haidenluma, on the coast of Haidenhaid, they tell the story of a charming princess and of her lover, fair and strong. Wandawind was the name of the princess, and she lived in her castle on the top of a hill. Every morning, at early dawn, Wandawind rose from a bed of roses to bathe in the River of Souls so that its rippling waters might ever be pure. For there, in the swiftly flowing stream, the souls of the departed were purified before they reported at the gate of Shadenshade for eternal peace and comfort.

One day, Wandawind, the charming princess, felt tired on waking. She walked down the hill but did not go in to bathe. The souls would be disappointed, but her head was heavy and her feet ached. She sat upon a rock to rest. For a moment she closed her weary eyes to see a dizzy, whirling world. Then she opened them. But in the brief interval something happened. She was now being carried in the arms of a ragged shepherd boy.

Loverlain was the name of the lad, and he lived on the plain. Loverlain had been walking along the bank of the river, following the soul of his father who had just departed. Sad had been the heart of the shepherd boy, and full of grief and love. His head had been lowered, his eyes upon the water. When he raised them, he beheld Wandawind prostrate on the rock.

Tired was the charming princess and heavy her eyes. Yet she opened them to gaze upon the wonderful shepherd lad who was carrying her up the hill to the castle. And as she gazed at him, her golden locks mingled with his hair of jet, and her azure eyes bathed in eyes that were black as night. And as they reached the draw-bridge, their lips came close together, locked in a kiss of love.

Now, Wandawind was a charming princess and Loverlain only a shepherd boy, so she returned to her chambers in the palace and Loverlain went back to the valley. But the lad could never forget the warmth of Wandawind's lips or the gaze of her dreamy eyes. He could neither eat nor sleep, always longing for the lovely princess, who lived in the castle above. One morning, when he heard that the princess was to marry the King of Radan, he came down to the rock where he had first found Wandawind and lay down to die. The shepherd boys of Haidenluma buried the body of Loverlain, but his soul remained hovering over the waters of the river.

And as Wandawind came down to bathe in the River of Souls

she heard a faint murmur in the waters. It was the voice of
Loverlain, speaking of love and of longing. And the charming
princess said to the shepherd boy : " They would not admit you
to the castle when you were living, but I shall admit your soul to
my body and take you along with me. Our souls will be for ever
united even as our lips were on that sunny morning when you
carried me up the hill."

So the soul of the shepherd boy entered the body of the lovely
princess, and people called her possessed. She now refused to
marry the King of Radan, for she was already living in marriage
with the soul of Loverlain. A fast was declared in all the land of
Haidenluma and a period of mourning on the coast of Haidenhaid. For the King of Radan was fully resolved to banish the
soul of a base shepherd boy from the body of a princess of the
blood.

And on the seventh day of mourning, the priests of Haidenluma
were all assembled in their temple that faced the sun and Haidenhaid. They lighted the black candles and opened the chest
wherein lay the sacred sword. For this sword could cut souls
and destroy them so that they might not live to enter the gate of
Shadenshade there to find peace eternal.

Loverlain's soul would not submit even under the edge of the
sacred knife. It would rather be destroyed altogether than forsake the happy abode of the charming princess. But Wandawind
would not have the soul of Loverlain destroyed. She asked it to
leave her body and to wait at the rock by the river.

So again were the priests of Haidenluma triumphant. Bugles
were sounded, tom-toms were played, and sirens were blown all
over the land, for again was Wandawind herself and her marriage
with the King of Radan could now take place.

All the land was happy, and there was no end to the joy and
clamour, which only increased with the fall of night. Fires were
made, and around them a happy people drank and danced. In
the midst of the festivities, as the waning moon crept from
beneath a heavy cloud, the face of Wandawind grew pale in
death, her soul departing to the rock below to meet the soul of
Loverlain. To this very day the two souls are for ever floating
over the waters of the river in eternal embrace.

And this is the end of the story. Because she defied the priests
of Haidenluma, the soul of the princess could never enter Shadenshade. But Wandawind would fain be worried, for what is life
on earth and eternal peace in Shadenshade in the face of love
triumphant ?

## II

This is also the end of the story of love as it emerged from the momentary passion of physical desire into the realm of the spirit. Love was born of physical desire, yet Loverlain dared to forego all desire, life itself, out of his love for Wandawind. And the princess went even farther, defying death itself for love. The spirit of love steps over life and transcends death, to remain like the Spirit of God, for ever moving over the waters.

Love could never have reached this stage were it not for the Spirit of God with which it had merged in the union of love and religion. That which once was brutal passion, mere physical hunger, was only little tempered by the social relationship and comradeship that proximity to the object of sex afforded. He who caught his woman in the field and raped her at his whim, was possessed of little more refinement when he was forced to keep her at his side for a while or compelled to associate with her in some social task. It was only when he came to do his loving in the temple that he discovered esthetic values in this prime force of his life. For just as music regulates sound, so have the temple requirements regulated man's sexual conduct within its walls. What was elsewhere a savage outbreak, animal fashion, was here reduced to an artistic accomplishment. In fact, it was in the temple that man made an art of his loving, an *ars amandi*, which Western man has well-nigh forgotten. And not until he relearns this sacred art will he be completely happy again.

In the temple there was an atmosphere of awe and admiration. One felt it toward the god and goddess, and this feeling was carried over to the priestess. Representing the divine being, she, too, was in a way divine. And as such she was to be treated accordingly. One's attitude toward her assumed a definite form. And the attitude toward the priestess affected the attitude toward women and love in general. They who came to cohabit in the temple unwittingly introduced a divine element into the act of cohabitation generally.

As the temple priesthood degenerated, and man began to look upon woman as a mere object of sex, religion again came to the rescue of love. For by that time it had established a new plane of living—a spiritual plane. Religion repaid sex by raising it to the high position to which religion itself had risen on the shoulders of love. With a spiritual concept of God and divine existence, man's attitude toward sex and love itself became highly spiritualized.

At base, love is still physical desire, sex, the hunger of the male for the female. But that is only its foundation. No edifice may be judged entirely by its foundation. One must look to that which has been built upon it. Upon the basis of sex, love has evolved disinterested friendship, cordial comradeship, and a communion of soul that is akin only to the communion man may achieve with God. Love, the physical force, has become the great spiritual power that makes for the creative arts, for the sense of beauty and of the higher values. And all this was brought about by the divine element that entered into love somewhere in its course of evolution. It was God's way in love.

### III

All this religion did for love. But even more was done by love for religion. In fact, one may doubt if, without love, religion would have survived the onslaughts of time and progress. With-

out love, religion would have remained a mixture of fear and magic. With the advancement of civilization, man's fears were bound to lessen. With the growth of the social organization, man came to look upon himself as the arbiter of his own destiny, and the instrument of magic was bound to become well-nigh powerless. A threatening god of fear could hardly dominate a modern, enlightened world. Here, love came to the rescue of religion. Love humanized religion. The god was no longer to be either feared, bribed off, or tricked by magic machination. He was no longer the terrible, vengeful master, and man his hateful slave. Love introduced intimate contact between god and man. Both worshipper and divinity partook of the same food, enjoyed the same revelry, and shared the same bed. In place of impersonal magic, intimate contact became the basis of man's attitude toward his god. The worshipper began to seek communion with his divinity, at first in concrete form, whether by consuming the god or feeding him with his own flesh, and in time, in symbolic form, through prayer and ceremonial. The voluptuous desire of love for union created the greatest value of modern religion—the desire and the attempt to commune with God.

In addition, love gave to religion the possibility of being its own reward. It made religion not only a means but an end in itself. Religion could not persist solely on the promise of a here-after. The promise of an after life may still have a powerful hold upon man, yet it is doubtful that he would go on praying daily if it were only for that. Prayer is largely its own end. Whether it brings the object prayed for or not it relieves the aching heart. The kingdom of heaven was acceptable on the basis of a kingdom upon earth. It was love that offered a kingdom here as a base for the kingdom to come. Before the heavenly bliss of joining one's God in heaven there was the earthly joy of meeting one's God here on earth. To melt away in the love for God, to be ever pining for Jesus, were in themselves the greatest boon from heaven. Communion with God lifted the burden from one's shoulder, rolled away the stone weighing down upon one's heart, gave the warmth of life to those walking in the valley of death, brought friendship to the lonely and solace to the loveless. Religion became lover, parent, and child to the weary soul, drifting in the sea of humanity. Whether in synagogue or church, mosque or pagoda, whoever came to worship in prayerful mood found his God awaiting in love the communal embrace.


IV

Pious souls need not be wary of this great force of love in their religion. They have more reason to be proud of it than to apologize for it. Love in religion has had, indeed, an humble origin, but so has had religion itself. Like religion, love has been evolved and elevated, refined and sanctified. To-day, it is difficult to choose the more divine : love or faith. To the refined, delicate, sensitive soul of modern times, love in its religious aspect offers greater spiritual depth and wider esthetic experience than the other elements in religion. Any movement to rob religion of its personal and emotional element and reduce it to intellectualism, whether theologic dogma or ethical precept, is an attempt on the very heart of religion to undermine its basis and to take away the reason for its existence.

The dogma, or ethical precept, was ever the concern of the theologians, but the ceremonial, as the bearer of the emotional content, is to-day, as it ever was, the key to the hearts of the faithful. What is the small white host that is offered by the priest at the communion table ? Is it merely a piece of bread or is it the body of Christ ? Are the bread and wine actually converted into the body and blood of Christ by his representative ?

The men and women who devoutly approach the communion table are little perturbed by these dogmatic problems. Theirs is a single purpose : to become more closely united with their God. Theirs is a belief in a Divine Being. He is their trust and their solace. It is He who is drawing their hearts to Him. Whether it is theologically the bread that bridges the chasm between the human and the divine, whatever it is that they receive from the hand of the priest, the moment it touches their flesh they are consumed by that divine presence for which they have been pining. All religious ceremonies of to-day are the expression of that int mate relationship that love introduced into religion. They who know religion know that no greater love exists and that there is nothing more all-inclusive in life than the love of God.

# BIBLIOGRAPHY

# ACKNOWLEDGMENTS

The author has drawn freely from a large number of books dealing directly or indirectly with eroticism in religion. These are listed in the following bibliography, and acknowledgment must, of necessity, be made to their authors *in toto*. From some of the books illustrations have been copied. These are indicated in the general bibliography by asterisks, and the author expresses his twofold indebtedness for their use. He is under special obligation to Grace M. Keeffe for her invaluable assistance in the preparation of the book.

# BIBLIOGRAPHY

Alexander, Hartley Burr. The Mythology of All the Races. Boston, 1916.

Alonso de Madrid. Arte para servir á Dios (In : Escritores misticos españoles). Madrid, 1911.

Auber, C. A. Histoire et Theorie du Symbolisme Religieux. Paris, 1870–71.

Augustine, St. City of God. London, 1609.


Baring-Gould, Rev. S. Lives of the Saints. Edinburgh, 1914.
Origin and Development of Religious Belief.

Baruzi, Jean. Saint Jean de la Croix et le Problem de l'experience mystique. Paris, 1924.

Baur, F. C. Symbolik und Mythologie ; oder, Die Naturreligion des Alterthums. Stuttgart, 1824–25.

Bayley, Harold. The Lost Language of Symbolism. London, 1913.

Bloch, I. Die Prostitution.

Braun, Julius, Gemalde der Mohammedanischen Welt. Leipzig. 1870.

Brinton, D. G. Religions of Primitive People. New York, 1897.

Brown, John P. The Dervishes. Philadelphia, 1868.

Buckley, E. Phallicism in Jaapan. Chicago, 1895.

Butler, E. C. Western Mysticism. London, 1922.


Cabbala, The. Ed. Adolph Franck. New York, 1926.

*Carus, P. The History of the Devil. Chicago, 1900.

*Carter, Frederick. The Dragon of the Alchemists. London, 1926.

Churchward, Albert. The Signs and Symbols of Primordial Man. London, 1830.

Crawley, A. E. The Mystic Rose. New York, 1927.

Creuzer, G. F. Religiones de l'antiquite. Paris, 1825–41.
Symbolik und Mythologie der alten Volker besonders der Griechen. Leipzig, 1836–42.

Cumont, Franz. Les Mysteres de Mitha. Paris, 1902.

Cuthbert, Father. The Life of St. Francis of Assisi. London, 1914.


Danzig, A. Chochmas Adam. Vilna, 1875.

Dean, J. B. The Worship of the Serpent. London, 1830.

Delacroix, Henri. Études d'histoire et de psychologie du mysticisme. Paris, 1908.

*Dictionary of Christian Antiquities. Boston, 1875.

*Didron, A. N. Christian Iconography. London, 1851.

Duchesne, L. Early History of the Christian Church. New York, 1923.

Dulaure, J. A. Les divinities generatrices chez les anciens et les modernes. Paris, 1825.

Dunlap, Knight. Mysticism, Freudianism and scientific psychology. St. Louis, 1920.

Dupouy, Dr. E. Prostitution in Antiquity. Cincinnati, 1895.

Edkins, J.   Ancient Symbolism among the Chinese.   London, 1889.
Ellis, Havelock.   The Dance of Life.   Boston, 1923.
    Studies in the Psychology of Sex, 6 v.   Philadelphia, 1910–11.
Emden, J. I.   Liturgy and Ritual.   Lemberg, 1901.
Encyclopædia Britannica.   New York, 1911.
Encyclopedia of Religion and Ethics.   Ed. by James Hastings.   New
    York, 1908.
Engels, F.   Der Ursprung der Familie.   Stuttgart, 1892.
Eusebius—Ecclesiastical History, with Valerius' Life of Constantine,
    Cruse's and Parker's trans.   London, 1847.


Faber, G. S.   Origin of Pagan Idolatry.   London, 1816.
Farnell, L. R.   Cults of the Greek States.   Oxford, 1896.
Field, C. H. A.   Mystics and Saints of Islam.   London, 1910.
Flaubert, Gustave.   Salambo.
*Forlong, J. C. R.   Rivers of Life.   London, 1883.
Foucart, Paul.   Les Mysteres d'Eleusis.   Paris, 1914.
Fowler, W. W.   The Religious Experience of the Roman People.
    London, 1911.
France, Anatole.   Thaïs.
Frazer, Sir James.   The Golden Bough.   New York, 1923.   London,
    1917.
    The Worship of Nature.
*Fuchs, E.   Geschichte der erotischen Kunst.   Berlin, 1908.


Garnett, Lucy M. J.   Mysticism and Magic in Turkey.   London, 1912.
Gennep, Arnold van,   Religiones, Mœurs et Legends.   Paris, 1908.
Goblet d'Alviella.   La migration des symboles.   Paris, 1891.
Goldsmith, E. E.   Life Symbols as Related to Sex Symbolism.   New
    York, 1924.
*Gruenwedel, A.   Die Teufel des Avesta und Ihre Beziehungen zur
    Iconographie des Buddhismus Zentral-Asiens.   Berlin, 1924.
Guyon, J. M.   Letters of Madame Guyon.   Translated and arranged
    by Mrs. P. L. Upsham.   New York, 1870.


Hall, Manley Palmer,   An encyclopedic outline of Masonic, Hermetic,
    Cabbalistic and Rosicrucian symbolical philosophy.   San Fran-
    cisco, 1928.
*Hannay, J. B.   Christianity, the Sources of Its Teaching and
    Symbolism.   London, 1913.
*Harrison, E.   Themis.   Cambridge, 1912.
Hartman, M.   Der Islamische Orient.   Berlin, 1905–10.
Herodotus, Rawlinson's trans.   London, 1862.
Higgins, G.   Anacalypsis.   London, 1836.
*Hoernes, M.   Urgeschichte der bildenden Kunst in Europa.   Wien,
    1898.
Horace.   Ed., A. J. Macleane.   2nd Edition.   London, 1869.
Howard, C.   Sex Worship.   Chicago, 1909.
    Sex and Religion.   London, 1925.

# BIBLIOGRAPHY 279

Hugel, Friedrich. The Mystical Element in Religion. New York, 1923.

*Inman, T. Ancient Pagan and Modern Christian Symbolism. New York, 1875.
Ancient Pillar Stones.

James, Wm. Varieties of Religious Experience. New York, 1928.
*Jameson, Mrs. Sacred and Legendary Art. London, 1857.
History of Our Lord. London, 1872.
Jennings, Hargrave. The Rosicrucians. London, 1870.
Jewish Encyclopedia. New York, 1903.

Kato, Genchi. A. Study of Shinto. Tokyo, 1926.
Knight, Richard Payne. A Discourse on the Worship of Priapus. London, 1894.
The Symbolical Language of Ancient Art and Mythology. New York, 1876.
Koran, The : commonly called The Alcoran of Mohammed. London, 1734. Translated by George Sale.

La Croix, Paul, Histoire de la Prostitution. Paris, 1851–53.
*Lajard, F. Recherches sur Le Culte, Les Symboles, Les Attributs, et Les monuments Figures de Venus. Paris, 1837–48.
Leuba, J. H. Psychology of Religious Mysticism. London, 1925.
Lévi, Éliphas, Les Mysteres de la Kabbale. Paris, 1920.
Lubbock, Sir J. The Origins of Civilization. London, 1870.
*Lundy, Rev. J. P. Monumental Christianity. New York, 1876.

Mackenzie, D. A. The Migration of Symbols. New York, 1926.
*Moll, Dr. Albert. Handbuch der Sexual Wissenschaften. Leipzig, 1921.
Morgan, L. H. Ancient Society. New York, 1877.

Nicholson, D. H. S. The Mysticism of St. Francis of Assisi. Boston, 1923.
Nicholson, R. A. The Mystics of Islam. London, 1914.
Studies in Islamic Mysticism. Cambridge, 1921.

O'Brien, H. Round Towers of Ireland. London, 1834.
Old and New Testaments.

Pausanias. The Description of Greece. Translated from the Greek, with notes by T. Taylor. London, 1794.
Phallicism, Article on, in Chambers' Encyclopedia of Religious Knowledge.
Philpot, Mrs. J. H. The Sacred Tree. London, 1897.
Pierre, Louys. Aphrodite. Paris, 1926.

*Ploss, H. and Bartels, M.  Das Weib. Berlin, 1927.
Preuss, J.  Prostitution und Sexuelle Perversitaten nach Bibel und Talmud in Monatschefte f. Prat. Dermatologie.

Quanter, Rudolf.  Das Weib in den Religionen der Volker.  Berlin, 1910.

Rade, M.  Die Stellung der Christentum zum Geschlechtsleben.
Reinach, S.  Cultes, mythes et Religiones.  Paris, 1905–23.
  Orpheus, a History of Religions.  New York, 1909.
Reitzenstein, F. E.  Urgeschichte der Ehe.  Stuttgart, 1908.
  Das Weib bei den Naturvolkern.  Berlin, 1923.
Renan, Ernest,  La Vie de Jesus.  Paris, 1867.
Roscher, W. H.  Lexikon der griechischen und romischen mythologie.  Leipzig. 1886–90.
Ruysbroeck, Jan van.  Flowers of a mystic garden from the works of John Ruysbroeck.  Translated from the French of E. Hello by C. E. S.  London, 1912.

Sabatier, Paul.  La Vie de S. François d'Assisi.  Paris, 1894.
Sacred Books and Early Literature of the East.  London and New York, 1911.  Ed. by Prof. C. F. Horne.
Sanger, Wm. W.  History of Prostitution.  New York, 1859.
Schroeder, T. A.  Erotogenesis of Religion.  New York, 1916.
  Heavenly Bridegrooms.  New York, 1918.
  Revivals, Sex and Holy Ghost.  Boston, 1919.
  Wildisbuch Crucified Saint ; a Study in the Erotogenesis of Religion.  New York, 1914.
Seabrook, W. B.  The Magic Island.  New York, 1929.
Sharpe, A. N.  Mysticism.  London, 1910.
Siedel, G.  Die Mystik Taulers.  Leipzig, 1911.
Springett, B. H.  Secret Sects of Syria and the Lebanon.  London, 1922.
Steinen, Karl von den,  Unter den Naturvolken Zentral Brasiliens.  Berlin, 1894.
Stern, B.  Geschichte der offentlichen Sittlichkeit in Russland.
Stocker, L.  Geistige Ehen im Urchristentum.
Stoll, O.  Das Geschlechtsleben in der Volkerpsychologie.  Leipzig, 1904.
Stone, L. A.  Story of Phallicism.  New York, 1927.
Summer, W. G.  Folkways.  New York, 1906.

Teresa, Santa.  La Via de la Perfeccior (In : Escritores misticos españoles.)  Madrid, 1911.
Tertullian.  Opera.  Ed. F. Oehler.  Leipzig, 1851–54.
Tylor,  Sir E. B.  Primitive Culture.  London, 1873.

Underhill, Evelyn.  Mysticism.  London, 1923.
  The Mystics of the Church.  London, 1925.
  The Mystic Way.  London, 1914.

Virgil. Ed. J. Conington. London, 1863–71.

Weber, C. J. Die Moncherei.
Westermarck, E. A. History of Human Marriage. London, 1891.
Westropp, H. M. and Wake, C. S. Ancient Symbol Worship. New York, 1875.
Wilson, H. H. The Vishnu Purana. London, 1840.
Wundt, W. M. Volkerpsychologie. Leipzig, 1900–09.

Zeller, E. Das Urchristentum.
  Religion und philosophie bei den Romern. Berlin, 1866.
Zohar, Hebrew trans., 5 vol. Leghorn, 1877–88.
Zscharnak, L., Der Dienst der Frau in den ersten Jahrhunderten der Christlichen Kirche.

# INDEX